D0962018

New Threats to Freedom

NEW
THREATS TO
FREEDOM

Edited and Introduced by
Adam Bellow

TEMPLETON PRESS

Templeton Press
300 Conshohocken State Road, Suite 550
West Conshohocken, PA 19428
www.templetonpress.org

Collection © 2010 by Templeton Press

The copyright for individual essays in this collection belongs
to the author of the work.

All rights reserved. No part of this book may be used or reproduced,
stored in a retrieval system, or transmitted in any form or by any
means, electronic, mechanical, photocopying, recording, or otherwise, without the written permission of Templeton Press.

Essay by Richard Epstein all rights reserved c/o Writer's
Representatives LLC, New York, NY 10011

Typeset and designed by Gopa & Ted2, Inc.

Library of Congress Cataloging-in-Publication Data

New threats to freedom / edited and introduced by Adam Bellow.
    p. cm.
  ISBN-13: 978-1-59947-351-2 (hardcover : alk. paper)
  ISBN-10: 1-59947-351-8 (hardcover : alk. paper) 1. Democracy—
Philosophy. 2. Paternalism—Political aspects. 3. Social values.
4. Freedom of expression. I. Bellow, Adam.
  JC423.B3437 2010
  323—dc22

                                                        2010003594
Printed in the United States of America

10 11 12 13 14 15   10 9 8 7 6 5 4 3 2 1

Contents

Introduction

Where Have All the Grown-ups Gone?

Adam Bellow

ON JUNE 8, 1978, Aleksandr Solzhenitsyn accepted an honorary degree from Harvard University. I happened to be sitting in the audience watching a friend graduate when he delivered his famous commencement address, "A World Split Apart." The writer had come down for the occasion from his house in a remote part of Vermont—an exile within an exile that served to insulate him from the temptations and distractions of his adopted society.

My father also had a house in Vermont and spent the summers there in self-imposed seclusion with his manuscripts and books. For many years there was no television, and the paper often came a day late. Long walks in the woods and conversations in the overgrown garden were the only entertainment. In general I understood the need for this kind of artistic withdrawal. But Solzhenitsyn's was much more severe, and it hinted at an ascetic strain that seemed distinctly foreign to our open, confessional culture.

Some commentators felt that he should have embraced his new home and become a proper American, cheerfully making the rounds of talk shows and going to baseball games. After the Harvard speech, a lot of these people probably wished he had stayed home.

"The Western world has lost its civil courage," Solzhenitsyn declared in a tinny, far-off voice one strained to hear across the sea of folding chairs. It was a hot and humid day in Harvard Yard, and the graduates sat sweltering in their black commencement garb as the stern chronicler of the Soviet gulag, speaking in Russian with the aid of a translator, bitterly attacked them, along with their parents, teachers, political leaders, and pretty much the whole Western world. Solzhenitsyn accused the West of blind arrogance, of material abundance coupled with spiritual poverty. Acknowledging the wealth and security provided by the capitalist welfare states, he warned that such security would be addictive and enervating. He dourly indicted the mendacity of the press, the decadence of art, the mediocrity of our leaders, and the broad conformity of opinion imposed more by fashion than censorship. Sounding a lot like someone else I knew—my dad—he spoke of the "revolting invasion of publicity . . . TV stupor . . . intolerable music."

Worst of all, the gift of freedom had been abused and debased in the West: "Destructive and irresponsible freedom has been granted boundless space." This perversion of the doctrine of rights had grown out of a benevolent humanism whose hallmark was the denial of evil. But evil did exist and in fact had grown stronger as we grew weaker. "Facing such a danger, with such historical values in your past, at such a high level of realization of freedom and apparently of devotion to freedom, how is it possible to lose to such an extent the will to defend oneself?"

Few of the privileged elite in attendance that day could have guessed that they would be seized roughly by the neck and have their faces rubbed in the dirt by this distinguished foreign visitor. Instead of the flattery and thanks they undoubtedly thought they deserved for inviting him there in the first place, he delivered a deadly blow to the *amour-propre* of the Harvard establishment.

As for me, I squirmed a little uncomfortably in my seat as the indictment rolled on. I had been up late the night before and was a bit hung over from too much drinking and partying. Part of me was decidedly irked at having to listen to yet another Nobel Prize–winning writer declaim against the shallowness and superficiality of my generation. Surely I got enough of this at home. But part of me respected what he had to say and knew he had a point. We *were* less serious than our fathers' generation. That's why it was good to have these cranky old codgers around to bang on about freedom and tyranny.

Thirty years later I sat in exactly the same spot, proudly watching my own daughter graduate, listening to Energy Secretary Steven Chu trying to enlist the Class of 2009 in the Obama administration's fight for conservation and sustainable energy. I understood, of course, that young people long to be enlisted in the service of higher ideals and that concern about global climate change has become the test of moral seriousness for this generation. I had nothing against the pursuit of these goals and I admired the willingness of my daughter and her friends to take personal responsibility for saving the planet. But I couldn't help observing that in raising their sights so much higher, they were expressing a certain blithe assurance about the permanence of freedom. Growing up in a world where the Cold War was a distant memory, they took it even more for granted than we had.

I also couldn't help reflecting on the abrupt disappearance of the discourse about freedom and democracy that had preoccupied the noblest minds of the twentieth century. As the son of a writer much concerned with these grand themes, I had grown up at the margins of this high-flown international debate and was familiar with its cast of characters and basic vocabulary. The destiny of man, the needs of the soul, the fate of free societies—this was heady stuff to hear debated at the dinner table or over the morning paper, mixed in with Jewish jokes and family gossip. But for me it defined what it meant to be a serious person.

Who offers such warnings today? Which writers and intellectuals have taken upon themselves the defense of freedom on a high moral plane? Where have all the grown-ups gone? Those of us who came of age during those years might be forgiven for asking this question.

Of course, the older generation had an advantage we do not (if one can really call it that)—namely an acquaintance with history. For them the Cold War was a mesmerizing drama, a globe-spanning confrontation between freedom and tyranny. To keep a distracted public focused on these issues, they held conferences, gave interviews, edited magazines, wrote articles and books, and testified before congressional committees. Mere words, one might say. ("What did you do during the Cold War, Daddy?" "I edited *Commentary*.") But words matter when the war is, at bottom, a war of ideas.

Many of us assumed that there would always be such people on hand to make the case for freedom and democracy. The loss of many of these outsized intellectual and literary figures in the first decade of this century leaves one wondering whether there are still any grown-ups around.

But here is a sobering thought: merely to ask the question is to assume responsibility for embracing the task oneself. Resistance doesn't come out of nowhere; it has to be fostered the old-fashioned way, word by word, through magazines and books, think-tank panels, conferences, and seminars. We are the grown-ups now, and we owe it to the next generation to provide a model of how to be serious about ultimate questions. This collection is a tentative first step in that direction.

First, however, a few disclaimers are in order.

This is not your father's Cold War anthology. The Soviet Union is gone, the captive nations are free, and the imminent threat of nuclear extinction has retreated. To be sure, some of the old threats remain, in different forms. Thus, the specter of Islamic totalitarianism has replaced those of fascism and communism. We have also recently been reminded how much of our personal freedom depends on economic prosperity. But on the whole we are remarkably free from external threats of the kind that characterized most of the twentieth century.

The contributors to this volume have steered away as much as possible from the drumbeat of current events and tried to focus their gaze on the field of emerging threats, or on current challenges to freedom that seem likely to endure. There is some criticism of the present administration, though not in a partisan spirit but from the perspective of its commitment to promoting freedom around the world.

The result is very far from comprehensive. Indeed, in making our assignments, my Templeton colleagues and I have eschewed a systematic plan and trusted in the passion and conviction of our authors—and believe me, they are passionate. To read these essays one after another is to enter a series of highly individual worlds of emphatic and intelligent concern. Each of these authors has thought deeply about his or her chosen subject and has approached it in a very personal and sometimes idiosyncratic fashion. No doubt we have overlooked important aspects of the subject; I can think of a number of topics not covered here. But this collection makes no claim to be exhaustive. Instead it is a modest attempt to revive a discourse about freedom that has gone out of fashion and to foster a proper attitude of resistance to the forces that threaten it.

Every generation has to meet this challenge, and it is primarily an intellectual one: resistance (for that is the point of this exercise) necessarily begins with an effort to grasp and define the precise nature of the threats we confront. For it is the essence of self-government that we must, as individuals, make sense of the world we inhabit, even as it changes dramatically from decade to decade.

Introducing such a volume is a daunting task, and I hope I may be excused from the usual reflections on the nature and meaning of freedom. My role as editor is not to define what freedom is or plumb its philosophical depths. What I can say is that as a result of assigning and editing these essays, I have concluded that in our time, threats to freedom are much less visible and obvious than they were in the twentieth century and may even appear in the guise of social and political progress. Another way of putting this is to say that the greatest threats to freedom have migrated from the *external* to the *internal*. They still exist outside of us, but their power to limit our freedom often depends upon our failure or reluctance to notice them.

This book tries to make us aware of these new threats and addresses how they affect us both collectively and as individuals, for the defense of freedom (today more than ever) is the job of the individual. Especially in the absence of outstanding figures like Solzhenitsyn, whose personal sufferings conferred both the duty and the authority to speak of such things, we are now more or less on our own. Each of us must therefore accept responsibility for confronting the new threats to freedom, which are on the whole much more insidious than they were a few decades ago. As such, they require not only extra vigilance on our part, but a real effort even to see that they exist.

Another anecdote may illustrate this point.

A few years after Solzhenitsyn's Harvard speech, I happened to be walking through Soho, then in its infancy as New York's fashionable art district, and came across an unusual installation that occupied a large display window on lower Broadway. The window (easily twelve feet across and six feet high) contained what looked like a large classical edifice in ruins—broken columns, heaps of rubble, the remains of a marble façade slowly effaced by the passage of time. Affixed to the columns were yellowed bits of parchment containing fragments of flowing script which I instantly recognized as phrases from the U.S. Constitution.

It was then that I noticed the movement of thousands of ants, busily swarming up and down the columns and poking about in the rubble. Suddenly the point came home to me: America was like a great and noble edifice constructed by giants who had long since disappeared. We who remained had dwindled in size to the point where we could not even see what they had built, let alone read and comprehend their founding documents. Instead we crawled around in the ruins looking for food.

This visual tableau, which I am tempted to call "Swiftian" for the way it used differences in physical size to symbolize diminished moral stature, perfectly embodied Solzhenitsyn's observation that human characters in the West had been weakened, hollowed out, and in effect made less interesting by decades of security and comfort.

Luckily for us, Solzhenitsyn turned out to be wrong about the strength of the communist threat. A decade later the Soviet Union collapsed, and the West emerged triumphant. But some of his statements about Western triviality and decadence seem as accurate as ever, and many of the concerns he expressed are echoed in this volume. Indeed, if anything they appear to have grown worse in the intervening decades.

Take this, for instance: "The defense of individual rights has reached such extremes as to make society as a whole defenseless against certain individuals." Or this: "Hastiness and superficiality are the psychic disease of the twentieth century, and more than anywhere else this disease is reflected in the press." Or this especially timely observation: "When a government starts an earnest fight against terrorism, public opinion immediately accuses it of violating the terrorists' civil rights."

Most of all, Solzhenitsyn was surely correct that many people will not sacrifice a fraction of their freedom, even in the defense of freedom. Instead they cling to their comforts and burrow deeper into the security of their domestic lives and personalized media bubbles. None of us is immune to this hobbitlike temptation, and real effort will be required even to make ourselves aware that threats to freedom still exist, let alone take responsibility for confronting them.

Yet despite the seriousness of the task, this is not a gloomy book. To the contrary, there is liveliness and engagement and optimism here. Above all, there is a spirit of resistance—and resistance gives us energy and purpose. Much as we admire the old Cold Warriors and seek to continue their struggle, we feel no need to emulate their sometimes grim sobriety. And just as the triumph of the West on largely material grounds suggests that "Western materialism" should be retired as a term of opprobrium, maybe we can also have a defense of freedom that is a little less apocalyptic and a little more hopeful, a little more fun.

I would even go further and suggest that we respond to the various new and old threats to freedom today not with fear and anxiety or by hunkering down in a defensive and critical crouch, but with an exuberant affirmation and assertion and expression of our freedom in as many dimensions as possible. This is something everyone can do, and it is not only the best use of our freedom but the best way we have of repaying the gift.

New Threats to Freedom

The Decline of
American Press Freedom

Anne Applebaum

IN 1949, when George Orwell wrote his dystopian novel *1984*, he gave its hero, Winston Smith, a job at the Ministry of Truth. All day long, Winston clips politically unacceptable facts, stuffs them into little pneumatic tubes, and then pushes the tubes down a chute. Beside him sits a woman in charge of finding and erasing the names of people who have been "vaporized." And their office, Orwell wrote, "with its fifty workers or thereabouts, was only one sub-section, a single cell, as it were, in the huge complexity of the Records Department."

It's odd to read *1984* in 2010, because it makes one realize that the politics of Orwell's vision aren't at all outdated. There are still plenty of governments in the world that go to extraordinary lengths to shape what their citizens read, think, and say, just like Orwell's Big Brother. But the technology envisioned in *1984* is so—well—1980s. Paper? Pneumatic tubes? Nowadays, none of that is necessary: it can all be done electronically, or through telephone calls, or using commercial pressure. In the modern world, censorship can take many forms, even reaching across international boundaries. And it has already begun to affect the American press, and American publishing, far more than is commonly understood.

To see what I mean, look closely at a decision taken by Yale University Press in the summer of 2009. Deep in the month of August, its editors quietly issued a statement confirming that there would be a change to the content of one of their forthcoming books, *The Cartoons that Shook the World*. The book was a scholarly account of the international controversy that followed a Danish newspaper's 2005 publication of twelve cartoons depicting the Prophet Mohammed. The book contained a significant amount of new material. Among other things, the Danish author, Jytte Klausen, argued that the controversy had been manipulated by Danish imams who showed their followers false, sexually offensive depictions of Mohammed alongside the real ones, which were not inherently offensive at all.

She also argued that others—including the Egyptian government—used the cartoons to create "outrage" in the form of riots, boycotts, and anti-Danish protests, which they deployed for their own political ends. She consulted with several Muslim scholars who agreed that the protests were not evidence of authentic Muslim religious anger, but were rather political games. Later, she would write that she had "good reason" to believe that the publication of the cartoons need not have been interpreted offensively, and that republication of them by a scholarly press was not threatening or dangerous.

Nevertheless, the Yale press, "after careful consideration," decided not to publish the cartoons. In a statement, the normally independent press declared that it had consulted Yale University, and that the university had in turn consulted "counterterrorism officials in the United States and in the United Kingdom, U.S. diplomats who had served as ambassadors in the Middle East, foreign ambassadors from Muslim countries, the top Muslim official at the United Nations, and senior scholars in Islamic studies." To the intense disappointment of Klausen as well as of the book's original editor—who had himself consulted lawyers and who supported printing the book—the university decided that the risk of terrorism was too great to allow the publication of the twelve cartoons.

Predictably, a minor controversy ensued. Some Yale alumni, myself included, signed a letter of protest. The *New York Times* and others printed angry criticism. But the university stuck to its decision, citing fears of violence and possible terrorist attacks on the Yale campus. John Negroponte, former CIA director, former ambassador to Baghdad, and class of '60, even applauded the Yale press for its "brave" refusal to print the images.

Equally predictably, the story faded. But Yale's decision to bow to pressure from unnamed and unknowable terrorists has further consequences. Although there was no direct threat—just a fear that someone, someday, might present one—the university has now set a standard for others. Yale's press is one of the best in the country: if its editors won't publish the Danish cartoons, why should anyone else? Indeed, one of Yale's strongest and most frequently cited arguments for not publishing the cartoons was the fact that most major U.S. newspapers refused to publish them in 2005. Now the bar is higher: if not only the *New York Times*, not only the *Washington Post*, but even Yale University Press refuse to publish them, then that makes it much harder for anybody else to treat the cartoon controversy as a legitimate matter for scholarly and political debate.

But Yale's decision was not an unusual one either. On the contrary, it is only one of a number of recent incidents that illustrate the increasing power of illiberal groups and regimes—not only Islamic terrorists but authoritarian foreign governments and the companies aligned with them—to place de facto controls on American publishers, newspapers, and media companies, constraining once-sacred American rights to free speech, and once-inviolable American traditions of press freedom.

Indeed, the vague threat of "terrorism" is only one tool that foreign entities use to control free speech, and it is not necessarily the most powerful. Yale's decision attracted a good deal of attention, but in fact the university was merely cowardly. It thought it was acting in the interests of its students' safety. By contrast, the motives of other Americans who have lately tried to suppress information on behalf of foreign entities are often murkier.

A case in point is another decision, also taken in the summer of 2009. At that time, *GQ* magazine was debating whether it should publish an article titled "Vladimir Putin's Dark Rise to Power," by Scott Anderson. The article, based on extensive reporting, argued that Russian security services had helped plan and execute a series of bomb explosions in Moscow in 2000. These explosions, which killed dozens of people, were blamed on Chechen terrorists. Subsequently, then-Russian president Vladimir Putin also used the explosions as a justification for the launch of the second Chechen war.

So conveniently timed were these terrorist attacks, in fact, that even at the time many in Moscow suspected the secret services had a hand in them, and much circumstantial evidence is available to support this thesis. Nevertheless, in Russia, discussion of this evidence remains officially taboo. Obviously, if Russian special forces acting on the authority of the Russian president were involved in killing Russian citizens, this is a very controversial matter indeed.

Eventually, Anderson's article making this case did appear in the September 2009 American edition of the magazine, but not anywhere else. Condé Nast, the U.S. media company that owns *GQ*, banned the article from appearing in the magazine's Russian edition, banned it from appearing in other foreign editions, and banned it from appearing on any Condé Nast website. In addition, the company ordered all of its magazines and affiliates around the world— magazines such as the *New Yorker* and *Wired*, among others—to refrain from mentioning or promoting the article in any way. In an e-mail sent to senior editors and later quoted by National Public Radio, company lawyers even forbade company employees to physically carry the U.S. edition of the magazine into Russia or to show it to any Russian government officials, journalists, or advertisers.

Clearly, Condé Nast's motives had nothing to do with security, and everything to do with Russian advertisers, many of whom are one way or another linked to the Russian government. And of course the company was made to look foolish: within days, Anderson's article was scanned, translated, and published in English and Russian on multiple websites. But perhaps that didn't matter. What Condé Nast seems to have wanted was to appear to be groveling before their Russian subscribers and advertisers.

In this, they succeeded. And, as in the case of Yale's decision, Condé Nast's humiliating act of self-censorship sets a precedent. If one of the largest and richest media companies in the country is not willing to take the chance of offending Putin, why should anyone else? The same, of course, is true for Russians: if American journalists writing about Russia in American publications cannot feel confident that their work will be supported, why should Russians, who risk so much more, feel any braver? Ultimately, a tame, censored Russian press is a disaster for the American companies that work in Russia and Americans who live there, since such a press will not dare to expose the culture of corruption that makes doing business in Russia so difficult for foreigners. But clearly, Condé Nast wasn't thinking that far down the line.

None of these flirtations with censorship compares, however, with the lengths to which American companies have been persuaded to go in aiding and abetting censorship in China. Once upon a time, visionaries predicted that, in the twenty-first century, authoritarian and totalitarian regimes would no longer be able to operate, so overwhelmed would they be by the flood of free information available on the Internet. China in particular was often cited as the perfect example, a place where free markets would bring free information that would ultimately destroy the communist regime.

If it hasn't worked out that way, the fault lies partly in the decisions of some of America's best-known media and software companies, many of which have collaborated with the Chinese government's increasingly sophisticated Internet censorship regime for much of the past decade. In fact, the "Great Firewall," the vast Chinese Internet filter, was originally created with the help of Cisco Systems, an American company. Among other things, Cisco provided the Chinese government with technology designed to block traffic to individual pages within a particular website, so that you can read about Tibet's architectural heritage and never know you missed the description of the Dalai Lama at all. Cisco shows no remorse: in a 2005 interview, a company spokesman told me that this is the "same equipment technology that your local library uses to block pornography," and besides, "We're not doing anything illegal."

Others have also complied. Since 2002, Yahoo! has been voluntarily controlling its own search engine in China. The company signed a "public pledge of self-discipline" when it entered the Chinese market, in exchange for being allowed to place its servers on the Chinese mainland. At around the same time, Microsoft agreed to alter the Chinese version of its blog tool, MSN Spaces, at the behest of the Chinese government. In practice, this means that Chinese bloggers who try to post a forbidden word—"Tiananmen," say, or "democracy"—receive a warning stating that "this message contains a banned expression, please delete."

After much agonizing, mighty Google also joined them. The company had been operating a Chinese version of google.com, with U.S.-based servers, for many years. But the service was difficult for ordinary Chinese users to access, so in 2006, the company decided to launch Google.cn. In order to be allowed to do so, it too pledged to abide by Chinese rules on banned websites. Anywhere else in the world, type the name of "Falun Gong," the banned Chinese spiritual movement, into Google, and thousands of results, chat rooms, and blogs turn up. On Google.cn, "Falun Gong" produces nothing.

What has been the result of this American compliance with Chinese edicts? Far from appeasing the regime, it appears to have emboldened the Chinese government to expand its censorship program. Pressure has been put on individual companies: in 2005, the Chinese government demanded that Yahoo! hand over the e-mail account information of a Chinese journalist who had leaked documents to a U.S.-based website—documents describing Chinese restrictions on media coverage of the fifteenth anniversary of the Tiananmen Square uprising. Yahoo! agreed to help; the journalist received a ten-year jail sentence for "leaking state secrets."

At about the same time, the Chinese government also demanded that Microsoft delete the writings of a free-speech advocate from its blog software. Microsoft complied with this request also, even though the company's servers are based in the United States. In other words, a Chinese government demand had forced an American company to change information on American servers based on American soil, possibly setting a precedent.

Since then, pressure has expanded over the system as a whole. Throughout 2009, U.S. sites such as YouTube (owned by Google) or Flickr (owned by Yahoo!) suddenly and inexplicably disappeared from Chinese servers, usually at a time when some politically sensitive event was taking place in China. (YouTube could not be viewed in China for many months, for example, after videos of Chinese soldiers beating Uighur demonstrators in the rebellious province of Xinjiang began to circulate on the service.)

More generalized harassment has also been directed at Google, which in the summer of 2009 was accused of "spreading pornography." As a result, both of its sites, google.cn and google.com in Chinese, were completely blocked. Off the record, the company suspects that the real source of these accusations is its main Chinese competitor, Baidu, which of course benefits directly whenever Google suffers from technical difficulties. But in the murky and corrupt world of Chinese business and politics—made murkier and more corrupt by the lack of a completely free press—this accusation was difficult to prove.

In June 2009, the Chinese made an attempt to go even further. The government issued orders requiring all personal computers sold in the country to include a special form of filtering software, Green Dam, designed to filter out "unhealthy information" from the Internet. Allegedly aimed, once again, at "pornography," the software would have allowed the government to access its citizens' individual computers, preventing them from reading a constantly updated list of banned websites. It would also have allowed the government to monitor the browsing habits of individuals. "It's like downloading spyware onto your computer," one Hong Kong Internet expert explained, "but the government is the spy."

Full of bugs, and liable to freeze screens, Green Dam would have made all personal computers more difficult to use in general. As if that were not enough, the time allotted to load the software onto new computers was very short—the original deadline gave manufacturers one month—which presented enormous technical problems to any hardware company selling in China. Nevertheless, two companies—Lenovo, based in China, and Acer, based in Taiwan—complied.

In this case, however, the U.S. companies—computer hardware

companies this time, and not merely makers of software and search engines—decided to fight back. Acting as a group, they went to the U.S. trade representative and the commerce secretary, who in turn protested to the Chinese government and threatened to take the issue to the World Trade Organization. After a few weeks, the Chinese government backed off. Although Green Dam remains mandatory in Chinese schools and in Internet cafes, personal computers are not forced to use it—at least not yet. But although that story ended more or less happily, it is worth pausing for a moment to imagine what would have happened had those U.S. companies not banded together, and had they not protested the Chinese government's demands. The software would have been loaded; everyone in China would eventually be forced to use a computer containing government spyware; and the Chinese government would have been strengthened, once again, in its resolve to force foreign companies to collaborate in the mass censorship and limitations on free speech that it places on its own people. U.S. companies would have maintained their ability to sell in China, but over time might well have lost out to the Chinese companies, which are more willing to work closely with the Chinese government to get the results it wants.

And, in the winter of 2010, another crisis showed exactly how this can and will happen: in January, Google announced its intention to pull out of China altogether. The company said that it had been subject to an extraordinary series of cyber-attacks, aimed at entering and spying on the company's servers—as well as gaining access to the email accounts of Chinese and Tibetan dissidents. The company decided to take a principled stand on the issue: its CEO, Eric Schmidt, told *Newsweek* that "this was not a business decision." But, in fact, it was not clear whether Google's announcement was made for moral reasons, or because Chinese cyberhacks threaten the company's critical intellectual property—software codes, documents—as well as its reputation for security.

As of this writing, Google's final decision had not been made, and the company said it was talking to the Chinese government. But the dramatic announcement, coupled with the "Green Dam" fiasco do make one thing clear: large American companies still have the power and strength to challenge the Chinese government, at least when they act together—or at least when they have the size and strength of Google. As the cases of Yale University Press and Condé Nast well illustrate, smaller American companies no longer necessarily have this power, or at least they do not have the courage to find out whether they do. For the record, I note that weakness in the face of rich authoritarians is not an exclusively American trait: the Finnish company Nokia and the German company Siemens have sold cell phone monitoring and silencing equipment to the Iranian government. But the American corporate involvement in China is broader and deeper than that of almost any other country.

I don't want to imply, by discussing all of these stories together, that they are exactly the same. Many nuances exist. Yale does seem to have agonized over its decision not to publish the cartoons; Google, too, has publicly agonized over how it should operate in China, and has argued in the past that at the very least the company can provide Chinese consumers with *more* information, if not *complete* information. Nevertheless, these stories do point, more generally, to something new: even a decade ago it would have been hard to imagine an American university press refusing to print something out of fear of foreign terrorism, or that a large and respectable American company would agree to participate in mass censorship at all.

Indeed, two decades ago, even three and four decades ago, the American press had a reputation for standing up to totalitarian regimes. Moscow correspondents for American newspapers regularly investigated, and then printed, stories that infuriated the governments of the Soviet Union and the Warsaw Pact; as a result, Eastern European dissidents sought out American correspondents. In 1972, *New York Times* correspondent Hedrick Smith and *Washington Post* correspondent Robert Kaiser conducted the historic first interview with Aleksandr Solzhenitsyn. In 1984, another *New York Times* correspondent hosted a party in Warsaw for Adam Michnik, one of the country's most notorious dissidents, on the occasion of his release from jail. Their bosses knew about these escapades, and approved: when Nick Daniloff, a correspondent for *U.S. News and World Report* was arrested and accused of spying in Moscow, the magazine retained former Secretary of State Cyrus Vance as defense attorney; Daniloff remembers getting "great support" from Mortimer Zuckerman, the owner of the magazine. There was no suggestion of conforming to the demands of these totalitarian regimes. Why should there be?

But the world has changed, the financial power of illiberal regimes has grown, the reach of international terrorism stretches further than it once did, and globalization has some unexpected consequences. Among other things, globalization means that consumers of the luxury goods so expensively advertised in Condé Nast magazines increasingly do not live in the United States—hence, the company's need to tailor its content to the tastes of the rich in Russia, China, the Gulf States, and other parts of the world that do not respect the rights of the free press or admire American traditions of investigative journalism. The kinds of pressures put on newspaper owners are much different from what they used to be.

This shift represents a major cultural change, and it is not one that a law or congressional resolution can correct. On the contrary, the only solution to the new threats to American press freedom lies in organized resistance, as in the case of the Chinese software edicts, and in the widening of debate on this growing threat. Talking and writing help, since many of these decisions are easy enough to justify on an individual basis. But companies confronted by the long-term consequences of their refusals to publish may eventually come to think differently. Sergey Brin, one of Google's founders, said even before the 2010 announcement that it was "a mistake" for Google to enter China, partly because of the continued pressure the company has experienced, but also partly because of the negative consequences on Google's image in its most important market, the United States. A company that once claimed its motto was "Don't Be Evil" proved itself willing at least to dabble in some very evil practices—and, as it turned out, subjected itself to serious security threats as well.

Fortunately, still enough Americans were committed to the principle of free speech to point this out. The more these issues are debated and discussed, in the U.S. media as well as in Congress, the more likely that companies will think twice before making the wrong choices. Attacks on press freedom have always been best countered with more press freedom. That, at least, hasn't yet changed.

2

The Closing of the Liberal Mind

Bruce Bawer

RECENTLY I WAS interviewed by telephone on an American radio program. Its host was a proud self-styled liberal who begins every show with a recorded rant about the evils of conservatism and the menace of the Christian right. I was there to talk about the dangers of Islam in the West, and I tried to make the point that when it came to threatening the liberal values he presumably held so dear, many respected Muslims in America and Europe make even the most toxic members of the Christian right look like amateurs. But he wouldn't listen. I told him about the Euro-Islamic "intellectual" and liberal darling Tariq Ramadan (of whom he had never heard), who has refused to reject the Koranic punishment of stoning adulteresses to death. But the host did his best to talk over me and dismiss the whole topic. I began to describe how life in Amsterdam, over the last decade, has become hell for gay people because of predatory Muslim youth gangs who know that according to the teachings of Islam homosexuals deserve to be killed. "So don't go to Amsterdam!" airily quipped the host (who himself is gay). Indeed, this man who routinely talks in apocalyptic terms about the perils of the Christian right dismissed categorically the notion that Islam might represent any kind of danger at all to anything he valued.

Note well: he didn't have any counterarguments; he didn't dispute my facts; he *simply didn't want to hear the facts.* After the interview, he made a sneering comment on the air to the effect that I'd been "picking on a minority," then took a call from a listener whom he plainly expected to agree with him but who—to my surprise and gratitude—chewed him out for having refused to let me have my say.

A few months earlier, I had gone to Washington, D.C., to speak about the same topic at a conference attended by State Department officials and foreign diplomats. This talk was far from the first I'd given about the subject. I had spoken to audiences around Europe—audiences of ordinary citizens who know what is going on around them, are concerned, and were receptive to my message. Not so the diplomats in D.C. From the moment I began to talk, I sensed resistance. The Q&A session instantly became a ritual of mass denial. One diplomat after another stood up to denounce me. I felt just a tad like the defendant at a Stalinist show trial. My talk had consisted totally of unquestionable facts—events that had happened in the West over the previous year or two which demonstrated that liberal values were being sold out in the name of multicultural sensitivity. But these diplomats sputtered with rage at me for having dared to recount these occurrences. They didn't deny the facts; they just didn't want to hear them. "These are just *anecdotes*!" one diplomat raged, as his colleagues nodded—seething, it seemed, at reality itself.

This was a roomful of people upon whose understanding of the world the safety and well-being of humankind depend. And yet their minds, like the mind of that radio interviewer, were quite simply closed to certain facts.

They aren't alone. Today, millions of self-styled liberals have closed their minds to aspects of reality that challenge their ideology—an ideology that is, in fact, radically *illiberal*. There are, as it happens, certain home truths about the world today that are utterly inconsistent with what passes for twenty-first-century American liberalism, and that threaten the self-images of people for whom being liberal means, among other things, being an orthodox multiculturalist. And for all too many twenty-first-century American liberals, alas, politics and self-image are intimately intertwined. Rather than endure a profound and disorienting ideological self-examination, many self-styled liberals have chosen to close their minds to plain facts—thus keeping intact their ideology, their self-image, and their self-satisfaction and contentment. This closed-mindedness is nothing less than terrifying.

Times have changed. A century ago, both the great Republican of the day, Theodore Roosevelt, and the leading Democrat of the age, Woodrow Wilson, were categorized as progressives. After World War II, leading major politicians in both parties were essentially in accord on vital questions. Yes, there were always extremists: on one side the fellow travelers and even outright Communists (Henry Wallace and *New York Times* correspondent Walter Duranty come to mind), and on the other the John Birchers. (At that time, of course, when southern reactionaries were Democrats, the far right was a bipartisan phenomenon.) But the intellectual leadership of both parties consisted of men who considered themselves, in some sense, liberals. The men who served as president during the three decades after World War II—the Democrats Truman, Kennedy, and Johnson, and the Republicans Eisenhower, Nixon, and Ford—all recognized Communism as a danger to freedom and the free world, terms they used without irony. NATO was introduced under Truman; JFK described the Soviet Union as "a slave state . . . embarked upon a program of world aggression." To listen now to the 1960 Kennedy-Nixon debates is to see two men between whom there was not a hairsbreadth of difference on the issue of Communism. All of these presidents also recognized America's racial injustice as a problem—and a threat to America's image abroad. Eisenhower, for example, supported *Brown v. Board of Education* and signed into law the Civil Rights Acts of 1957 and 1960.

Congress, too, saw the world as it was. When I think back to the men who dominated the Senate when I was a boy, I think of Everett Dirksen of Illinois, a Republican who staunchly supported the Vietnam War—but who also helped write such landmark civil rights legislation as the Civil Rights Act of 1964 and the Open Housing Act of 1968. Another leading Republican, New York's Jacob Javits, also supported LBJ's civil rights and Great Society initiatives. New York's Daniel Patrick Moynihan was a Democrat—indeed a liberal lion— but was also a strong anti-Communist and an influential critic of welfare policies that encouraged dependency. (For him, those views were not antithetical to liberalism; on the contrary, they were, in his view, part and parcel of his liberalism.) Then there was Henry Jackson, a state of Washington Democrat who was very strong on national defense and who in 1974 fiercely opposed Nixon's policy of détente with the Kremlin, arguing that the United States should stand foursquare not only for Americans' but also for the Russian people's freedom.

For men like these, being a liberal—being an *American*—meant standing up for freedom, both at home and abroad, against every form of oppression and totalitarianism. Part of what kept men of honor on both the left and right from being too far apart on this question during most of the late twentieth century was that the majority of them were veterans who had fought Nazism, fascism, and Meiji imperialism in World War II. Resisting Soviet Communism during the Cold War was only a natural extension of that effort on behalf of human freedom.

They were liberals, in short, in the sense that the United States of America itself is a liberal phenomenon—the original liberal state, the first nation to be founded explicitly on the principle of individual liberty and on the idea that governments derive their legitimacy from the consent of the governed. And even if nineteenth-century America, say, represented something considerably short of a perfect realization of the constitutional ideal, the history of the Republic, from that era straight on until a time within living memory, was in large part a history of the increasing realization of the promise of universal liberty enshrined in the Republic's founding documents. In this sense, leading mid-twentieth-century Americans of all stripes plainly saw themselves as upholders of liberal values—of values that we would now identify as classical liberal values—because constitutional values *were* liberal values.

That was then.

Fast forward past the race riots of the 1960s and 1970s, past Vietnam, Watergate, Carter, Reagan, Bush the elder, and Clinton, and fade in on September 11, 2001. A new generation is at the helm. On a sunny morning, America is viciously attacked by religious totalitarians—and the response of all too many self-styled liberals is to blame America. For some, the blame-America rhetoric comes easily and reflexively, the words beginning to form themselves even as the towers are falling. Others, however, after an initial flush of natural human anger at the attackers, gradually recognize the implications of this jihadist assault and recoil from the ancient, alien values to which they feel themselves being summoned—honor, responsibility, commitment, sacrifice—as well as from the grim and overwhelming fact that American freedom is once again under serious assault and needs defending. Not that this retreat is difficult for them; on the contrary, it is rooted in the very mind-set on which they were raised.

For unlike Truman and Ike, JFK and Nixon, Moynihan and Jackson, Javits and Dirksen, they are the children of the New Left of the 1960s and '70s. In its time, of course, the New Left was—politically—a marginal phenomenon. Yes, it was sufficiently powerful a force to divide the Democratic Party and lose elections for them, but it was far from strong enough to even come close to winning the presidency. The one Democratic presidential nominee prior to 9/11 who can unquestionably be identified as a member of the New Left was George McGovern, whom Nixon beat in a landslide.

But while the New Left never won the White House, many of its young members, as they grew into middle age, came to wield extraordinary cultural and educational influence. They conquered Hollywood; they moved into the academy. Veterans of groups like the SDS (Students for a Democratic Society) became high-school teachers and professors of history and social science and set about inculcating students in New Left values. And as an older generation of educators retired, and were replaced by the disciples of their New Left colleagues—who were now the Establishment—the victory became complete and the message unitary and unchallenged. Meanwhile the takeover of Hollywood proceeded apace. Beginning in the 1970s and '80s, films that treated Communists with admiration and made heroes out of the victims of the Hollywood blacklist became common. One Hollywood picture after another left historyless young audiences convinced that Joe McCarthy had been the most dangerous man of the 1950s (forget Stalin) and that America's actions in Vietnam had been the most inhuman atrocities in history; meanwhile, films like *Three Days of the Condor* and their progeny, right up to the recent Jason Bourne series, encouraged a paranoia about the U.S. government, and especially the CIA, that was straight out of the New Left playbook. Over the decades, this paranoia gradually became the default Hollywood posture toward the U.S. government, so that young people were increasingly fed a diet of films whose politics liberals and conservatives alike would have considered absolutely repulsive at the height of the Cold War.

Among the outlooks served up to young people was the New Left's deep-seated suspiciousness toward anti-Communism. Why be so concerned about the alleged evils of the USSR, after all, when the real danger to the world's well-being was the United States of America? If the bedrock tenet of Cold-War liberals had been that the United States, for all its failings, was on the whole a massive force for good in the world, young people who went to school and college and movies in the closing decades of the twentieth century unwittingly imbibed a directly antithetical philosophy. Even the fall of Communism in Europe—and the obvious satisfaction of Eastern Europeans at their liberation—made little impression on the products of the New Left's comprehensive indoctrination. Communism, schmommunism: Americans under a certain age had been taught that the greatest evil in the world was racism, and that the United States, exterminator of Native Americans and enslaver of Africans, took second place to no other nation in the extent to which racism poisoned the very blood in its veins. And as European Communism faded into the past, America produced a generation of young people whose ignorance of and indifference to the reality of Stalin and the gulag reached unprecedented levels—as reflected in their increasing eagerness to don Che Guevara T-shirts, hammer-and-sickle caps, and the like. These were, note well, not activists, radicals, neo-hippies, neo-SDSers; they were just ordinary, run-of-the-mill, young turn-of-the-century Americans, many of whom would doubtless describe themselves as relatively apolitical.

When 9/11 happened, then, their reactions were predictable enough. They had been bred to be suspicious of the United States and its military, to have no particular respect or appreciation for American liberty, to equate totalitarianism (if the word meant anything to them at all) not with any political system abroad—especially not in places where the people were poor and dark-skinned—but with America, Washington, the Pentagon. When they saw America invading Muslim countries, they didn't see a free country defending its freedoms from patriarchal tyrants; they saw an imperial hyperpower acting like a racist bully.

To be sure, when the United States invaded Afghanistan, while some on the left railed about American warmongering, others sat by and waited to see what happened—many of them inhibited by the fact that the United States enjoyed the support of the United Nations and the participation of a broad coalition of Western powers. Then the United States invaded Iraq—and hordes of self-styled liberals, rather than simply questioning the strategic wisdom of this decision (a thoroughly legitimate position), demonized the United States, its president, and its troops while finding nice things to say about Saddam Hussein, a totalitarian monster if ever there was one. The "liberal" mentality of the moment was reflected in such epiphenomena as the popular anthology *Poets against the War*, throughout which the idea that America might be in any way preferable to Saddam's Iraq was consistently ridiculed: one poet sneered about "the myth of democracy"; another asked, "Who are the Good Guys now? Who are the bad?"; another called America "this place that has spit on everything I know to live." By contrast, the poets' images of life in Saddam's Iraq were uniformly idyllic: "She rises in the glow of a red sun / to make strong coffee. . . . She sits / drinking slowly, beneath her lime tree." To the mass graves and child prisons, the good "liberals" of twenty-first-century America had closed their minds entirely.

So the first decade of the new millennium rolled along. Mahmoud Ahmadinejad, another bloodthirsty dictator, spoke at Columbia University and was applauded by New York liberals who compared him favorably to Bush the younger. And as Russia sank back into brutal despotism, and North Korea rattled its sabers, and Iran inched closer to nuclear-strike capacity, and China and Burma tortured human-rights activists, and Saudi Arabia and Syria funded terrorists, and Iran executed gays, and Sudan committed mass genocide, and Western Europe steadily morphed into a province of the Islamic world, with what were the bright-eyed young "liberals" all preoccupied? The rights violations purportedly taking place at Guantanamo, an American camp for jihadist prisoners of war, and a few instances of abuse of jihadist inmates by U.S. soldiers at the Abu Ghraib prison in Baghdad. To criticize Zimbabwean "president" Robert Mugabe's dictatorship in the presence of many a twenty-first-century American liberal was to be a racist; to bad-mouth Venezuela's Hugo Chávez— to their minds, like Fidel Castro, a hero of the people—was to be a champion of Yankee imperialism south of the border.

The closing of the liberal mind has its roots in the 1960s and '70s. But it took 9/11 for it to go fully mainstream and to become the default attitude on the left. Not until after 9/11 did American liberals, en masse, pull the shades, close the blinds, turn up the music, and choose to pretend that what was happening out there was not really happening at all. Not until after 9/11 did the average American liberal, confronted with a totalitarian enemy every bit as appalling as the Soviet Union, retreat into willful ignorance.

To get a sense of how widespread a phenomenon the closing of the liberal mind has become, all you need to do is watch any episode of *The Daily Show* with Jon Stewart or *Real Time with Bill Maher*. What's most revealing about these shows is not the hosts or guests or comedy bits; it's the audience response. The audiences, composed almost entirely of people who consider themselves liberals, follow very strict rules about what does and does not draw a laugh. The criteria are purely ideological. They won't brook any witticism that takes a jab at Obama, however gentle, even if told by Stewart or Maher, both strong Obama supporters. Conversely, they will laugh at any joke, however easy and cheap, whose point is that Sarah Palin is the world's biggest idiot or that Dick Cheney is evil incarnate. They will reflexively cheer any guest who makes a statement, however foolish or obvious, that falls into what they know to be P.C. territory; they will reflexively boo or hiss at anyone who says something, even if demonstrably 100 percent factual, that falls into the category of Uncomfortable Truths They Know They Are Not Supposed to Acknowledge.

9/11 was a test for the baby-boom and post-baby-boom generations. They failed. Talk about freedom, and they'll look at you with a condescending smirk. Criticize Islamic ideology, and they'll grow visibly uncomfortable at being in the presence of such bigotry. Talk to them about responsibility and sacrifice, and they will look at you as if you are some out-of-touch old codger or some character out of the *Iliad.* They call themselves liberals, but they have effectively aligned themselves with the most illiberal regimes on the planet.

The radicalism of this transformation cannot be overstated. Americans are, or used to be, a pragmatic people. They were never, in considerable numbers, captives of *any* fact-defying ideology. What mattered was the testimony of their senses; what mattered was getting things done, making things better, solving problems, figuring out what worked and what didn't. Whether they called themselves liberals or conservatives mattered infinitely less than the fact that they shared this sensible, practical, eyes-wide-open approach to the world. But today the ideological malady that afflicted the most extreme of 1960s radicals has infected millions of rank-and-file Democrats. The refusal to acknowledge the facts on the ground because they conflict with political correctness, with multiculturalism, with orthodox New Left ideology, is a phenomenon that has deep roots but that came into full bloom only after 9/11. Yes, there were people like Michael Moore in the last third of the twentieth century—radicals who poured out crude, bilious rhetoric in which America was always the villain and the "other" always the hero and/or victim— and they were heroes to a relatively limited segment of the younger generation and to the radical chic crowd (the Leonard Bernsteins, the

Jane Fondas); but they didn't write truth-defying books that became number one best sellers and they didn't make outrageously dishonest documentaries that broke box-office records. Now they do. For there are millions out there who have closed their minds, and who are eager to listen to, and vote for, anyone who congratulates them for doing so.

3

The New Dogma of Fairness

Peter Berkowitz

IN 1980, the Democrats' platform declared, "The Democratic Party has long stood for an active, responsive, vigorous government. . . . In all of our economic programs, the one overriding principle must be fairness." Almost three decades later, on the campaign trail in 2008, candidate Obama frequently invoked fairness to justify raising taxes on the wealthy and correcting policies that benefited Wall Street at the expense of Main Street. As he explained in Ohio in October of that year to Samuel Joseph Wurzelbacher, soon to be known across the country as Joe the Plumber, "When you spread the wealth around, it's good for everybody."

Accordingly, progressives insist on fairness in housing and health care. But progressives hardly believe that the requirements of fairness are exhausted by governmental regulation of the market and redistribution of wealth. Fairness, they further contend, requires government to protect an expansive right to abortion, to pursue an aggressive affirmative-action program, to promptly legalize same-sex marriage, to drastically reduce worldwide carbon emissions, and, of course, to reform health care by placing one-sixth of the nation's economy under federal supervision.

In short, fairness is the name progressives have given their chief political goal. Indeed, they seem to believe that fairness and progressivism are one and the same. This rhetorical and intellectual conflation has consequences. By imposing on a concept that seeks to stand above partisanship an exclusively partisan meaning, progressives exacerbate political polarization and compound the difficulties of thinking accurately and speaking clearly about freedom's presuppositions.

Fairness is among our simplest and most complex concepts. Little children are quick to understand and demand it even as the wisest never cease grappling with its implications. In a liberal democracy, opinions about fairness are inextricably bound up with beliefs about freedom, or the rights that all citizens equally share. Keeping claims about fairness and freedom in harmony is, for a liberal democracy, an abiding political challenge. Over the last forty years, however, the new dogma of fairness championed by progressives has increasingly gained currency in America and threatened the balance.

The new dogma holds that fairness has comprehensive public policy implications that can be derived from theory and which enjoy the status of truths of reason. Fairness's concrete content of invariably turns out to be progressive, requiring greater state action, particularly through government regulation of economic life and the redistribution of income, to ensure a more substantive equality among citizens. This dogma has been elaborated abundantly in scholarly books and articles over the last several decades and has become solidly entrenched as conventional wisdom in the academy.

The trouble does not consist in bringing considerations of fairness to bear on the rough-and-tumble of democratic politics. When all is said and done, fairness is another name for justice, or giving each his or her due. Rather, the trouble is that the new fairness doctrine masks the complications and dissolves the controversies that surround the application of our convictions about justice to politics. It does this by equating a single debatable interpretation of fairness with justice, delegitimating alternative interpretations as unreasonable, and suppressing empirical considerations vital to the formulation of responsible public policy. A good start in restoring the balance can be made by appreciating the controversies embedded in claims about fairness.

Even before we can begin to teach fairness to them formally, children seem already to have acquired a rudimentary understanding of it. "Me" and "mine" are invariably among their first words. And of course what toddlers, or grown-ups for that matter, believe to be theirs they believe belongs to them of right, regardless of whether they can articulate the theory—from might makes right to giving each one's due—that underlies their claims.

Children are especially keen to get what they believe they deserve and to demand that they get treated equally or that other kids not receive more of some good thing than they do. Parents and teachers build on this moral sense to socialize and civilize children. That the fundamental ideas about fairness that come easily to children reflect enduring principles facilitates the process. That the fundamental ideas often conflict, because children sometimes deserve different things, unavoidably complicates it.

Furthermore, children tend to apply their fundamental ideas about fairness in self-serving ways. The young demand what they deserve except when they deserve something bad, or when equal treatment would get them more than they deserve. And they insist on equal treatment except when they believe they deserve something special, or equal treatment would leave them with less than others. The anger and resentment that frequently accompany children's demand for fairness is understandable. Fairness implies a universal and objective standard, but sometimes it can't be met. In addition, children invoke it selectively, out of self-interest, to get more good things or fewer bad things for themselves. Children's abuse of the term dramatizes the temptation to make unreasonable and unfair demands for fairness.

If all goes well, we learn as we grow older to apply the requirements of fairness, to ourselves and to others, in a reasonable and fair or adult manner. Ascent to the adult perspective begins with seeing things from others' point of view. Eventually it involves an appreciation that determining who deserves what and ascertaining the shape and content of equal treatment frequently depend on shifting circumstances, complex calculations, and subtle judgments. At the core of the adult view is the understanding that "desert" and "equality" are open to a variety of reasonable interpretations, and that reasonable interpretations of both can bring them into sharp conflict.

Put differently, justice involves, as Aristotle observed, treating like cases alike and different cases differently. The difficulty consists in knowing what counts as a like case and what counts as a different one, or, what factors are morally relevant to classifying cases properly. If eight-year-old Tony is allowed to stay up until nine o'clock, isn't it only fair that twin sister Abby also be allowed? But what if Abby requires more sleep than Tony in order to get up for school in the morning? And if Abby is allowed to have a fudge brownie for dessert, doesn't fairness require that Tony be allowed one, too? But what if Abby eats all her vegetables and is slender and fit as a fiddle and Tony prefers pasta and pizza and is pudgy and out of shape? As most any parent can attest, achieving fairness in the family is an endless and exasperating task. How much more endless and exasperating will be the task in a continent-spanning nation of more than 300 million citizens that promises freedom and equality to all?

To be sure, fairness in the family and fairness in politics differ in crucial respects. Citizens are not family members. But for both fairness involves treating like cases alike and different cases differently, along with the host of challenges that arise in identifying the factors relevant to properly distinguishing the like cases from the unlike ones. And both require the reconciliation of competing principles— giving each what he or she deserves and treating each equally—at the heart of our conception of fairness.

In a liberal democracy, in which both conservatives and progressives affirm the bedrock principles of individual freedom and equality before the law, questions about fairness inevitably revolve around the kinds of freedom the state will safeguard and the kinds of equality the state will guarantee. Answers tend to divide along partisan lines.

While conservatives emphasize freedom and progressives stress equality, in practice the divisions are not always clear-cut, in part because conservatives also cherish formal equality and because progressives are devoted to individual freedom in a variety of spheres. Conservatives generally think government should interfere as little as possible with individual freedom, particularly religious, political, and economic freedom; that the equality that the state is charged with protecting consists in impartial treatment under the law; and that firm limits should be maintained on the measures government may undertake to protect citizens from misfortune and their own foolish conduct. Progressives, for the most part, think that economic freedom should be aggressively regulated; that the state must guarantee a high level of substantive equality, even if it means compromising freedom by limiting choice and personal responsibility; and to do so the state must substantially redistribute wealth so that all the citizens enjoy a certain minimum level of material well-being and financial security.

The contest between the conservative understanding of fairness or justice and the progressive view cannot be settled once and for all within the terms posed by liberal democracy because both draw on intuitions and principles fundamental to liberal democracy. The new dogma of fairness, however, is determined to end the debate. It seeks to accomplish this by reducing fairness to the progressive interpretation, and by devising stratagems to suppress and silence rather than engage the conservative perspective.

One could see such a stratagem at work in the recent talk about reviving the federal policy known as the Fairness Doctrine. Introduced in 1949, at a time when access to the airwaves was severely limited, it served a salutary purpose, requiring broadcasters to air both sides of controversial political issues. In the past few years, however, congressional Democrats have publicly contemplated bringing it back on the grounds that conservative dominance of talk radio must be balanced by left-leaning talk radio. Of course in the age of cable TV, satellite radio, the Internet, blogging, Facebook, and Twitter, the original reason for the Fairness Doctrine—the scarcity of opportunities for broadcast to the public—has disappeared. Progressives' barely disguised intention in contemplating the revival of the Fairness Doctrine was to weaken their right-wing adversaries where they were prevailing in a competitive market, and strengthen left-wing allies through government restrictions on consumers' choices.

Progressives' determination to co-opt the word "fairness" exclusively for the progressive political agenda has a history. The appeal to greater fairness became a familiar refrain in post-1960s America. By the end of the 1970s, progressives led by Jimmy Carter had managed to define the Democrats as the party of fairness. Certainly, the left took the lead in passing laws—the 1964 Civil Rights Act and the 1965 Voting Rights Act—obliging the federal government to ensure more energetically that individual rights, especially of minorities and women, were respected. Through LBJ's Great Society programs, progressives placed themselves at the forefront of government efforts to meet the needs of the poor, the sick, and the elderly.

At the same time, in the name of fairness, progressives effected a transformation in the meaning of equality and of rights. Traditionally, equality was understood in terms of rights that all shared, and rights were understood negatively, to protect spheres of individual freedom from government action. For example, the Bill of Rights prohibits Congress from making laws interfering with freedom of religion, speech, press, assembly, and so on. Such positive obligations as it imposes concern the formal legal process that is due in matters of crime and punishment. Progressives, however, championed a new conception of rights—entitlements—which imposed positive obligations on government. They argued with increasing success in the 1960s and 1970s that the job of government was not merely to ensure equality before the law, but to use law and public policy to bring about greater substantive equality in social and economic life. The classic case is welfare.

Conservatives resisted this rights revolution. They defended the claims of formal equality, rejected many of the new interventions of the federal government as contrary to the principles of federalism, criticized welfare programs for providing perverse incentives that encouraged single mothers and fathers not to marry and able-bodied men and women not to work, and attacked the high taxes that supported entitlements as a drag on the economy and an impairment of individual freedom. Yet progressive politicians, professors, and pundits portrayed conservatives as not just opposed to the progressive theory of government on constitutional and pragmatic grounds but as adversaries of fairness itself.

One of Ronald Reagan's historic achievements was to go beyond restoring the case for individual opportunity, limited government, and growth-oriented economic policies in terms of efficiency and also to vindicate them as requirements of fairness. In addition to the right to participate in the political process, what individuals were owed from government, according to Reagan, was the room and security to develop their talents, earn a living, care for their families, and contribute to their communities. He regarded the cultivation of private virtue as a public good. While Reagan recognized government's obligation to provide a safety net for the less fortunate, he rejected any policy that smacked of equality of result.

In fact, both fairness as equality of opportunity and fairness as equality of result have roots in the American political tradition and in the bedrock principles of liberal democracy. Consider affirmative action. Equating equality with equality of result, progressive proponents have argued since the 1970s that the state should take race into account in hiring and promotion decisions, and universities should take it into account in admissions decisions as well, to correct for disadvantages caused by the long and ugly history of government-enforced discrimination. Race and sex are also relevant in such decisions, they maintain, because the state has an interest in fostering a diverse labor force. In contrast, equating equality with equality of opportunity, conservative critics contend that the state must be color-blind in doling out benefits and burdens because each citizen deserves to be treated as an individual and no citizen should be given an advantage or deprived of an opportunity because of race. The color of one's skin, they emphasize, is morally and politically irrelevant to the determination of individual merit.

Both left and right have a point. When a state devoted to liberal and democratic principles is responsible for tilting the playing field, the state should level it. But a liberal democracy should not itself tilt the playing field to advantage favored groups and classes. The hard question is what counts as a level playing field. And it cannot be answered without a heavy admixture of empirical evidence, a careful consideration of concrete circumstances, and pragmatic analysis of government's competence to intervene effectively. In some cases progressives have the better argument about fairness, and in some cases conservatives have it, but in many of the hard cases that have roiled our politics, fairness involves a synthesis of progressive and conservative concerns. Unfortunately, in both the academy and in the present Obama administration, the need for a synthesis is not merely resisted but determinedly obscured by insisting that fairness requires progressive outcomes.

Harvard philosophy professor John Rawls (1921–2002) developed the most theoretically sophisticated expression of the progressive ambition to equate fairness with the progressive understanding of justice. He devoted his career to the task and in the process became the most influential philosophy professor of his generation. One of his earliest professional papers was called "Justice as Fairness" (1957), and the last book he wrote, published more than four decades later and a year before his death, was titled *Justice as Fairness: A Restatement* (2001). In between, he published two major works, *A Theory of Justice* (1971) and *Political Liberalism* (1993), which were devoted to elaborating the equation. They became the two most discussed books of political theory of the last fifty years.

To be sure, few officeholders or policy makers have read Rawls, let alone with care. Many have never heard of him. But his thinking permeated the atmosphere of the colleges and law schools in which they were educated. His approach and arguments make explicit premises and reasoning that underlie progressive thinking, and the ambiguities in his thoughts about fairness reflect ambiguities common to much progressive thinking.

According to Rawls, justice concerns the principles that free and equal citizens would adopt to govern themselves if they thought rationally about their situation. It has two basic parts: fundamental and inviolable liberties, and an obligation on the part of the state to adopt "measures ensuring for all citizens adequate all-purpose means to make effective use of their freedoms." In fact, virtually all conceptions of justice in a liberal democracy recognize fundamental rights, and obligations on the part of the state to provide for those who can't provide for themselves. The main task of Rawls's justice as fairness is to articulate abstract principles that structure the public debate about politics. But it also claims to derive policy from the proper principles. Suffice it to say, however, that "justice as fairness" builds a great deal of the government intervention and redistribution that it purports to derive into the words "adequate," "all-purpose," and "effective," and infuses the formal reasoning that is supposed to structure public debate with considerable substantive content. So it is no surprise that the Rawlsian is rare who has derived even a single public-policy position from Rawls's theory that does not more or less harmonize with the progressive political agenda.

Rawls acknowledges that "justice as fairness" is but one of the many political conceptions of justice that deserve consideration in a liberal democracy. But he makes no such concession about his understanding of fairness. His concession about justice, moreover, is unconvincing. By equating his favored conception of justice with fairness itself, and by demonstrating throughout his half-century career in academic philosophy a decided lack of interest in other interpretations of justice, Rawls powerfully signaled that the progressive understandings of fairness did equal justice.

A legion of second- and third-generation Rawlsians, today representing a major, if not the dominant, school within academic political theory, developed an offshoot of the theory of justice as fairness they often called "deliberative democracy." Many variants have been put forward, and the approach has been extended to international relations and international law, but all respond to a common problem, develop a common solution, and embody a common conceit.

The problem was that despite the pride they took in their democratic bona fides, the professors regarded as dictates of justice as fairness progressive policies—on abortion, affirmative action, welfare, taxes, and others—that frequently failed to command majority support.

The professors' solution was to argue that the policies their theories demonstrated were fair and just were democratic in a higher sense: they reflected the choices people should make and would embrace but for poor education, and passions and prejudices corrupted by the imperfections of social life and the inequities of the market economy.

The professors' conceit was to suppose that their own education was adequate and that their theory yielded rational truths unsullied by rationalizations of their own passions and prejudices. Pleased with their analytical abilities and persuaded of the purity of their moral intentions, the deliberative democrats rarely considered the illiberal and antidemocratic implications of a theoretical approach to politics that systematically disdains the expressed preferences of majorities of their fellow citizens, and which not only appoints professors as guardians of the fair and the just but also equates this self-aggrandizing arrogation of power with greater democracy.

A similar sensibility, which equates fairness with the progressive agenda but obscures the gap between the progressive agenda and popular preferences, has become visible in the Obama approach. It can be seen in candidate Obama's carefully choreographed efforts to present himself as not only a determined Democrat and devoted progressive but also a moderate, postpartisan pragmatist; in Chief of Staff Rahm Emanuel's "Rule one: Never let a crisis go to waste"; in a massive stimulus bill sold to the public as necessary to jump-start the economy but loaded with nonstimulus social spending; in health-care reform bills defended by the president as cost-cutting measures and required to address the economic crisis, but which are destined to generate massive deficits over the next decade and beyond and diminish individual choice; and in the president's and his Supreme Court nominee then Judge, and now Justice, Sotomayor's repeated insistence in the years before her Senate confirmation hearings that empathy was a crucial judicial virtue coupled with her repudiation of empathy's importance in her testimony before the Senate Judiciary Committee. The pattern involves a concerted effort to conceal the inspiration, ultimate aim, and full cost of positions, policies, and programs that, though advanced in the public's name, would not, if forthrightly explained, garner majority support.

It is an awkward orientation for progressives. For the sake of fairness it treats the public as too simpleminded or mean-spirited to adopt the correct policies for the correct reasons. It overlooks that government is often a bad judge of what citizens deserve and poorly equipped to ensure equal outcomes. And in seeking to expand government's responsibility for managing citizens' lives, it diminishes citizens' freedom.

Most important, the progressive equation of fairness with progressivism itself suppresses the vital lesson that parents seek to impress on children: life is often not fair, and frequently neither parents nor politicians possess the wisdom or power to make it so. And frequently neither parents nor politicians possess the power to make it so. To be sure, we are not merely creatures of our circumstances, in many undertakings we can honor the claims of fairness, and numerous injustices can be rectified by individual initiative and appropriate government action. But to make fairness itself the be-all and end-all of public policy is to ensure a citizenry that is never satisfied and that is constantly consumed with anger, indignation, and resentment. For progressives in America to go further down that road by making a partisan interpretation of fairness government's "one overriding principle" is to inflame partisanship by teaching that those who embrace individual freedom for all but differ about its political requirements are enemies and monsters.

Understood exclusively in progressive terms, as the dominant perspective in the academy and the Obama administration favor, fairness threatens freedom. To fortify freedom, the ambiguities of fairness must be fairly understood.

4

The Urge to Regulate

Max Borders

IN THE SOUTH, making barbecue sauce is an art. Having come up from North Carolina's red clay, I learned how to make sauce at my father's hip. From the tomato-based sauce of the foothills to the vinegar sauce of the flats, I've become a master sauce-maker—at least in my own mind.

I was also raised in a family that still cans food. I don't know why people can things using jars, but they do. Old ladies bring the fruits of their labor to church basements in the fall, for example. From persimmon jams to pepper jellies—tomatoes, green beans, and pickles. Canning is an inheritance of folk wisdom—from a time when the only assurances about the cleanliness and quality of one's food came from an unbroken seal, a discerning nose, and bonds of community trust.

Canning is part of a dying tradition of localism and sharing. Neighbors engage neighbors in what we might call slow trade. You bring a jar of tomatoes today. I stop by with a jar of creamed corn next month. People claim to cherish these traditions, yet they often blindly support policies that are at odds with them. The question is why.

A couple of years ago, my wife and I began trying to think of ways to earn extra money. We lived in northern Virginia. I was a writer, so living was expensive. At the time she worked as a nanny, but would soon lose that income due to the arrival of our son. Because we're from North Carolina, we started thinking about what people back home would've done to earn extra money—people like our parents and grandparents. We thought of all the folks we knew who were enterprising, albeit in an old-timey way: the woman who would take in ironing, my grandfather who mowed lawns until he died, and blue-hairs who would can vegetables.

As I mentioned, I make pretty good barbecue sauce. So my wife and I started thinking we could sell it at the farmers market up the street from us. It was nothing fancy, just tables in an Arlington parking lot. At this particular market, people sell different things—but mostly fresh produce from farms in the extended area. Other folks there had started putting out jams, salsas, homemade breads, and so on. Some good stuff, too. But no barbecue sauce.

So we looked into selling our sauce. We got so excited, in fact, we got busy cooking straightaway—scaling up my recipe for larger batches and, of course, canning. Using my laptop, I made a "Curly Q" label with the image of a pig with a screw-tail. (N.C. barbecue is mostly pork, but my sauce is good on chicken and beef, too.) Finally, after some phone tag, we got in contact with a representative from Arlington County. She proceeded to explain what would be involved in selling our sauce at the farmers market. The following conversation is accurate to the best of my memory.

"First, you'll need to contact the County Board of Health to come out and inspect the kitchen where you prepare the sauce," she said.

"But it's just our apartment. We're just talking about canning sauce in Mason jars—you know, like old ladies do."

"Well, they'll have to inspect where the food is prepared."

I know deep down that no degree of cleaning, reorganizing, or whatever would get our 1940s-built apartment up to code. But heck, maybe I could suffer the indignity and give it a try. *With a little research and some lead time,* I thought. . . . I decided to hear her out.

"Then, we're going to have to see a business license."

"Business license?"

"Yes."

"But it's just my wife and me. We're making barbecue sauce. If we sell a hundred cans, we might make all of a hundred dollars. That's not really a bu—"

"Well, that's not all."

"Really?"

"No, the county needs proof of business insurance."

I looked at the phone as if it were some alien device transmitting gibberish. For a moment, I considered taking the woman to task. I wanted to launch into a speech about what farmers markets are supposed to be, about what community is, and about an era in this country where "buy at your own risk" actually meant something to both buyers and sellers. . . . But she was just a functionary. A cog. She was enforcing the requirements of a wiser, more powerful, and more benevolent bureaucrat.

I thanked her for her time and hung up.

So this is what had become of home canning? Forget Atlas. Grandma has shrugged. Maybe she has gone underground to run kerosene pickles on the black market. I realize this may sound flip. But what was the relevant difference between my hawking Curly Q on Columbia Pike and old ladies trading their wares—in kind—in the recesses of the Presbyterian fellowship hall? I found it sad that there might be greater barriers to entry for a poor person to sell homemade sauce than to pick up a welfare check.

One Sunday, a week or two later, my wife and I strolled up to the farmers market. We noticed one lady selling greenhouse tomatoes. But she was also selling homemade salsa. We bought a couple of the tomatoes and asked the seller if she had had to jump through any hoops to sell the salsa. "No," she replied, but soon clammed up. She'd only recently started putting the salsa out (though her space had been reserved for a while). If she knew anything about the county regulations on prepared food, she feigned ignorance.

I looked around and noticed a couple more tables where people had begun putting out such fare. While there were no "buy at your own risk" signs, I doubted health inspectors had been out to many of these people's homes in rural Virginia. Did the vegetable sellers need business insurance? I admit I was angry. But I didn't want to let my indignation spoil everyone else's gray-market commerce even though my Curly Q jars were collecting dust.

Milton Friedman said we should never question people's motivations. We should only study the consequences that follow from proposed policies. I disagree. Not because questioning someone's personal motives yields much in changing his mind. In this sense, Friedman may be right. Rather, I disagree in the broader sense: in order properly to confront the regulatory urge, we should try to understand its manifestations, as well as its origins.

What makes people want to control others? What's the nature of this urge to regulate and to ban? It's a human urge, to be sure. But no two people are disposed to it in quite the same way. The urge is stronger in some than in others, and wherever you find it you'll find a multifaceted phenomenon.

As far as I can tell the urge to regulate has five main motivating facets:

Paternalism. The root of the urge is the assumption that other people are too stupid or lazy to look after themselves or act responsibly. In other words, they are like children who require the supervision of a watchful and benevolent parent. This paternalistic attitude is clearly implied in the maze of regulations we encountered when we applied for a license to make and sell barbecue sauce. One also finds it in the warning labels on baby seats and microwave ovens, which are clearly written for idiots. One might think this rather elitist disposition is at odds with egalitarian values like fairness and equality. After all, the parent-child relationship is unequal. Often, though, regulators are egalitarian and paternalist in equal measure.

Utopianism. A close cousin of paternalism, utopianism comes from a tendency to idealize the world in a certain way. The utopian imagines the world otherwise and believes it can be made, by force if necessary, to conform to the way he imagines it. Sometimes it can be so fashioned and sometimes it can't. But generally, utopians fail to consider the trade-offs required to achieve their particular ideal. We might wish for a world that is completely free of pollution, poverty, or salmonella poisoning. We can imagine that and even agree it would be a nice outcome. In our minds, we conjure worlds in which no one ever suffers or in which all social problems are solved and markets never "fail." But these worlds usually involve ignoring both real-world facts and competing values. You might even say that it involves something close to blind faith. The utopian replaces God with government, but still expects miracles.

Linear thinking. Suppose the utopian described above has a vision involving a specific goal. Because she is also a rationalist, she is single-minded about the means. She can't imagine their unintended effects or see other ways to solve a problem. The obvious path is the logical one. In encountering a social problem, the linear thinker gloms onto the most convenient explanation or scapegoat. The temperance movement of the early twentieth century is a good example. Prohibitionists thought the easiest way to solve social problems associated with alcohol abuse was to ban alcohol. Ultimately, liquor was driven into the black market, gangland rumrunners killed each other over territory, and alcoholics still managed to get whiskey and gin. Economics says smuggling and gangs are a by-product of policies that make profits higher due to riskier trade. Yet regulators in the War on Drugs continue undeterred. Linear thinking yields a kind of myopia, and the problem boils down to this: life is rarely a matter of simple cause and effect. Sometimes there are multiple causes. Other times the apparent effects are really just side effects of a deeper underlying problem. The linear thinker has difficulty parsing these distinctions in order to see things holistically. Nonetheless, when utopia lies on the horizon the linear thinker plows ahead.

Greed. Believe it or not, the desire for profit can be a facet of the regulatory urge. Economist Bruce Yandle reminds us that bootleggers were in the picket line with Baptists in the days leading up to Prohibition. Why would this be so? The bootleggers knew most of their competitors would go out of business if they helped get alcohol banned. Imagine the profits they could reap. And profit they did. Earnings were so high, in fact, that it was worth it to stay in business despite harassment from the law. Today, greed fuels all manner of campaigns to regulate this or ban that. Energy companies with heavy nuclear or natural gas interests will fare better than coal companies in a carbon tax environment. (Why else do companies like Duke

Energy back alarmist environmental organizations lobbying for CO_2 regulation?) Larger companies know they can absorb regulatory costs better than upstart competitors, so they tend to cheer regulations that will hurt the competition. Economist Mark Crain found that "on a per employee basis, it costs about $2,400, or 45 percent, more for small firms to comply than their larger counterparts."[1] Even hairdressers know they can create barriers to competitors if they lobby to make licensure requirements stricter for new entrants. There's nothing wrong with self-interest per se, but when greed drives someone to rig the rules in her favor, it becomes corruption.

Moralistic self-promotion. Where paternalists and utopians mostly have good intentions, the moralistic self-promoter does not. The politician may don the mask and borrow the language, but his aspirations are almost always to retain office and expand his authority. This facet of the regulatory urge is similar to greed, except the politician's profit is power. He craves it for its own sake. Moralism for the sake of self-promotion is not exclusive to the politician. Anyone who values prestige and power can take on the mantle of righteousness. But politicians corner the market. None of this is to say there are no idealists in politics. But idealists tend not to survive very long in an environment that rewards collusion and compromise.

With different people motivated by different facets of the urge running around loose in society, things get interesting. Alliances form. The regulatory state grows and grows.

This human propensity probably lives in our DNA somewhere, forged in the evolutionary fires by ancestors trying to bring order to their clans. Hunting and foraging out on the steppe must have been a chaotic affair. And still we rage for order. So what's new about the urge as a threat to liberty? It's not so much the urge itself, but the extent to which the state can now interfere with every aspect of our lives. And this is not sustainable. The ecosystems of contemporary life are not designed to be fixed or regulated like machines from a bank of rheostats in Washington. Indeed, they're not "designed" at all. That's what ultimately makes control by a central authority a fool's errand.

Still, for many people the reach of the regulatory state causes no great offense. Some demand it: "The government needs to do something" falls so easily from people's lips nowadays. But as economist Bryan Caplan reminds us, some beliefs have practical consequences for the believer, while others don't. For example, a belief "about the relative merits of evolution and creationism is unlikely to make a difference to one's career outside of the life sciences, but maintaining that faith-healing is more effective than modern medical science may be deadly."[2] Likewise for anyone's belief in the power of the regulatory state to lower the risks associated with living in America: the practical consequences and personal costs of a given regulation may be small. Unfortunately, mistaken beliefs, shifted costs, and foolhardy regulations add up—and rarely go away.

Today, regulation gets lost among all the other inconveniences, annoyances, and struggles of life, which is how it gets mistaken for a necessary evil. A minor cost here and a hassle there are easy to dismiss, especially when it's someone else's hassle. After all, we still enjoy more prosperity and variety than we could have dreamed just a hundred years ago, despite the growth of Leviathan. But are we prepared to abort a million more prosperous futures with just a few penstrokes? Might we reach a point of critical mass beyond which awaits economic sclerosis? As of 2005, regulatory costs hit an estimated $1.13 trillion—almost 10 percent of U.S. GDP. And that doesn't include the burden of state and local regulation.

There's nothing earth-shattering in my tale. Still, I think it points to a loss of the little things in life. What simple pleasures, elements of community, and ground-floor opportunities have just been regulated away? A lot of people have stories like mine. In other words, this isn't something that affects only conservatives and nostalgic libertarians. It affects everybody.

Take slow foodies and "real milk" lovers. They share common sentiments with environmentalists in that they value what they believe to be eco-friendly, natural products. But even organic food enthusiasts sometimes find that they just want government to leave them alone. Joel Salatin raises grass-fed beef, free-range chickens, and more on a diversified farmstead in the Shenandoah Valley. In an article for *Acres* magazine—"Everything I Want to Do Is Illegal"—he writes:

> Every time a letter arrives in the mail from a federal or state agriculture department my heart jumps like I just got sent to the principal's office. And it doesn't stop with agriculture bureaucrats. It includes all sorts of government agencies, from zoning, to taxing, to food inspectors.[3]

Ultimately, Salatin wants nothing more than to offer people "honest food, honest ecology, honest stewardship." But he's thwarted at every turn.

Purveyors of unpasteurized milk or cheese—hardly coldhearted capitalists—would like to sell dairy products whose quality is improved by microorganisms. Trouble is, these microorganisms are destroyed in the process that makes the products suitable for sale according to government nannies. (We don't hear about the French dropping like flies due to a want of controls on stinky cheese, but I digress.)

The regulatory state amounts to a regressive tax that penalizes small independent producers and protects the status quo. It is a cost of doing business for large corporations, can be burdensome for small businesses, and is sometimes an insuperable obstacle for the poor. A handful of examples come to mind:

▶ "The State Council of Higher Education for Virginia recently declared that studios offering yoga teacher instruction must be certified. That involves a $2,500 fee, audits, annual charges of at least $500 and a pile of paperwork." (From the *Washington Post*)[4]
▶ "Hoping to raise money for a family trip to Disneyland, [Daniela Earnest] opened a lemonade stand Monday. But because Daniela didn't have a business license, the city of Tulare shut it down the same day." (From the *Fresno Bee*)[5]

▶ "A Consumer Product Safety Commission regulation intended to safeguard children against dangerous toxins is hurting business at small toy stores and thrift shops across the country. The regulation requires that retailers test and label children's products to prove they are not hazardous. . . . While their bigger corporate competitors have less difficulty adhering to the standards, smaller stores—especially resellers or thrift shops—are finding it costly to comply." (From *Inc.*)[6]

▶ "Natasha Lima-Younts can't see how she's putting anyone's life at risk. She's been an interior designer for more than 20 years. She started her own business, and hired dozens of employees. She has an extensive portfolio and magazine features about her work. What she doesn't have is a state license." (From Reason Online)[7]

▶ "In the 1940s, under a mayor who soon would take his New Deal liberalism to Washington—Hubert Humphrey—[Minnesota] capped entry into the taxi business. By the time Paucar got here in 1999, 343 taxis were permitted. He wanted to launch a fleet of 15. That would have required him to find 15 incumbent license-holders willing to sell their licenses for up to $25,000 apiece." (From the *Washington Post*).[8]

I could be accused of picking out small instances while ignoring greater social protections. After all, though I might never have done anyone harm with my Curly Q sauce, it takes only one careless person to sell someone spoiled food, give someone diarrhea, or—heaven forbid—put someone in the hospital.

If God conducted some grand cost-benefit analysis, God would be able to tell us exactly what harms are really being prevented by regulations, controls, and bans, and then measure these against all the markets—large and small—that are regulated away in the process. But no such analysis is possible. We have to appeal to worlds that might have been to get an idea of what we're actually losing.

In my imagined world, there are no regulatory barriers to my selling Curly Q at the farmers market. One of my customers buys the sauce and really enjoys it. He owns a pig cooker—the kind that has to be hauled on a trailer. He happens to cook Boston butts for families at kids' ball games. We strike a deal to replace his store-bought sauce for Curly Q. In this parallel world, our partnership is mutually beneficial. People at the ball games love the meat and the sauce. Together we earn local fame. Soon I'm able to save up the working capital to rent an industrial kitchen and scale up my operation—enough to sell sauce not only to the cook, but to local grocers. My business continues to expand. Eventually, my sauce becomes such a hit that I become a mini-magnate. *Forbes* names me the "King of Barbecue." Curly Q finds its way to shelves around America alongside Bull's Eye and K.C. Masterpiece. I retire a philanthropist at thirty-six.

The probability of all this actually happening is vanishingly small. But my wife and I might certainly have saved something for our little boy's college tuition. We might have supplemented our income without going into debt. And what community might we have helped to build? How many people would have enjoyed better barbecue sauce at their picnics? As everyone knows, most successful ventures come from modest beginnings. Cottage industries are at the genesis of wealth creation. If my story is one among millions, how many millions of big dreams (and small) have been regulated away on behalf of the precautionary principle?

The point is not so much to dwell on the past as to wonder about the freedoms, the values, and the possible worlds that government interference destroys. Regulation raises the costs, thus reducing the likelihood, of these better worlds coming into existence. In the language of economists, these are the opportunity costs. And they are innumerable.

Notes

1. W. Mark Crain, "The Impact of Regulatory Costs on Small Firms," *Small Business Research Summary*, no. 265 (September 2005): 1.
2. Bryan Caplan, "Rational Ignorance v. Rational Irrationality," http://www.gmu.edu/departments/economics/bcaplan/ratirnew.doc.
3. Joel Salatin, "Everything I Want to Do Is Illegal," *Acres: A Voice for Eco-Agriculture* 33, no. 9 (September 2003): 1.

4. Maria Glod, "Va. Yogis seek rapture not regulation," *Washington Post*, August 24, 2009.

5. Eddie Jiminez, "California city shuts down girl's lemonade stand," *Fresno Bee*, August 6, 2009.

6. Caitlin McDevitte, "A Sticky Situation for Second Hand Toy Stores," *Inc.*, March 3, 2009.

7. Nick Gillespie, "Throw-Pillow Fight," reason.tv, http://reason.tv/video/show/throw-pillow-fight (accessed April 2, 2009).

8. George F. Will, "Cabs and Cupidity," *The Washington Post*, May 22, 2007.

The Isolation of Today's Classical Liberal

Richard A. Epstein

To ME, the most important domestic threat to political liberty in the United States is that neither political party exhibits a deep internal commitment to the principles of private property and freedom of contract or association, or to the legal rules, social practices, and institutional arrangements needed to implement these principles in our daily lives. Nor are there today any significant broad-based political movements that articulate these principles in an intelligent and restrained fashion. To be sure, Glenn Beck, Rush Limbaugh, and other lions of talk radio on the right often sound their libertarian clarion calls. Yet too often they fail this key test: however sound their instincts, their denunciations are too personal and too vehement, and their substantive positions too simplistic, to command real respect.

This tenuous state of affairs forces the conscientious small-government classical liberal into political isolation. What is needed, now more than ever, are political leaders like Ronald Reagan who can once again make first principles fashionable in political debate. But from where will they come? Not from the Democratic Party whose Obama incarnation advances a reckless interventionist agenda in regard to health care, labor, financial institutions, international trade—even lead paint. At every juncture, the Democrats are obsessed with the endless multiplication of rights—the right to housing, to education, to health care, to welfare, and to (union) jobs. This unwise reincarnation of Roosevelt's Second Bill of Rights never candidly addresses the heavy taxes and regulatory thickets that are the inevitable by-product of such dubious ventures. Nor do they recognize how redistribution through regulation saps the initiative and energy of a free people and divides a nation against itself. Yet sadly, rising deficits and declining public morale fall on deaf ears in the White House.

It is, however, more painful to observe the strong statist impulses on the Republican side of the aisle. Most disappointing is the widespread unwillingness of Republican leaders to mount a full-scale assault on the deadly Democratic troika of open-ended entitlements, progressive taxation, and market regulation. No party can stand on principle if its key members rejoice in the destructive tangle of ethanol import restrictions and domestic subsidies that undergird Republican strongholds in the farm states. To be sure, the Republicans are now resisting the egregious Democratic effort to nationalize the health-care system. But their defensive zeal has not been matched by a concerted effort to deregulate, say, the legal barriers to the interstate sale of insurance, which, by lowering price, could improve both quality and access to care. More distressingly, the social conservative wing of the Republican Party flexes its statist muscles on a wide range of moral questions relating to gay rights, where on the issue of gay marriage Democrats exhibit better small-government instincts. Small-government libertarians will keep the Republicans at arm's length so long as social conservatives dominate the party.

Thus far this essay has spoken in generalities. It is time to make them more concrete. To do so, I shall explore the antilibertarian impulses in two areas: labor markets and gay rights. To many, these questions seem unrelated. But in fact a coherent classical liberal theory should block government interference in both markets.

Labor Markets

One of the most pronounced differences between the Bush and Obama administrations lies in their respective attitudes toward organized labor. The Bush administration commendably held organized labor at arm's length. The Obama administration embraces it with open arms. At no point does Obama disagree with any of labor's provincial aims. Its only qualms go to the amount of political capital it can afford to spend on the labor agenda as it relates to free trade, the Employee Free Choice Act, and the minimum wage. This Democratic position is beyond redemption. The Republican alternative is far better, but still less than perfect. It is useful to identify both its commendable strengths and its serious shortfalls.

On the positive side, the Republicans have stood firm against the misnamed Employee Free Choice Act. The EFCA features two dangerous reforms. The card-check system calls for the recognition of a union in the workplace on the strength of signed cards without the benefit of a secret ballot election. That provision invites massive union coercion. And once the union is in place, it no longer runs the risk that it will fail to obtain a contract through collective bargaining. Instead, EFCA's second main provision allows a panel of arbitrators appointed by the Department of Labor to craft two-year labor "contracts" that cover all aspects of the workplace relationship. Two easy steps thus lead to the partial nationalization of unionized firms. The risk is especially great in those industries that cannot walk away. Retail, restaurants, and hotels join the manufacturers who flee overseas. They have to brave the union thicket or close down. With labor markets showing 10 percent unemployment, now is not the time to pass legislation that will drive new businesses from the field.

Notwithstanding their opposition to EFCA, Republicans remain far too kind to the National Labor Relations Act first adopted in 1935. The present system of collective bargaining is far better than EFCA, but it still embodies two mistakes of monumental proportions. First, it allows majority unions to prevent dissident workers from dealing directly with their employer. Second, in a conscious exemption from the antitrust law, it allows unions to present a united negotiating front against employers. This one-two punch often leads to two outcomes, both bad. The first is disruptive strikes. The second is onerous labor contracts. Agreements negotiated under the NRLA during the 1960s and 1970s are no laughing matter. By overreaching, they have destroyed much of the domestic automobile and steel industries in the United States.

The Republican Party's tactical refusal to promote competitive labor markets undercuts its current case against EFCA. Now the differences between the old NLRA and the new law are just matters of degree. The Republican posture also lets powerful unions parlay their strength in other areas. Led by such misguided stalwarts as United Steelworker president Leo Gerard, unions work overtime to block international free-trade agreements. They also pressure local officials to use zoning laws to block the entry of nonunion firms like Wal-Mart and Target in low-income areas desperate for new business blood. Finally, its wishy-washy intellectual posture makes the Republican Party ineffective in resisting the growth of public unions. Strong teachers' unions have created an unresponsive public school monopoly that fights against market-based innovations like charter schools and vouchers. Strong prison and transportation unions have likewise been able to shake down local governments for unsustainable pension and health-care benefits. California and New York could both bring their bloated budgets into balance if they could shrink public pensions down to the size of private plans.

Similarly, the weak Republican response to minimum-wage agitation makes it easier for the Democrats to enact substantial wage increases. The usual benign hope is that natural increases in market wages will dull the impact of higher minimum wages. But three minimum-wage increases of $0.70 each in July 2007, 2008, and 2009 have increased a $5.15 minimum wage by about 40 percent at a time when real wages are at best stagnant. Thus black, teenage male unemployment has moved from just under 40 percent to just over 50 percent in the second half of 2009, just as basic theory painfully predicts.

At root, the dominant Republican sentiment in favor of *smaller* government has not offered a vigorous defense of *small* government, period. Yet nothing short of this will restore competitive vigor to labor markets. Republican stall tactics may slow the rate of increase in labor market regulation. But they also cut the party off from its libertarian roots. A little more backbone would go a long way. But as matters now stand, a classical liberal is estranged from the substantive approaches of both political parties.

Gay Rights

The same sense of uneasiness applies to the question of gay rights. At first look, the controversies over gay rights seem to raise human rights issues that work at right angles to these labor market questions. Not so. Recall that the classical liberal theories of associational freedom are not limited to purely economic affairs—as if it were possible to cleanly separate economic from social rights. Rather, associational freedom rests on this strong presumption: in all domains of human activity, our axiom should be: consensual arrangements yes, coerced relationships no.

By common consent disputes over gay rights revolve around two key issues. The first is the contentious question of marriage. The second is whether to extend existing laws that prohibit discrimination in such areas as housing and employment to cover acts of discrimination on grounds of sexual orientation. Most current thinking links these together through a single question of whether, tout court, one supports or opposes gay rights. Conventionally, therefore, liberals who favor gay marriage offer vigorous support for extending antidiscrimination laws to cover cases of sexual orientation. Similarly, conservatives who oppose gay marriage are skeptical of any antidiscrimination law based on sexual orientation.

Both sides are wrong. The small-government libertarian rejects both pairings because they work at cross-purposes with the principle of freedom of association in all areas of life. When, therefore, anyone mentions that issuing marriage licenses is a traditional and accepted government function, my uneasiness extends not to the word "marriage," but to the word "license." What classical liberal political theory gives the state power to license any consensual behavior between two (or more) individuals that involve sexual relations or anything else? In American constitutional history, the courts have not been consistent libertarians. Until recently, they have allowed the legislature to invoke the "morals" portion of the police power to snuff out individual liberty on matters of sex, marriage, and procreation, even when they do not involve the use of force or fraud against third parties.

My current project is not to overturn the long-standing constitutional position that legislation can regulate on public morals. Just that approach was taken, without historical warrant, by Justice Kennedy in the much-debated 2003 case of *Lawrence v. Texas*, which struck down all statutes that, in the absence of any health risk, criminalized acts of sodomy performed in private between consenting adults. *Lawrence* is dubious constitutional law, but Kennedy's decision is nonetheless instructive because it closely tracks the classical liberal approach to intimate personal relations.

More specifically, as a matter of first principles, the libertarian inquiry asks from whence comes the state power to license marriage, an institution that long antedates the modern state. Taking deep offense to gay marriage does not justify stopping the practice. After all, the fact that you take mortal offense at my political views offers you no right to suppress my speech. A sensible society does not let some stop the speech or conduct of others solely by working themselves into a white heat. To be sure, state power can properly be used to block the spread of venereal disease or protect children against abuse. But these legitimate interests apply evenhandedly to all couples. They do not translate into some categorical disadvantage to consensual gay relationships.

This position rests on a recognition of the dangers inherent in the state's permit power. This government monopoly is far more dangerous than any private cartel because it is not eroded by free entry. The person who cannot get a license from his or her home state can't get that license from someone else—unless he or she is prepared to pack up and move on. No state needs the power to put ordinary people to such stark choices. It is therefore exceedingly important to reject the social conservative claim that the state has a special interest in the "protection of marriage." Religious institutions should not be protected from competition by rivals any more than ordinary businesses.

To be sure, protection against the use of force that disrupts voluntary arrangements is needed in both economic and social arenas. No one should be allowed to drag a married couple apart. That is because the use of force shrinks the domain of choices for all individuals and if left unabated leads to the Hobbesian war of all against all. In contrast, competition expands the range of choices to all individuals. Economists see force as a negative sum game that leaves all persons worse off. They see competition as a positive sum game that leaves everyone better off. The proper response to personal distaste is to turn away, not to bring out the heavy artillery of the state. If gay people cannot ban straight marriages, then straight people cannot ban gay marriages.

On this logic, liberals who defend gay marriage can rightly sport their impeccable libertarian credentials. But they quickly lapse into their customary statism by championing laws that prohibit discrimination in housing and employment by reason of sexual orientation. Both housing and labor markets are highly competitive, so why regulate at all? There may be only one place to get a marriage license, but there are literally thousands of prospective employers. Some fraction of them are happy to hire gay workers. No anti-gay person has a stranglehold on labor markets, which let gay workers gravitate to the people who like them the most without having to do business with those who disapprove of them. It is regrettable, therefore, when a political majority feels so insecure in its own beliefs that it is prepared to create the very condition that it deplores by using the monopoly power of the state to decide which kind of employment relations are acceptable and which are not. Here, as with gay marriage, it is not acceptable to say that those who do not like the rules can leave the jurisdiction. The monopoly power of the state is equally bad when it bans gay marriage and when it requires forced associations.

And yes, in competitive markets, we can't blink at the obvious challenge. The same view applies to any private discrimination on grounds of race, sex, and religion. Private parties can sort themselves out on those grounds in either work or play. We don't need special exceptions to boost up affirmative-action programs that embody the "right" kind of discrimination; freedom of association is enough to let private firms have their way, free of the threat of state coercion. As with gay marriage, mere offense—now by different groups—should never allow political majorities of any persuasion to persecute businesses that don't toe the proper line.

In both the long and the short run, the private sector works far better without state coercion. The harder case asks whether gays should be allowed in the military, where the state acts as an employer, not as a regulator. This heated dispute is not for courts to resolve. But whatever the public sentiment on the issue fifteen years ago, times have changed. On practical grounds of military necessity, the United States should jettison "Don't ask, don't tell," and open up the military service to gays and lesbians. The massive fears of social disruption have not been realized anywhere else, and military authorities should be able to defuse tensions by sensible management techniques. Indeed, as a matter of logistics and operations, integrating women into the military raises far more challenging issues because of the obviously relevant physical differences. The time for a change in policy is now at hand.

Constitutional Complications

In closing, let me address the large issue of whether this classical liberal solution is entitled to constitutional protection against legislative interference. I have already noted that the broad power to regulate morals cuts against the libertarian position on gay marriage. But no such tradition exists for other kinds of personal interaction. Yet the program to protect all forms of associational freedom has badly stalled. Politically, a strong left-right alliance has resisted claims of personal liberty in the economic sphere on the ground that all key questions of social and economic policy are best solved by legislative and not judicial determination.

More concretely, the American left opposes judicial intervention on issues relating to private property and economic liberties. At root their belief stems from the deep suspicion that private property and competitive markets are cloaks that allow dominant business interests to exploit the poor. The left views zoning laws and rent control on the one side, and collective bargaining and antidiscrimination laws on the other as correctives against private abuses of economic power. It therefore works overtime to neutralize the explicit textual protections afforded property by a twofold strategy. Step one involves giving narrow definitions of the constitutional provisions that speak of individual liberty and private property. Liberty only protects people against arbitrary arrest, and private property only protects them against expropriation of their land or chattels. Under these restrictive definitions, people no longer have any basic constitutional right to use and dispose of their labor and property as they see fit. Consistent with this view, the state's police power allows it to suppress competition and promote monopoly, as with the labor and zoning statutes. To the modern liberal the ultimate expression of the Supreme Court's folly is its 1905 decision in *Lochner v. New York*, which invalidated a statute that limited the workday for certain kinds of bakers to ten hours per day.

Many conservative thinkers have rightly denounced maximum-hour laws as disguised economic protectionism by union bakers against their nonunionized rivals. (Nonunion bakers worked in the night, slept on the job, and then collected the bread in the morning.) But conservatives won't connect the dots because they insist that courts lack the institutional competence and democratic legitimacy to override legislative judgments, except when the government position is so absurd that just about everyone would reject it. So long as many people believe that the risk of economic exploitation warrants a government response, the conservative justice will sit on his hands.

Once again I dissent from both the liberal and conservative positions. Constitutional deliberation starts not with supposed matters of institutional competence, but with the explicit text and basic structure. Judicial deference exposes individuals to protectionist decisions that arise when Congress and state legislatures fall victim to factions, just as Madison feared in Federalist 10. The core commitment to competition has remained strong on matters of freedom of speech and religion. It has also worked wonders by preventing unwise state legislation from balkanizing the American common market by excluding goods and services that come from out of state.

Our greatest judicial achievements, then, lie in the area in which courts have given their most vocal support to open competition. The conservatives give no explanation why the judicial successes in preserving interstate competition can't work in dealing with issues pertaining to the freedom of contract, speech, and religion. The tools to do so are already at hand. What is needed is a renewed conviction that the venture is worth undertaking. Today's dire circumstances offer no reason for holding to the failed policies that have brought about the situation.

New waves of excessive government intervention should not be allowed to pose mortal threats to the freedom of individuals and groups alike. Yet just that gloomy prospect is lurking in Congress's misguided efforts to pass revolutionary legislation boosting the rights of unions through such initiatives as the ill-named Employee Free Choice Act, and the jingoistic-sounding Affordable Health Care of America Act, which if enacted will drive out of business all private health-care providers, by forcing them to provide ever more services at ever lower prices. As this is written, the surprise victory of Republican Scott Brown in the Massachusetts senatorial race has dampened the short term prospects of the misbranded Employee Free Choice Act, any one of the countless versions of health-care reform legislation, or onerous and ill-conceived cap-and-trade regulation. Any of these could be revised with a switch in political fortunes. And populist reform of the banking industry is still a very live possibility. Only a bipartisan commitment to defending private property and contractual freedom within the constitutional framework can reverse this nation's otherwise inexorable decline. We must work hard to make that day come by all possible means in every disputed area. For that is what it will take to reconnect the now-isolated libertarian with mainstream American politics.

6

Single Women as a Threat
to Freedom

Jessica Gavora

"FREEDOM IS the desire of every human heart." That was the go-to line George W. Bush used to defend his doctrine of fighting terrorism by spreading democracy.

More than a few times, Bush was taken to task for assuming that goat herders in the Diyala Province yearn for freedom as much as suburbanites in Cleveland. But the skeptics missed a demographic much closer to home: Single moms in Indianapolis. Divorced female office managers in Pasadena. Widowed retirees on Staten Island.

If freedom is defined as individual liberty untrammeled by government regulation and uncorrupted by government provision, single women—never married, divorced, or widowed—are not big fans. They support, more than other women and more than men, bigger and more activist government. They back more than other women and men the government regulation of business and markets. They believe more than other women and men that government should intervene in their lives to protect them from big and powerful interests. And they disagreed more than other women and men with George W. Bush's "forward strategy of freedom." As a consequence, single women are surpassed in their loyalty as a Democratic voting group only by African Americans. They delivered a whopping 71 to 29 percent majority for Barack Obama in 2008.

But unmarried women's ambivalence about individual liberty goes deeper than any single candidate. As traditional marriage declines, the ranks of single women are growing, and increasingly these women are substituting the security of a husband with the security of the state. Liberty is a casualty in either case, of course. But a husband who's a plumber can't raise taxes. A husband who's the government can, especially if you want him to help out more raising the kids.

With little fanfare, the United States passed a significant demographic milestone in 2007: that year, for the first time, the U.S. Census reported that the majority of American households were headed by unmarried people. This historic demographic shift was the culmination of a trend that has been building for years. Since 1960, the percentage of the population that is over fifteen and unmarried increased from 32 percent to 45 percent. If the trend continues, swinging singles will be the majority of Americans in less than fifteen years.

Of this emerging majority of unmarried Americans, single women are dominant, both existentially and politically. Because women live longer than men, there are about 10 million more single women than single men, and their ranks are growing. Between 2000 and 2006, the number of single women grew at twice the rate of married women, either because they are delaying marriage longer, never getting married at all, or taking more time to remarry after divorce.

This story of women living and raising children without husbands is the story of the decline of traditional marriage. As in Western Europe, marriage in America has become so passé that demographer Tom Smith of the University of Chicago describes the United States as a "traditional" society that has now become a "modern family system."

A modern family system is one in which the rate of divorce is increasing, along with rates of cohabitation and out-of-wedlock births. It is a society in which an increasing number of households have no children under eighteen, the percentage of homes with children headed by two married people fell by half since 1972, and the percentage of homes of unmarried couples with no children doubled in the same time.

The modern family system is one in which, according to Smith, "family values follow family structure." On the range of social issues, from the acceptability of cohabitation and premarital sex to the effect of working mothers on children, Americans in traditional families tend to have more traditional values, and Americans in "modern"—read single-headed—family arrangements have more permissive or liberal values. The presence and number of children only magnify this effect, with children making traditional families more conservative and single families more liberal.

More than those in traditional families, modern American families also look to government to provide for their needs and protect them against perceived threats. They equate government that keeps taxes low and stays out of its citizens' lives as government that favors the few over the many. Thus, they generally believe that government regulation of business is necessary to protect the vulnerable masses against the powerful few. By wide margins, they believe that government should protect those in need, even if it means going into debt to do it.

The only thing that hasn't changed about the modern American family is that it is still overwhelmingly headed by women. Ninety percent of single parents in America today are women, a number that is virtually unchanged since the early 1970s. The problem—or the opportunity, depending on where you stand—is that these struggling, female-headed, "modern" American families are more numerous than they've ever been before.

How can growing numbers of impoverished single women heading families be considered in any sense an "opportunity"? Ironically, the answer to this question begins with welfare reform. Ending the federal entitlement did a predictably unpredictable thing: It took single women raising children off the list of national problems to be "solved." The 1996 law has been hailed as a historic retreat of the welfare state, and, in fact, 60 percent of recipients have moved off the welfare rolls since the law was enacted. Welfare spending declined as millions of single mothers moved from welfare to work, and with the public dole has gone the public controversy. Democrats were happy to no longer be the party of welfare queens, and Republicans were content not to puncture the surface of their rare victory for smaller government.

But the one change welfare reform pointedly has not accomplished is the benefit most promised by reformers on the right and on the left when it was enacted: ending the culture of dependency and irresponsibility that caused poor, unmarried women to have more and more babies. During the height of the "crisis" of illegitimacy that gave rise to welfare reform in the mid-1990s, 33 percent of American babies were born out of wedlock. Today, that number is an astonishing 40 percent.

The unwed mothers of today are older and whiter than they were fifteen years ago. Most single mothers today, for instance, are not teenagers but are well into their twenties. And the number of middle-class white women becoming unmarried mothers is increasing.

Still, overwhelmingly, the single women having babies in America today are poor and from a minority group. While 28 percent of the white women who gave birth in 2007 were unwed, nearly 72 percent of black mothers and more than 51 percent of Latinas were unmarried. And the single white women who gave birth were mostly poor and working class.

Sociologist Barbara Defoe Whitehead blames the relative public silence about the record numbers of poor, single women having children on a "new and harsh libertarian bargain" with the American underclass. In Whitehead's formulation, the public has agreed to stay out of the personal lives of unmarried mothers as long as they agree not to stick the public with the tab for their offspring. It's a plausible theory, but a closer look shows that the post–welfare reform bargain isn't very libertarian and isn't much of a bargain. True, the taxpayers are spending less on welfare qua welfare, but that doesn't mean that today's single mothers are suddenly self-sufficient. Other, much more expensive, federal programs have moved into the breach.

As welfare spending declined following the 1996 law, participation in other federal means-tested programs for the non-elderly has gone up. As of 2003, the Earned Income Tax Credit (EITC), Supplemental

Security Income (SSI), food stamps, and Medicaid each served more low-income Americans than traditional welfare ever did. What's more, these social-safety-net programs are much, much more expensive than traditional welfare. At its height, Aid to Families With Dependent Children cost around $20 billion. In 2008, the taxpayers spent $714 billion on means-tested welfare or aid to the poor. And President Obama is expected to increase federal welfare spending by one-third in his first two years.

The end result is that poor, dependent, single mothers are still very much with us. But now they're no longer welfare queens; they're the working, deserving poor. Barack Obama acknowledged as much during the 2008 campaign. "Before welfare reform, you had, in the minds of most Americans, a stark separation between the deserving working poor and the undeserving welfare poor," Mr. Obama told the *New York Times*. "What welfare reform did was desegregate those two groups. Now, everybody was poor, and everybody had to work."

Welfare reform did put a lot of poor women to work. But it also did something else: it combined with rising numbers of unmarried women to transform government-dependent women—particularly single women raising children—from a social pathology to be cured into a voting cohort to be courted.

The political implications of this growing, statist, single-female cohort are profound. Eager Democratic strategists fixate on the fact that there are currently 49.5 million female citizens over eighteen who are single, separated, divorced, or widowed. This group is not to be confused with the different species of "moms" who turn up in the crosshairs of political strategists and pundits each election cycle. "Soccer moms," "security moms," "hockey moms," and others are *married* moms, generally white, and they are true swing voters. Unmarried moms, as we've seen, don't swing. They stick. And they constitute 26 percent of all eligible voters, a bigger national electoral pool for Democrats than African Americans and Latinos combined.

Emphasis on *eligible* voters, however. Despite the fact that they reliably pull the lever for Democrats, single women, in the eyes of the professional Democratic political class, don't do it nearly enough. Strategists have long known that married people go to the polls with more regularity than singles. And even though single women vote more than single men, they still typically lag married women in turnout by double digits.

And so it was for good reason that, until the 2000 presidential election, Democrats generally wrote off the single female vote as not worth the effort. But in that razor-thin contest, liberals noticed for the first time that 22 million of their most reliable cohort of voters failed to vote. Most maddening was the fact that 6 million single women who were registered to vote nonetheless failed to punch a chad for Al Gore that year, far more than enough to have won him the White House.

The Democratic Party's answer to this missed electoral opportunity has been to attempt to mainstream being a single woman in America, to make it cool and fresh and new. In the 2004 election, Democratic strategists and the sympathetic media began to subject single women to an extreme political makeover. They started with labeling. Because focus groups told them that unmarried women regard the word "single" as a depressing reminder of their inability to land a man, they rechristened them simply "unmarried" or, even better, "women on their own." When some pundits tried to call them "Single Anxious Females" (SAFs), liberal advocacy groups quickly countered with more palatable evocations of *Sex in the City* voters.

Democrats also began to create ostensibly nonpartisan advocacy groups dedicated to registering and delivering single women to the polls. These groups scoured voting rolls and cross-referenced census data. And they did more. They gave away free manicures, hawked lingerie emblazoned with "Give Bush the Pink Slip," and provided free day care on election day. They ran ads featuring Hollywood starlets breathily proclaiming they like to "do it"—vote—"in the morning."

The Democratic project to "validate" single women is given

urgency by this interesting political fact: Although single women vote overwhelmingly Democratic, their condition is not permanent. According to the University of Chicago's Tom Smith, once divorced and separated people get married again, they start to vote like married people again.

Take the 2004 presidential election. Among married people, George W. Bush had about a 12 percent advantage. Among divorced voters, John Kerry had a 3 percent margin, and among separated and never-married voters, his margin exploded to 35 percent and 25 percent, respectively. But among voters who were remarried, Bush was once again the winner, by 15 percent, a number remarkably similar to that of married voters. Something about the institution of marriage, even if it's the second or third time around, makes people vote Republican.

But underneath the pink superficiality of the political courtship of single women is a more profound and more ominous shift. The political constituency in question is poor. Fully half of unmarried women have household incomes of less than thirty thousand dollars annually, compared to just 15 percent of married women. To mainstream such economic inequality is not to ask why it exists, but to use the power of the state to erase it or, in the very least, mitigate it. Thus have Democrats sought to transform the expansion of government services that necessarily attend to expanding numbers of single women and mothers from a regrettable but necessary government function into the unquestioned entitlement of a new and proud American demographic.

This approach in many ways is simply a continuation of the moral and political argument that has justified the welfare state since its inception. That society should step into the breach when mothers lose their husbands was the genesis of welfare. As the years went by, "losing" a husband was supplanted by "never finding" one. Still, single motherhood was always treated as generally a thing to be avoided.

In the current campaign, any acknowledgment that remaining single is a less than ideal situation for women, or that raising children in such an environment is anything less than these women's inalienable personal choice, is gone. Democratic strategists include single women as part of an emerging Democratic majority that includes other identity-politics groups defined not by their personal life choices but their inherent characteristics. Hispanics and African Americans can't change who they are, nor should they want to. Single women are a different call; they can change. Still, liberals talk breathlessly of single women becoming for the Democratic Party what evangelical Christians are for the Republicans: a large, awakened, reliable force for liberal social change.

So single women are pro-statist, for good reasons. But are they anti-freedom? When freedom is defined in traditional, individual—one could even say masculine—terms, there is evidence that women as a gender are, in fact, fearful and suspicious of freedom. A study of the countries emerging from communism after the fall of the Berlin Wall and Soviet communism found that in country after country, from Russia to Poland to Bulgaria, women were less welcoming than men of political freedom and free markets. In particular, women were more eager than men to suppress free-speech rights and political organizing among people with whom they disagreed.

In this country the gender gap has been a fixture of our politics for decades. Underlying it is a significant preference among American women for security before individual freedom. George W. Bush briefly won the allegiance of so-called security moms during an interregnum in which security against jihadists briefly trumped security against insurance companies. Still, American women consistently show less attachment to traditional aspects of individual liberty like free speech, free markets, and Second Amendment rights.

But maybe it's not women who are the problem. Maybe it's our definition of "freedom." Despite the best attempts of feminists, liberal politicians, and media to convince them otherwise, when you ask American women if they feel free, they answer in the affirmative more often than men. Among women and men who are identical in income, education, race, religion, politics, marital status and number of children, men are about 10 percent less likely to say they are free. Men are also less likely than women to think that Americans in general are free.

How to account for the fact that American women feel freer than their patriarchal oppressors? Arthur Brooks of the American Enterprise Institute has speculated that this difference in perceived personal and societal freedom is due to women defining freedom in a more personal and spiritual way. Women who attend church regularly, for instance, feel significantly more free than women who don't. For women more than men, freedom seems to be a state of mind—a sense of contentment that is summoned from within rather than a feeling of limitlessness that is experienced from without. And if that's the case, it follows that women would look first for the security that allows them to make this personal journey.

What are the public policy implications of this female preference for security over liberty? Nowhere is it more in evidence than in the quantum expansion of the nanny state known as health-care reform.

No issue plays more centrally to the insecurity of women—particularly single women—than health and health insurance. During the heat of the debate in 2009, First Lady Michelle Obama called health-care reform "the next step" in the women's movement, and the political facts bear this out. Women, particularly during their childbearing years, consume more health care than men. They go to the doctor more and are more attentive to their own health and, critically, the health of their children. As a consequence, long after the American people's opinion of Obamacare dipped negative, American women remained believers.

And here, again, single women are leading the charge. Marriage and health-care coverage, like other advantages of middle-class life, are directly related. Single women not yet old enough to qualify for Medicare are about 60 percent more likely to lack health insurance than married women. They are four times more likely than married women to be on Medicaid.

For single women, the health-care reform of overwhelming choice was the so-called government option. They failed to achieve this, of course. But the fact that women's groups accepted restrictions on government funding of abortion in exchange for the more limited government guarantees in health care is a sign of where their priorities have shifted. Ideological feminist touchstones like abortion are being supplanted by the need for the state to fill the traditional role of a husband.

Another, less obvious realm in which the freedom averseness of women is changing American public policy is in the area of high finance. Bolstered by new research linking testosterone levels to greater risk-taking in financial decisions, a meme broke out in 2009 in the enlightened confines of places like the World Economic Forum in Davos that men—not reckless borrowers or politicized quasi-governmental lenders—were responsible for the global financial meltdown. Nicholas Kristof suggested in the *New York Times* that the financial calamity might not have occurred "if Lehman Brothers had been Lehman sisters." The *Financial Times* even called for Norwegian-style gender quotas on corporate boards as a way to put a halt to the testosterone-fueled mayhem.

Gender quotas on American corporate boards aren't likely to happen soon. But women like Harvard law professor and chair of the congressional financial bailout oversight panel Elizabeth Warren have led the charge by the Obama administration for the creation of a Consumer Financial Protection Agency on the grounds that it would "protect families." The new agency would create a vast new bureaucratic apparatus with the sole purpose of shielding Americans from risk in financial transactions, including determining which of us are "sophisticated" enough as financial consumers to qualify to purchase more complex products. It would be, in essence, the female answer to the masculine "problem," putting consumer protection before profit making, and security before risk.

It's increasingly clear that security, for women, can be found in government or it can be found in marriage. And if the goal of feminism can be said to supplant the latter with the former, feminists have only been partially successful. For despite decades of agitprop aimed at convincing women that marriage is a prison, married women are 10 percent more likely than single women to say they feel free. For women, there's something about saying "I do" that liberates.

Maybe that's why, even among the ranks of America's post–welfare reform, low-income, single mothers, marriage remains a personal life goal. Liberal academics and writers attempting to explain the persistence of single motherhood despite the yearning for marriage inevitably point to economic reasons: under- or unemployed men, or the desire to have sufficient resources for a lavish wedding and comfortable postnuptial lifestyle. But others have pointed to a more plausible, if less politically correct, reason: men who are unmarriageable not because they lack money, but because they lack character. Studies of post–welfare reform groups of single mothers are filled with poor women complaining not of men's lack of earning power but of irresponsibility, drug and alcohol abuse, criminality, and what sociologists euphemistically call "multiple partner fertility." For these women, gaining a husband isn't gaining a partner with whom to build a stable, secure life; it's gaining a problem. And so they find elsewhere the resources they need and the security they seek.

Perhaps President Bush was right after all: freedom *is* the yearning of every human heart. It's just that for women in general, and single women in particular, freedom isn't the liberty to live their own lives but the security to do so. The political project to substitute government for the role husbands once played in the lives of American women sacrifices our traditional notion of freedom for this feminized version. It may or may not succeed. Whether it does, it seems, hinges on American women's continued belief that, for all his faults, the guy dozing on the couch at least can love them, which is something the state can never do.

7

The Loss of the Freedom to Fail

Michael Goodwin

AT FIRST GLANCE, the idea that we are losing the freedom to fail sounds like a reason to celebrate. It prompts visions of Utopia, or at least of Lake Wobegon, Garrison Keillor's imaginary town where all the women are strong, the men are good-looking, and the children are above average.

It is perhaps even stranger to claim that we should actually fear losing the freedom to fail. Most of us are hardwired to avoid losing, and giving up the prospect does not logically seem a sacrifice. Losing the chance to fail should also mean we're guaranteed to win, right?

Wrong. Misguided social perfectionists have given failure a bad rap, and too many of us have bought into their foolish view. Declaring failure a cruel and permanent blot on the self-esteem of those who don't measure up, the new social perfectionists are making a run at banning the idea of losing. In their vision, failure has no place in the civilized world, so they are determined to eliminate it.

The bid certainly has appeal, and the movement enjoys a growing and diverse congregation. Part of the popularity is owed to the seductive wrapping of compassion, which promises to soften life's blows if not prevent them altogether. It's not just that you should be able to have your cake and eat it too. You should be able to have your cake, eat it, and not get fat. You should also have a house you can't afford.

These are the salad days of the compassion industry, which is stimulating an entitlement mania for individuals and, lately, tax-payer bailouts for both irresponsible borrowers and businesses deemed "too big to fail." Planned safety nets built on universal contributions, like Social Security, are one thing, but emergency bailouts of whole industries and millions of homeowners are quite another—especially when those who played by the old rules of thrift and sacrifice are forced to pay for the rescue of those who didn't.

The economic meltdown of 2008 and 2009 put on vivid display this clash of old versus new American values. What started as a housing bust turned into a credit and financial crisis. With the collapse of Wall Street investment banks Lehman Brothers and Bear Stearns, widespread fears of a return to the Great Depression understandably led to calls for Washington to do something to stop the slide.

Bankruptcy laws were written for this very kind of moment, but many who bet the farm and lost demanded exemptions as America's addiction to borrowing swiftly morphed into an expectation of bailouts. The government obliged, as first hundreds of billions, then trillions of taxpayer dollars and guarantees were poured into the breach. Time and again, the argument was that failure of key firms or industries would bring down the system.

When it came to individual homeowners, proponents of promiscuous aid argued that government had an absolute duty to help virtually all those facing foreclosure. Everybody had a stake, we were assured, in preventing failure.

Letting someone fail when we have the power to prevent it seems so robber-baron-ish, so social Darwinist, especially when the shock waves could ripple across the country. This Gilded Age comes equipped with safety nets for those in danger of losing their gilt.

These days wherever you look, failure is an endangered experience. Unions, once the champion of the oppressed, increasingly fight for rigid protections that put the lazy worker on an equal footing with the productive one. Consider that Detroit automakers had a jobs bank program that paid extra workers for not working, sometimes for years. No wonder the companies went bust.

But Detroit's policies pale next to the social promotion movement that has turned much of our nation's educational system into a global joke. Instead of demanding that students meet academic requirements that will prepare them for college or the workforce, today's educrats find it easier just to pass little Johnny along, even when he is illiterate. And when Johnny gets bigger and still can't read, they pass him along again, sending him out into the world, which usually finds it has no use for him.

All this is done, of course, in the name of compassion. Armies of psychologists and other captains of the self-esteem movement wail that holding Johnny back until he is actually ready for the next grade will destroy his psyche. In the real world, self-esteem comes from mastering new skills and achieving goals. But the antifailure forces have turned the idea on its head: They think they can give Johnny self-esteem first, and only later ask him to earn it.

As the late William Henry III argued forcefully in his ground-breaking 1994 book, *In Defense of Elitism,* "We have taken the legal notion that all men are created equal to its illogical extreme, seeking not just equality of justice in the courts but equality of outcomes in almost every field of endeavor."

This disastrous egalitarianism, which Henry blamed on a multi-cultural movement to delegitimize individual accomplishment, led by those who couldn't compete, is now so entrenched that many of Johnny's teachers are themselves products of the same social promotion disaster. Naturally, flunking bad teachers—and booting them out of the schools where they don't belong—runs afoul of ironclad union protections. Better that all students should just be passed along so teachers can keep their jobs.

Nationally, upward of 60 percent of American high school graduates entering two-year community colleges do not meet entrance standards and need remediation work.

The New York City experience is as instructive as it is disheartening. In 2008, four years after the city supposedly ended social promotion policies, nearly 75 percent of high school grads entering the City University's community colleges needed remediation in reading, writing, or math. Many needed it in all three. That is the case even though the community colleges have open enrollment, meaning the only requirement for admission is a high school diploma.

As part of the so-called reforms, Mayor Bloomberg's education department created report cards for schools and promised teacher and principal bonuses in schools that met benchmarks. Talk about grade inflation! For 2008, 97 percent of the schools received either an A or a B, forcing the cash-strapped city to pay out as much as $35 million in bonuses. The scam—that's what it is—recalls the joke among factory workers in the waning days of the Soviet Union: we pretend to work and they pretend to pay us.

So it is in many of America's schools, where every tough new standard is hollowed out by an even stronger push to make sure nobody fails to meet it.

Nearly all education officials and politicians clamor to raise student achievement and the graduation rate because they understand a solid education is needed for someone to be a productive citizen in the twenty-first century. These proponents, in effect, recognize the value of success.

But they want it guaranteed and without allowing the chance for failure. By lowering standards and bending the rules to boost the graduation rate, they are creating a Potemkin village of success. There is still massive failure, but it will be revealed only later.

The fraud is a perfect illustration of the doomed and misguided zeal to sandpaper failure from American life. Students waste their educational years and are not forced to develop the knowledge and skills that will prepare them for life after school. Most realize they have been duped only when they collide with a wall that hasn't been lowered to meet their stunted abilities. Had they been allowed to fail earlier, they would have a far better chance of leading productive lives as adults.

Yet there is a winner in this scam: bad teachers. Here, too, failure is not an option. Those who can't do the job are almost all protected by tenure rules that make it nearly impossible to fire them. In most years, only about 1 percent of New York's eighty thousand teachers are given an unsatisfactory rating in the annual pass-fail review. Match that against the 40 percent of students who do not graduate on time and the others who do get diplomas but need remediation, and the only honest conclusion is that thousands of teachers should not be allowed near a classroom.

Wait, it gets more infuriating. Because of union protections, those few teachers who do fail reviews usually face no penalties. Many of the worst still manage to find jobs teaching and inflict their poison on another class of children. A former chancellor dubbed their survival "the dance of the lemons."

Some are paid not to work in a program similar to the automakers' jobs bank. It's called the "rubber room," and New York pays at least seven hundred teachers a year not to teach, at a cost of about $200 million. They sit in unused classrooms and offices, reading newspapers, sleeping, or watching TV, waiting for adjudication of various issues or for a classroom vacancy. They might as well be waiting for Godot.

The overarching truth is that one of the great achievements of the American Experiment, the democratization of learning, is being sabotaged by a regressive monopoly that is little more than an adult jobs program. Bureaucrats and unions, aided and abetted by feckless politicians, conspire to resist any form of competition, including merit pay for teachers and principals and union-free charter schools. Virtually anywhere they have been allowed, charter schools yield better results with students from the same demographic who fail to learn in nearby unionized schools. Ditto for most inner-city parochial schools, especially those run by the Catholic Church, which send 98 percent of their students to college.

Someday, the public at large will figure out it is being hoodwinked and overthrow the educational monopoly strangling public schools. When that day comes, all of America's children will have a true chance to succeed.

Let it not be said that the antifailure mob has overlooked any opportunities to work its mischief. One growing focus is youth sports, where bureaucratized compassion has found an enemy in the very idea of competition. It may seem to the uninitiated that competition is the point of sports, but apparently that is not so. The new idea taking hold in our culture of noncompetitive sport is that kids can play games without winning or losing. That way, nobody believes they are better or worse than anybody else.

The website for a Wisconsin T-ball league makes it clear that the goal is to "develop individual player skills in a noncompetitive environment" and emphasizes "There is no score keeping of any kind." The manifesto goes on to list thirteen "Performance Goals" ("Players will demonstrate knowledge of Tee Ball rules"), eight safety rules ("No Sliding"), and twenty other rules, including three for coaches. There are sixteen more rules under "Play of the Game," starting with the command to "Make the game fun." Five more specifications about the size and shape of the field, and it's "Play Ball" —sort of.

Anyone tempted to credit the adults behind such fiddle-faddle with a simple excess of compassion should resist. Ending the freedom to fail is a mean-spirited attack on the freedom to succeed. Without failure, how can we know success?

Certainly the dictionary doesn't know. The definition for "failure" is generally described as the opposite of success. Thus, failure is something or someone "unsuccessful." It is a "lack of success" and "nonperformance." To "fail" is to "fall short of success."

The point is more than mere wordplay. Failure and success are as inseparable as two sides of the same coin. Just as we don't know pleasure without pain, fullness without hunger, or black without white, we can't define success without its opposite. It's true; you can't have one without the other. Someone who is not free to fail is not truly free to succeed.

Adults who must compete in the real world, where there are rewards for success and penalties for failure, understand this integral relationship. Carrots and sticks are the commonsense way of managing virtually any enterprise and moving it toward a goal. Those who reach their goals are winners, and our society heartily celebrates them.

But we can't measure success unless we are also willing to measure failure truly and accurately. Failure is prevalent in every human endeavor, and to pretend otherwise—through social promotion or endless bailouts or a stubborn refusal to keep score—is to create a false Utopia that will eventually destroy any organization in its thrall. That's why a staple of management gurus is the idea that those who cannot produce must be fired, both as a deterrent to others and as a spur to the entire organization.

The head of a major cable television network scoffs at the notion that failure should be avoided. This successful executive, who asks that she and her company remain anonymous, has found an unusual way to inspire her creative talent to keep taking chances: she gives an annual "Failure Award."

By rewarding the best idea that nonetheless flopped, she aims to reinforce the message that playing it safe is a dead end in the fast-changing, competitive business of TV programming. With consumers having hundreds of choices at the click of a remote, she believes her company can stay successful only if it takes risks in the conceptual, developmental, and operational stages. The ideas that wash out are more than offset by the hits the process yields.

Perhaps no business superstar has thought more deeply about the relationship between success and failure than Lew Frankfort, the chairman and CEO of Coach, the leather goods maker. Now in his thirtieth year at the company, Frankfort left a management job in government because he found the rules and low expectations stifling. "It wasn't a meritocracy," he said.

Rising through the ranks at Coach, then a sleepy unit (oddly enough) of Sara Lee, Frankfort took the brand public in 2000. Its growth since then has been a phenomenon, with sales of about $3 billion a year through hundreds of stores in the United States and twenty other countries. It is the leader in the "affordable luxury" category of handbags and other goods, with a global market share double its closest rival.

Success certainly has its rewards. Frankfort, whose father was a New York City detective, has made as much as $86 million in a single year, through salary, bonuses, and stock options. He lives very well, enjoys expensive toys, and gives generously to educational and other causes.

Yet he can't shake an abiding fear of failure, or the sense that it plays a major role in his success. "I've always been motivated by a drive for excellence and a simultaneous fear of failure. It's a very wicked combination because no matter what I do, what level of achievement I have, I won't be satisfied, and I will always be afraid I'm going to fail on the next level," he tells me.

Frankfort relays this conflict in matter-of-fact tones as we sit in his airy office atop Coach's headquarters in Manhattan. It is a beautiful, warm spring day, but he is talking about vivid fears that come in the night, in what he calls "failure dreams."

One of these takes place in the suburban New Jersey home where he and his wife Bobbi raised their three children. Out one window is a serene pastoral view; out the other and down a hill, it's the gritty Bronx neighborhood where Frankfort grew up. Sometimes he wakes in a panic, frightened his home is sliding down the hill, back into the Bronx, signaling, he believes, a fear he'll lose all he has gained.

Frankfort believes the fear of failure is common among successful people, even if many of them do not acknowledge or understand the dynamic playing out in their own heads. He sees the fear of failure as far more prevalent in America than in Europe and thinks it has its roots in our mobile society and the sense that anything is possible in America.

The last point is especially relevant given the growing chorus that wants our nation to adopt many of the rigid government controls and extensive labor protections common in Europe. The entrepreneurial, market-driven nature of our capitalist system, which has made America the world's lone economic superpower and a magnet for strivers from around the globe, is under fierce attack as fundamentally flawed, with the painful recession cited as the latest proof.

While additional regulations are inevitable on new and exotic trading instruments, wholesale calls to smooth out capitalism's uneven results run against the grain of the failure-success correlation Frankfort describes in himself and other high-achieving Americans. Similarly, the urge by many bureaucrats and leftist organizations to slap excessive curbs on risk and executive compensation is another manifestation of the movement to reduce the freedom to fail by limiting the freedom to succeed. As usual, it's a doomed trade-off.

Frankfort incorporates the fear of failure into his management rules at Coach. The company expects rapid innovation and production—it introduces new products every month—and needs talented people who can function under intense pressure. Those who meet the demands are rewarded with annual bonuses, and top achievers are publicly recognized and given shares of company stock.

There are losers, too, in what Frankfort calls Coach's "performance family." He states, "What we have come to believe is that the people who are the long-term best performers take calculated risks. Those who are more security minded will tend not to get ahead as much and will be the less innovative people."

In other words, those whose fear of failure inhibits them usually cannot meet the performance standards Coach requires. They are among the 6 or 7 percent of new hires the company terminates within the first twenty-four months, a level Frankfort finds acceptable and comparable to the bottom 5 percent Jack Welch famously weeded out at GE.

Frankfort holds himself to those standards, telling me in 2009, "I am not getting a bonus this year, and no one in my group is getting one. Not because we lost money or didn't do well, but because we did less well than last year and less well than our plan."

Perhaps there is a land over the rainbow where everyone always wins and nobody ever loses. Perhaps we will get there one day. In the meantime, in this world, we are stuck with the verity that success and failure are inseparable. "In order to succeed, you must first be willing to fail," goes an old saying. So it was, and so it remains, no matter how much we wish and pretend otherwise.

8

The European Union as a
Threat to Freedom

Daniel Hannan

PICTURE A MAP of the world. Where do you expect to find the biggest threats to American liberty? In Iran? In Red China? In the more radical Arab states? Among Latin American *anti-yanquistas?*

Come off it: think of the economic and military imbalance. There are plenty of people in those parts of the world who dislike American values. But none of them is exactly challenging you for supremacy.

No, far more invidious in the long run is the development of the European Union (EU), an organization founded under American tutelage, and which spent its first three decades as a more or less reliable ally, but whose ideology is now drifting farther and farther from that which underpins American democracy.

I don't mean, of course, that the EU will pose a direct military threat to the United States. Although some extreme Euro-integrationists daydream about a united Europe acting as a counterbalance to the American *"hyper-puissance,"* most mainstream European politicians support NATO. The danger is subtler, coming, as it does, from allies. It isn't to be found in bombs or even, very much, in trade disputes. It resides, rather, in a profound difference in what the Germans call Weltanschauung: one's way of looking at the world.

Where American policy tends to favor the dispersal of power, European policy favors its concentration (the EU, for example, uses its trade and aid policies to encourage other states to form themselves into regional blocs on the European model). Where America tends to side with the masses, the EU prefers to deal with the elites.

Where the United States, other things being equal, tries to uphold national sovereignty, the EU likes global technocracies: the International Criminal Court, the Kyoto process, and so on. And, where the sympathy of the American is with personal liberty and limited government, the European shudders at what he sees as the heartlessness and chaos of the American model.

Small wonder, then, that the EU should be such an inspiration to those in the United States who want a different model of domestic government: those, that is, who want higher taxes, a stronger state, universal welfare entitlements, government-run health care, and the rest.

American leftists generally support the EU in foreign policy, which is fair enough. This essay is not aimed at them. It is aimed, rather, at everyone else: not just American conservatives, but the broad mass of apolitical people who feel that they live in a free country and who want to keep it that way.

Look again at that map. Let your eye rest on the areas more regularly cited as threats to the United States. In all of them, you will find that Brussels is taking a very different line from Washington.

In China, the EU continues to isolate Taiwan and has declared its willingness in principle to sell arms to the Communist regime (although, as yet, no arms have been sold). In Cuba, Brussels refuses to do business with the anti-Castro dissidents and angrily denounces the American embargo. In Israel, the European Commission is determined to keep funneling money to Hamas, despite its own rules on not financing proscribed terrorist organizations. In Iran, European foreign ministers have spent fifteen years pursuing a policy of "constructive engagement" in the hope of jollying the ayatollahs out of their nuclear ambitions.

At first glance, these disagreements might seem unrelated. Look a little more closely, though, and you will see that they are aspects of the same difference in outlook. In each case, Europe tends to favor stability over democracy, America democracy over stability.

Why the EU Is Undemocratic

All states, all polities, all unions grow according to the DNA encoded at the moment of their conception. The United States was the product of a popular revolt against a remote autocracy. Its founders were determined, above all else, to prevent the concentration of power. Accordingly, American democracy has tended to develop along what we might call Jeffersonian lines: jurisdiction is dispersed; decisions are made as closely as possible to the people they affect; decision makers, wherever practical, are accountable.

The EU, too, is a product of its time. Its founders were chiefly concerned with preventing wars. They looked back with horror at the plebiscitary democracy of the 1920s and 1930s: in their eyes, it had been the precursor to fascism and war. Whereas the United States' founding fathers saw representative government as a guarantee against tyranny, the EU's saw it as a prelude. They fretted that, if voters were given unconstrained powers, they might fall for demagogues. They aimed to trammel democracy: to ensure that public opinion was mitigated by a class of sober functionaries.

Accordingly, they designed a system in which supreme power was vested in the hands of unelected civil servants. The only EU institution that can propose legislation is the European Commission, a large bureaucracy that answers to twenty-seven appointed commissioners, one from each member state.

When critics attack the EU as hypocritical over its readiness to cozy up to unpleasant regimes in Beijing, Havana, or Tehran, they are missing the point. The EU is simply extending its foundational principles to its foreign policy. Just as it is prepared to swat aside referendums within its own borders when they go the "wrong" way, so it has little time for the idea that a foreign government is at fault simply because it lacks an electoral mandate.

You will often hear people talk of the EU's "democratic deficit" as though it were an accidental design flaw. It wasn't. The men who conceived the plan for a united Europe—above all Robert Schuman and Jean Monnet—understood that their scheme would never come to fruition if each successive transfer of power from the national capitals to Brussels had to be referred to the voters for approval. That is why they were careful to make the European Commission—"the motor of European integration," as it calls itself—invulnerable to public opinion. A lifelong servant of that system will naturally have more sympathy with unelected regimes overseas than would an elected politician.

Why the EU Is Anti-Israel

Sympathy—in the literal sense of fellow feeling—is an important factor in diplomacy. Consider the Israel-Palestine dispute. An American politician, looking at the Middle East, is likely to feel sympathy with Israel as the country that most resembles his own: a parliamentary democracy based on property rights and the rule of law, a state founded in adversity which elected its generals as its first leaders. But to the Euro-sophist, who dislikes "coca-colonialism" and feels that the French farmers who stone McDonald's have a point, things look very different. To him, Israel represents an incursion of precisely the same globalized culture that he resents in America. Just as his sympathy is with the settled European smallholder threatened by Wal-Mart, so it is with the Bedouin in his flowing robes.

In my ten years in the European Parliament, I have often wondered why Israel seems to provoke anger out of all proportion to its population or strategic importance. It is the subject of endless emergency debates and condemnatory resolutions. The EU takes very seriously its role as the chief financial sponsor and international patron of the Palestinian regime. Americans often put the phenomenon down to anti-Semitism, but this won't quite do. There *are* anti-Semites in Europe, of course; but many of those who are angriest in their denunciations of the Jewish state have honorable records of opposing discrimination at home.

So why does Israel find it so much harder to get a fair hearing in Brussels than in Washington? Partly because the EU sees its role as being to counterbalance the United States. Partly, too, because of demographics: we are forever hearing about the "Jewish lobby" on Capitol Hill, but it is rarely mentioned that there are more than three times as many Muslims in the EU as there are Jews in the United States.

The single biggest disadvantage that Israelis have in Brussels, however, is one that they can't do anything about. The story of Israel represents the supreme vindication of the national principle: that is, of the desire of every people to have their own state. For two thousand years, Jews were stateless and scattered, but they never lost their aspiration for nationhood: "Next year in Jerusalem." Then, one day, astonishingly—providentially, we might almost say—they achieved it.

Looked at from an American perspective, it's a heartening story. But, to a convinced Euro-integrationist, national feelings are transient, arbitrary, and ultimately discreditable. Simply by existing, Israel challenges the intellectual basis of the European project. As one Christian Democratic member of the European Parliament (MEP) put it in a recent debate, "Why is Israel building walls when the rest of us are pulling them down?"

1787 versus 2004

Such attitudes are hardwired into the EU: its spokespersons today are faithfully reciting its founders' creed. To grasp the extent to which the United States and the EU diverge in their design, look at the key documents. The U.S. Constitution, with all its amendments, is seventy-two hundred words long; the EU constitution, now newly adopted under its new name of the Lisbon Treaty, is seventy-six thousand words long. The U.S. Constitution is mainly concerned with the rights of the individual; the EU constitution with the power of the state. The U.S. Constitution sets out broad principles, such as the division of power between legislature and executive, and the role of the states; the EU constitution busies itself with such minutiae as the rights of asylum seekers and the status of disabled people. The U.S. Declaration of Independence promises the right to "life, liberty and the pursuit of happiness"; the EU Charter of Fundamental Rights and Freedoms promises the right to "strike action," "affordable housing," and "free healthcare." The U.S. Constitution begins, "We, the people"; the Treaty of Rome, the EU's inaugural charter, begins, "His Majesty the King of the Belgians."

The most telling distinction, though, can be found in how the two documents were adopted. The U.S. Constitution came into effect when it had been separately ratified by specially elected conventions within the participating states. The EU constitution was repeatedly rejected in referendums—surely the modern equivalent—and was implemented anyway.

When the EU constitution was first drawn up in 2004, its authors had the American precedent firmly in mind. The chairman of the drafting convention, the former French President Valéry Giscard d'Estaing, called it "our Philadelphia moment" and compared himself to Thomas Jefferson (inaccurately as well as immodestly, since Jefferson wasn't in Philadelphia at the time: he was, as Giscard might have been expected to know, ambassador to France). Several of the member states promised to put the text to their peoples in referendums.

It turned out, not for the first time, that the citizens of Europe didn't see things quite the way their leaders did. The constitution was rejected in referendums, first by 54 percent of French voters, then by 62 percent of Dutch voters.

At this point, you might have expected EU leaders to take the document off the table and come up with something different. But that isn't how the EU works. There is never a Plan B in Brussels: Plan A is simply resubmitted over and over again until it is bludgeoned through. Thus, the EU leaders scrambled the text of the constitution and renamed it the Treaty of Lisbon. No substantive changes were made—none. As Giscard himself put it, with admirable frankness, the lawyers had simply rendered his clauses "unreadable." In the meantime, though, all the promises of referendums were quietly dropped, and the new version was pushed through by parliamentary ratification.

Only Ireland, whose national constitution requires referendums in cases of this kind, held a vote. Irish people duly did what voters anywhere else would have done, with 53 percent of voters rejecting the text. Needless to say, Brussels again refused to take no for an answer and forced the Irish to vote again. It was eerily reminiscent of that poem by Bertolt Brecht that ends, "Wouldn't it be easier to dissolve the people and elect another in their place?"

Why Europeans Seldom Vote

If you think that quotation is too harsh, look at what is happening to turnout rates. Of those Europeans who had taken the trouble to register to vote in the June 2009 elections to the European Parliament, no fewer than 57 percent declined to cast their ballots on the day. The figure is all the more remarkable when we consider that voting is compulsory in some member states, that others sought to boost participation by holding municipal elections on the same day, and that Brussels had spent hundreds of millions of Euros on a campaign to encourage turnout. (One of its gimmicks was to send a ballot box into orbit, which critics joyfully seized upon as the perfect symbol of the EU's remoteness.)

Not that the abstention rate should have surprised anyone. As the figures below show, there has been an unbroken decline in turnout since the first elections to the European Parliament were held in 1979.

Table 1. Turnout at European Elections (percent)

1979	62
1984	59
1989	58.4
1994	56.7
1999	49.5
2004	45.6
2009	43.1

The statistics are a serious embarrassment for Euro-integrationists. In the early days, they used to argue that the high abstention rate was a consequence of unfamiliarity, or a function of the relative powerlessness of the new institution. Give the European Parliament more authority, they contended, and it would attract a higher caliber of candidate. Let it make a real difference to people, and they would take more of an interest in it.

That theory has now been pretty comprehensively disproved. For thirty years, the European Parliament—like the EU in general—has been steadily agglomerating power. Yet people have responded by refusing to sanction it with their votes. Back in 1979, when no one really knew what the European Parliament was, and Euro-elections were treated as a series of miniature referendums on national governments, people voted willingly enough. Now that they have a sense of what the EU is about, they want nothing to do with it.

The response of most MEPs is, if not in so many words, to blame the voters. In the weeks that followed the poll, I listened as my colleagues demanded better information campaigns, more extensive propaganda. Europe was more important than ever, they insisted, and national electorates had to be made to see it.

This is to beg the question. The idea that people could be made to love Brussels has been comprehensively refuted by the empirical data. Euro-integrationists have tried giving the EU serious powers. It now runs agriculture; fisheries; industrial, social, and employment policy; trade; and a chunk of taxation, and is gaining substantial powers in the fields of defense, foreign affairs, and criminal justice. According to the only comprehensive study, carried out by the German Federal Justice Ministry, the EU is responsible for an almost unbelievable 84 percent of legislation in Germany (and therefore, presumably, in all the other states, too). Euro-enthusiasts have even bestowed on the EU the attributes of statehood—a parliament, a currency, a passport, external borders, a flag, a national anthem—but people stubbornly refuse to see themselves as Europeans. They continue to offer their primary loyalty to their national institutions, to which they are bound by ties of language, culture, and history.

To put it another way, there is no European *demos*—no unit with which we identify when we use the word "we." Almost nobody feels European in the same way that someone might feel Canadian or Japanese or Norwegian. Representative government cannot work except in a unit where people feel enough in common one with another to accept government from each other's hands. Take away the *demos* and you are left only with the *kratos*: with the power of a system that must compel by force of law that which it cannot ask in the name of civic patriotism.

Europeans ought to be familiar with the pattern. There have been plenty of multinational states in this part of the world: the Habsburg and Ottoman empires, the Soviet Union, Yugoslavia. But none of them was a democracy. As soon as their peoples were given the right to vote, they used it to opt for national separation.

Repatriate the American Revolution

What, then, is my solution? How about this? Instead of starting from the proposition that there must be a political union in Europe, and then casting around for ways to bring the electorates around to the idea, why not start with what people want? People evidently feel that government is too remote, that they have little bearing on the decisions that affect them. So why not copy some of the ideas that address these concerns: localism, states' rights, devolution, direct democracy? Why not drop the idea of a federal Europe and limit the EU's jurisdiction to a handful of cross-border issues, notably trade? Why not close down the European Parliament and much of the EU bureaucracy and reduce the European Commission to a small secretariat, more in line with what happens in Mercosur, NAFTA, ASEAN, and other regional trade blocs?

Euro-enthusiasts usually dismiss this idea as "Americanization" which, in their minds, pretty well closes down the arguments. But, in Britain at least, we might more productively think of it as reimporting our own revolution.

I realize that this may strike American readers as a curious notion. Most of the accounts of the American Revolution written by later

generations of U.S. historians tended to present it as a national rising—as, indeed, the War of Independence. But go back to the sources
and listen to how the patriot leaders were arguing *at the time*. They
saw themselves, not as revolutionaries, but as conservatives. In
their eyes, they were asking for nothing more than what they had
always assumed to be their rights as freeborn Englishmen. It was
the Hanoverian court, they believed, that was revolutionary, unbal-
ancing the ancient constitution by seeking to impose an autocratic
settlement.

Which brings me to my nation's present tragedy. The grievances
laid against George III by the colonial leaders—the levying of taxation without consent, the passing of unjust laws, the sidelining of
the legislature, and the concentration of power in the executive—
have come about in our own time. And the main force behind them
is European integration. In order to sustain a system that lacks popular support, the twenty-seven member states have all had to sacrifice
a measure of their domestic democracy.

Britain's greatest export, our supreme contribution to the happiness of mankind, was the idea that laws should be passed only by
the people's elected representatives. Our fathers carried the seeds of
that idea to far continents, where it found fertile soil. But in Britain,
the ancestral tree is withering. It is time to bring back the liberties
that flourish in our former colonies. It is time to repatriate the revolution.

Why Americans Should Care

Why should any of this matter to Americans? For three reasons.
First, as I hope I've demonstrated by now, the EU is a troublesome
diplomatic partner, not out of perversity, but because it is seeking to
export its ideology.

Second, the United States has not been impartial about this ideology. For half a century, more or less regardless of which party has
controlled the White House or Congress, the State Department has
been actively and uncritically supportive of European integration.
Diplomats the world over have a tendency to act according to strate-

gic assumptions whose justification has since ceased to pertain, and this is such a case.

From the 1950s to the 1980s, the State Department saw the European Economic Community (EEC, as it then was) as the economic wing of NATO: a bulwark against Soviet expansionism. When the Berlin Wall collapsed, and Europeans no longer needed to worry about the American guarantee, the EU (as it now became) started to take a much more anti-American line. I remember visiting France during the referendum on the Maastricht Treaty in 1992. The official posters from the governing Socialist Party showed a caricatured Texan in a Stetson hat squashing the globe and carried the caption, "*Faire l'Europe c'est faire le poids*" ("Building Europe gives us weight"). It was the first sign of a new and different European attitude to foreign policy. Yet, through diplomatic inertia, successive U.S. administrations have continued to support a project that has long since ceased to be friendly to America.

Above all, though, the United States should be true to its own Constitution and to the vision of its founders. They believed that, although the new republic should be reluctant to entangle itself in alliances, its sympathy should be with the democratic case.

This, surely, is the attitude that the United States ought to adopt toward the EU today. No one is asking Washington to intervene actively against the process of political unification: the peoples of Europe will do that themselves. But it is surely not too much to ask the administration to stop lending its support to a project that is as deleterious to the interests of ordinary Europeans as to those of the United States.

America was founded as an ideal, as an inspiration. When Barack Obama became president, he conjured, albeit in different words, John Winthrop's vision of the New World as a city on a hill. American authority, he told the cheering crowd, would rest on the rectitude of her example, not the supremacy of her armies. How strange, then, to see the Republic going in the opposite direction and reimporting from the Old World the centralized forms of government that its founders thought they had escaped.

9

Bad Political Theatre

Alexander Harrington

IN PREREVOLUTIONARY FRANCE, Beaumarchais' *The Marriage of Figaro* brought out into the open criticism of the aristocracy. In 1852, Harriet Beecher Stowe's *Uncle Tom's Cabin* (of which numerous stage adaptations were produced) stirred up opposition to the fugitive slave law and won people over to the abolitionist cause. Many believers in the politically transformative power of art would cite the Group Theatre's production of Clifford Odets's *Waiting for Lefty*, which sent its audience out into the street shouting "Strike!"

I imagine the Group Theatre's audience was predisposed to shout "Strike!" and I do not know whether these demonstrations translated into political action. But such works as *Uncle Tom's Cabin* and *The Marriage of Figaro* are unusual. Political art rarely has political effects. Also, political art is, more often than not, inferior art. Most of the greatest works of literature present human beings in all their complexity without tailoring that complexity to fit an agenda.

Nonetheless, a political play can be an aesthetically and/or viscerally powerful work of art, despite being one-sided and didactic and, therefore, intellectually unchallenging. Political satire is often very funny and entertaining. And while it is rare for political theatre to have immediate practical consequences, it can serve a political purpose. Producing dissident theatre in authoritarian societies that brutally repress artistic expression is an act of courage that may be one of many small acts of defiance that can, in the long run, bring about change. Even if such plays are presented only to audiences in agreement with the play's views, under such oppressive circumstances, there is something to be said for building the morale of the opposition. When presented to an audience that does not share the play's assumptions, a political play can challenge political beliefs and open minds. However, in relatively comfortable and relatively free liberal democracies, like the United States, theatre that panders to its audience's political assumptions has the opposite effect: it enforces conformity and shuts down debate.

Political theatre has been around since the first plays were performed in ancient Greece. Aristophanes wrote wickedly funny, farcical political and social satires, attacking the demagoguery and patronage of Athens' democratic politicians, the Peloponnesian War, and the dramatic innovations of Euripides. His plays aren't profound art, but they're great entertainment. For his part, Euripides penned what may be the first work of "victim art." Performed shortly after the Athenians killed all the military-aged men and enslaved the women and children on the neutral island of Melos, Euripides' *The Trojan Women* is a relentless catalogue of atrocities inflicted on the Trojans by the Greeks.

Shakespeare's major history plays (*Richard II; Henry IV, Parts 1 & 2;* and *Henry V*) pack emotional and intellectual power. For centuries, audiences and critics have debated the rights of and wrongs of Henry IV's overthrow of Richard II, Prince Hal's rejection of Falstaff, and whether *Henry V* is a nationalist glorification of war or a condemnation of it. The characters are richly drawn, contradictory human beings: Richard II, who bares his soul in gorgeous poetry when the identity of divinely anointed king is stripped from him; Henry IV, who may or may not have intended to seize the crown from self-sacrificing or self-serving motives, and who is prematurely aged by the civil strife brought on by his usurpation; and the charming, amoral, glory-debunking Falstaff, who loves Prince Hal not wisely, but too well.

Under the surface Shakespeare is probably saying that Machiavellians are most fit to govern. I have no idea whether he is proselytizing for cynical governance or simply presenting a sad fact of life. And, even if the plays are advocating for a particular political philosophy, the audience has much to wrestle with before they find

Shakespeare's message (if they ever do), and are caught up in and moved by deeply human stories.

Bertolt Brecht is probably theatre's most famous political artist. Though he described his plays as didactic, they are not simplistic. He never depicts the world as he believes it ought to be, nor does he show the struggle of the oppressed. He presents the world as it is, hoping to spur the audience to think, "That's not the way. . . . It's got to stop." Many of his characters—Galileo, Mother Courage, Azdak— are amoral survivors. His *Threepenny Opera* is a funny, entertaining, scathing satire. His other major works suffer from excessive length, and in the case of *The Caucasian Chalk Circle* and *The Good Person of Szechuan*, from being faux-naïve renderings of folk tales; they are inferior not because they're one-sided but because they're boring.

Brecht is not alone as a left-wing theatre artist. At least since the end of World War I, the perspective of Western political playwrights has run the gamut from left-wing to liberal. America's major politi- cal playwrights have all been critical of capitalism and bourgeois society—Clifford Odets, Lillian Hellman, Arthur Miller, Edward Albee (Tennessee Williams is the least political of the lot). Since the '60s there has been an explosion of plays that, inspired by the Afri- can American and later civil rights movements, focus on identity politics. The antiwar youth movement gave birth to a generation of plays aiming to *épater le bourgeoisie*. This latter group of plays is not worthy of comment, since shocking the establishment is rarely anything other than an adolescent exercise. Giving voice to politi- cally and culturally underrepresented groups is valuable, but as long as a play's primary purpose is to challenge an injustice, it is unlikely to be interesting, particularly when it is performed for sympathetic audiences. Also, playwrights belonging to traditionally oppressed groups should give themselves freedom to address other issues and ideas. As Edward Albee once said, "There are gay playwrights and playwrights who happen to be gay."

Arthur Miller, who was called before the House Un-American Activities Committee (HUAC), wrote both good and bad plays. Per- haps from populist motives, he set himself the task of writing the tragedy of the common man. He fails in *Death of a Salesman*, which is only political insofar as it criticizes American society's focus on making it in business, not because its protagonist is a common man, but because he is self-deceiving and never gains awareness. On the other hand, *All My Sons*, which is far more anticapitalist, is a potent tragedy of the common man, which goes after the failings of both pragmatism and idealism and ends with the revelation of an unintended kin-murder straight out of the Greeks.

Miller's most overtly political major play is *The Crucible*, which uses the Salem witch trials as an allegory for McCarthyism and HUAC. It is still performed in high schools across the country. I saw a production at a community theatre in South Carolina. Does this mean that these high school students and South Carolinians are all Communist fellow travelers? No. Taken out of the context of the 1950s, *The Crucible* is about suffering for one's beliefs, be they Communism or the right to life.

Joseph Papp was a political man of the theatre who actually accomplished tangible good. Determined to bring free Shakespeare to the people of New York, he challenged and defeated Robert Moses, one of the most powerful politicians in New York State, in order to do so. Papp also produced one of the defining pieces of sixties' countercultural theatre: John Rado, Gerome Ragni, and Galt McDermott's *Hair*. While having thrilling music, the play's political and cultural ideas are simplistic, adolescent, and petulant. Yet the sixties' counterculture did produce some truly challenging political theatre. LeRoi Jones's *Dutchman* was deeply unsettling to the white liberals, leftists, and bohemians who made up its audience. Similarly, Barbara Garson's notorious *MacBird* went after not only the much-maligned Lyndon Johnson, but the Kennedys and, by extension, the Democratic Party—not something with which everyone in her New York left/liberal audience would be comfortable.

Perhaps the most prominent of today's political theatre artists is Tony Kushner. Yet his landmark *Angels in America* is not really that political. Yes, its being a Broadway play focused on gay characters was significant, and the play does equate with the capitalist selfishness of the Reagan era a man who is too much of a physical coward to tend to his AIDS-infected lover. However, *Angels in America* is primarily a philosophical play about living in a world in which all faiths have been abandoned. It fails, not because it's political, but because it's too frivolous to contend with the issues it raises.

Kushner's translation of Brecht's *Mother Courage* was part of The Public Theatre's 2006 summer season of plays presented in response to the Iraq War at Central Park's Delacorte Theater. *Mother Courage* was preceded by Moises Kaufman's staging of *Macbeth* and followed by a free reading of David Hare's Iraq War play *Stuff Happens*. What purpose did this antiwar programming serve? Opponents of the war did not have to win the hearts and minds of New York theatregoers. The audience was not challenged but affirmed in their beliefs, and inspired to contempt and satisfying displays of antipathy. As the *New York Times* reported, "At a performance of *Stuff Happens* a few weeks ago the audience guffawed and at times jeered when the actor playing Mr. Bush delivered his lines."

The fact that *Stuff Happens* elicited this crude and simplistic response says more about the audience than it does about David Hare. The play strives to be a tragedy of moral compromise, and, on the page (I have not seen a production), it succeeds. The tragic protagonists are Tony Blair and Colin Powell. Blair's moral reason for his unswerving support of the Bush administration is that he is trying to build a world order in which military intervention is used to stop atrocities like those in Rwanda and the Balkans. Colin Powell's opposition to invading Iraq is made very clear in the play, and he is shown emphatically and successfully persuading Bush to use diplomacy and go through the United Nations. Hare refrains from facile Bush bashing: Hare's Bush is an enigmatic man of few words who gives off a sense of strong inner conviction.

In contrast, Judith Thompson's *Palace of the End* is an anti–Iraq War play that pandered not only to its New York audience's political prejudices, but its class and regional prejudices as well. The play consists of three monologues delivered by the disgraced Abu Ghraib prison guard Lynndie England, the deceased British weapons inspector David Kelly, and Nehrjas Al Saffarh (wife of a leader of the Iraqi Communist Party), who was tortured by Saddam Hussein's secret police and later killed by a U.S. bomb in the 1991 Persian Gulf War. In the Epic Theatre Ensemble's New York production directed by Daniella Topol, the trajectory of the play became obvious as soon as it began. On one side of the stage was the Soldier (it soon became clear who she was), drinking a fast-food soda and singing KFC's jingle. At the other end was a tastefully dressed woman whose area of the stage had beautiful Middle Eastern architecture, and on the carved table next to her was an elegant brass teapot. I knew right away that we were going to move from American trailer-trash brutality and fast-food sodas to Arab virtue and brass teapots. The play did not disappoint. England was presented as a stupid lower-class thug who had tortured a crippled girl as a child and was unrepentant about what she had done at Abu Ghraib. The closest Thompson comes to giving this Tobacco Road Neanderthal any humanity is to have her say she was hazed by the male soldiers, and express a twinge of conscience when remembering the dignity with which one of her victims refused to acquiesce in his own humiliation.

The play is not without its virtues. We all easily fall into looking at war as an "issue" to be intellectually debated. Kelly's story of the rape and murder of a fifteen-year-old Iraqi girl by U.S. soldiers and the dramatic narration of other horrific acts makes these abstractions specific. Unfortunately, the juxtaposition of the gross England to the saintly Al Saffarh reduces the play to the most simplistic kind of agitprop. And it is not effective agitprop. In addition to being performed in New York, it was performed in Los Angeles and Florence, Italy. If the play had been performed in more conservative communities in America, the big-city-intelligentsia contempt for the rest of the country that is evident in the Lynndie England monologue would have turned people off from the start.

This problem points up the fact that it is not sufficient to simply present a political play to an audience that does not share the play's perspective; it needs to raise issues in such a way that the audience will listen. While I was teaching at Clemson University in South

Carolina, playwright Suzan-Lori Parks initiated a project called *365 Days/365 Plays* in which she wrote a play a day for a year and then gave professional and amateur groups across the country the rights to present seven of the plays in a given week. One night a group of Clemson students presented seven of the short plays in a public square in the city of Greenville. "George Bush Visits the Cheese and Olive" involved Bush looking for weapons of mass destruction and evildoers under a table at a chain restaurant. The actor playing Bush wore a mask of the president's face. As I stood on the street watching, a family passed by, and the mother said, "It's just a bunch of liberals making fun of the president; keep walking."

A political performing artist who *has* gotten people to listen, and who has challenged assumptions (including mine) is Michael Moore. While some conservatives may have seen his earlier documentaries *Roger and Me* and *Bowling for Columbine,* I doubt there were many in the audience for *Fahrenheit 9/11,* his highly partisan film about the invasion of Iraq. I saw it with a friend who is an unquestioning liberal. She never had a moment of ambivalence about the Iraq War. Despite having opposed the invasion as, at the very least, premature, I thought war opponents who chanted "No blood for oil" were simplistic. Sitting in the movie, my friend, along with the crowd, laughed when she was supposed to laugh, gasped in horror at the appropriate moments, and even clucked her tongue when Republicans were speaking. I, too, gasped when Moore showed close-ups of Iraqis wounded and killed by U.S. bombing; an image of a child's arm ripped open to release gory pulp stays with me to this day. I was given a glimpse of what war really is and forced to question my intellectualization of war. As we left the theater, I said to my friend, "It was a very good thing that I saw this movie, and a very bad thing that you saw it."

Not every recent political play has focused on Iraq. *My Name Is Rachel Corrie* (culled by actor Alan Rickman and journalist Katherine Viner from the writings of the American activist who was killed by an Israeli bulldozer in Gaza) is about the Israeli-Palestinian conflict. This is an issue on which New York lefties and liberals strongly disagree. The mere scheduling of the play created such a furor that, in an act of craven pandering, New York Theatre Workshop canceled its production.

So is *My Name Is Rachel Corrie* a play that would have challenged the assumptions of pro-Israel New York liberals and leftists? On the page, there are a few isolated moments at which it has that potential: descriptions of the home life of Palestinian parents and children, specific details of the brutalization of Palestinians, such as the destruction of wells. However, there is a problem with the play: Rachel Corrie. This woman, who had more courage than I will ever have, comes across as a caricature of the most strident and Puritanical of leftists.

One recent play that has successfully challenged its downtown New York liberal-left audience is Young Jean Lee's *Church*. The play, which premiered in 2007 at the experimental theatre venue P.S. 122, presents an evangelical Christian service. After the house lights go out, the audience hears José, the only male clergy member of this congregation in which everyone is addressed as "reverend," say,

> Your spiritual bankruptcy is reflected in your endlessly repeating conversations about your struggles to quit smoking, quit drinking, quit junk food, quit caffeine, quit unsatisfying jobs and relationships—and this is what you talk about when you're trying to be deep. You claim to care about suffering in the world and take luxurious pleasure in raging against the perpetrators of that suffering, but this masturbation rage helps nothing and no one. . . . Let go of these superficial earthly ties and deliver yourself in humility to the Lord.

When the stage lights come up, Reverend Karinne asks the audience for prayer requests. At the performance that was recorded for the DVD I viewed, an audience member named Raphael mischievously requests a prayer for gay marriage. Reverend Karinne responds, "Send your prayers to Raphael, and everybody who wants gay marriage; pray for tolerance and acceptance."

Later, Reverend Weena, punctuated by the chanting of the congregation, asserts that the congregation shares the values of the downtown New York audience:

> We believe that all of Jesus' political beliefs are right and just and that we must stand against racial discrimination, homophobia, anti-abortion, commercialism, war, and indifference. (chant: God is life) We believe that is sin to engage in masturbation rage against the perpetrators of this evil without doing anything concrete to create change. We believe that pontificating and making art about political subjects doesn't count as concrete action and is a form of masturbation rage (chant: Jesus Christ is Lord). We believe that it is sin to attempt in self-help therapy; it is just as wrongful as living a polluted and dysfunctional lifestyle if one is only focused on the self. (chant: The spirit is love. Rev Karinne: Dear God please have mercy on me)

Before this, Reverend José has said,

> Now, Jesus didn't go around picking on people for drinking too much or having pre-marital sex or being homosexuals. He wasn't interested in condemning people for their personal lives. Jesus was interested in things we experience as clichéd abstractions: police brutality, illegal immigrants in prison, the child living in poverty, trying to do his homework without electricity. . . . All the greatest evil that has been done in this world has been perpetrated by people who are prospering and terrified, just like you.

After the penultimate sermon, the congregation dances to some surprisingly infectious Christian pop.

Church not only challenges its audience, it has the potential to make secular audiences reconsider their prejudices. *Church* might also challenge religious audiences. While I doubt many conservative Christians would accept the notion that Christ wanted people to stand against homophobia, it might call into question focusing on sexual morality and hostility toward homosexuals.

Brecht once wrote,

> The theatre must in fact remain something entirely super-fluous, though this indeed means that it is the superfluous for which we live. Nothing needs less justification than pleasure. . . . Yet, there are weaker (simple) and stronger (complex) pleasures which the theatre can create. The last named, which are what we are dealing with in great drama, attain their climaxes rather as cohabitation does through love: they are more intricate, richer in communication, more contradictory, and more productive of results.

Brecht was not being entirely sincere in writing that the theatre was superfluous, for he goes on to write that one of the "stronger pleasures" of theatre is "construct[ing] workable representations of society, which are in turn in a position to influence society." For me, the difference between a weaker pleasure in the theatre (say *The Mikado*) and a stronger pleasure (*Richard II*) is the difference between sitting at home watching sitcoms and playing a sport. The stronger pleasure develops your muscles (in the case of theatre, intel-lectual muscles) and is invigorating and exciting. It is good for *you*, not for society. So, if a play is not going to change the world, why (even when your ideas are under attack) should it make you intel-lectually flabby and intolerant by pandering to your beliefs?

Changing attitudes and encouraging tolerance is the only kind of change that we can reasonably expect art to bring about. Plays that pander to prejudices (including preconceived assumptions as well as irrational hatreds) have the opposite effect; they encourage intol-erance toward the beliefs of others. Within the liberal to left-wing community, which makes up a disproportionate percentage of the audience for serious theatre, liberal/left political plays foster intel-lectual conformity.

Although I am not a conservative, I once tried to put together a "Waiting for Righty" festival of plays that would challenge the political assumptions of New York theatregoers. A friend of a friend said to me, "Alec, why do you want people to hate you?" Though she spoke partly out of concern for me, she completely missed the point that theatre does not "belong" to one side or the other and that its political role, if any, is to challenge dogmatic beliefs and force people to think for themselves. Only when it does that can it be said to contribute to freedom in a meaningful way.

10

The Rise of Antireligious Orthodoxy

Mark Helprin

All men shall be free to profess, and by argument to maintain,
their opinions in matters of religion, and . . . the same shall
in no wise diminish, enlarge, or affect their civil capacities.

THOMAS JEFFERSON,
Virginia Bill for Religious Freedom, 1786

HALF A CENTURY ago from the east bank of the Hudson, you could
see white excursion boats regularly steaming through the wide Tap-
pan Zee and toward the mountain walls of the Hudson highlands.
One Friday afternoon near the end of the school year, I was there at
Eagle Bay in the bright sunshine with two other rising ninth-graders.
Our blazers, ties, and briefcases, the tell of private school boys, might
as well have been signs on our backs saying, "Please beat me up."

As we descended from the New York Central tracks to the river,
we saw a boy and a girl on the beach. She was sitting near the water,
legs extended and crossed, back straight, elbows locked, her palms
planted on the sand, and her face turned toward the sun. She may
not have grown up to be a beauty, but at thirteen, lightly sunburnt,
auburn-haired, with a beguiling chipped tooth, and her chest thrust
out self-consciously, she was as gorgeous as the light, and we were
drawn to her like iron bolts to an electromagnet.

Not that we would have been untoward, but we were discouraged
because accompanying her was an Irish kid with swollen muscles, a
buzz cut, and a nose as turned up as if his face were pressed against
glass: her bodyguard. Reacting to our approach as if we were four
thousand Zulus, he circled like a hornet. He was a liege man to her

boyfriend, who was some sort of kid bigwig, and his sacred duty was to prevent her from contact with boys such as us. She had other ideas, however, and, over and above her budding sexuality, she charmed us almost to death with her version of ascending to what she took to be our class, which was to speak and act like Margaret Dumont in a Marx Brothers movie.

She actually held out her hand and said, "Pleased, I'm sure." I actually kissed it, and my lips feel it to this day. Thus was lit the fuse of her escort, who related in vigorous language what he would do to us if we didn't leave, because she "belonged" to kid bigwig. Though it would have been three against one, for some reason rather than fight him we anxiously expatiated upon the Magna Carta, the First Amendment, riparian rights, and the self-evident truth that this lovely girl, whose sweet-smelling skin was making me dizzy, could not be anyone's property. After we presented our disquisitions as breathlessly as if to a cocked crossbow, he simply shouted, "Don't give me none a dat college stuff!"

Perhaps he was not Richard Dawkins. But like Richard Dawkins, he was restricting a particular question to a register of consideration limited so as to render an answer to his liking. Commanded not to depart the realms of his logic, were we to do so we would suffer coercion for defying its terms. What happened to us then is analogous to the contemporary means by which freedom of spiritual conscience is attacked for departing the limits and dictates of a self-contained system of thought, that of reason, which when honorably employed is admirable in part as a means by which to identify questions it is impotent to address, but when dishonorably employed glories in the limits of other approaches while admitting none of its own.

Since time immemorial, insistence upon a sole path to truth has been essential to intolerance. Though traditionally directed toward unbelievers and the improperly faithful, intolerance is catholic in its applicability and, just as a hurricane draws energy from warm seas, is now sustained by the exercise of its powers against believers. After a long tryout in the totalitarian states of the previous century, where, due not to its nature but to theirs, it was violent—as is not the prospect here—this intolerance is new to the free West.

The intolerant will tell you in the same breath both that they are not and that they have every right to be; that historically and by nature religion is intolerant, and therefore should not be tolerated. They are correct in that they do have a right within the limits of the law to the intolerance they condemn in others. This might be reassuring were it not for the fact that their intent in testing the law is to transform it into an instrument of opinion with which to extend its limits. In the academy, media, and the great secular cities, the varieties of religious experience that have not petrified into politics and social service are mocked and challenged, as any traditional Catholic, Evangelical Protestant, or Orthodox Jew can attest. As the fashionable redefinition of morals proceeds at a white-hot pace, the biggest prize goes to whatever new turn of thought implies that the sentiments and achievements of every civilization up to this morning are reprehensible by default. Ancient, once ubiquitous, and in the West increasingly the province of lower classes, religion is a prime target. And how would a right-thinking, rational person explain the sins common to diverse faiths often at each others' throats—opposition to abortion on demand, to euthanasia, same-sex marriage, utilitarianism, and so on—except to note that their adherents are so unpolished as to believe in God?

Thus threading through the ranks of political infantry charges a philosophical cavalry, its recently popular tracts of disproof held forward like lances to pierce the hearts of the idiots who stand defenselessly on faith. Their thesis has trickled down to the point where signs on buses tell you it's okay not to believe in God. Admitted, but what of signs that said, "It's okay not to be gay," "It's okay not to be black," "It's okay not to be a Jew"? While true, these statements are more than the simple expression of a point of view. Accurately perceived, they are an ugly form of pressure that while necessarily legal is nonetheless indecent.

Must belief be accepted like race, sex, or sexual orientation, accidental characteristics impossible to erase? No, but one is born, even if not indelibly, to culture and creed. Then, who is to say that the ability to apprehend transcendence is not as innate as are musical ability or the navigational prowess of birds? And although the common wisdom is to give every biologically determined predisposition a free pass, why should a meticulously explored, brilliantly cultivated belief receive less deference than, say, the genetic accidents that produce sexual predators of children?

Campaigns against transcendent belief are an old story, begun before the Enlightenment but there born into the open, nourished by the triumph of science, and, after the elimination in the West of the last remnants of theocracy, freed to seek predominance. We are now in the cardinal period, when what once was the imposition of belief and marginalization of unbelievers threatens to become an equally repulsive mirror image. Constitutional neutrality has been subjected to continual abrasion with the object of using state power to ban religion from public questions. This and a more freewheeling cultural assault are attacks upon the individual's private conception of reality, a fundamental natural right, and the deepest commitments of conscience.

The partisans here opposed offer in their defense a valid critique of pure tolerance. Were deep commitments of conscience, conceptions of reality, and traditions of ancient lineage harmful, imperious, or absurd, attacking them would be virtuous. Thus the case against religion, bypassing tolerance, rests upon three accusations: that historically it has been destructive; that it is incompatible with democracy; and that belief in God is unsupportable.

Innumerable soapboxes, dorm rooms, and dinner tables have heard over and over that religion, opiate of the masses, represses sex, causes war, and is the source of countless other bad things. For Marx it is an opiate in that it masks the pain that would otherwise spur the oppressed to throw off their chains. Characteristically monotonous and cruel, as well as totally blind to the spirit, he disregards the chains of suffering, disappointment, and death, which cannot ultimately be thrown off and for which an opiate is forgivable. Even were religious comfort only illusory, what kind of creature would seek what kind of victory in denying it to, for example, a woman facing the death of her child? And though religion has often shared in the faults of history, it has both philosophically and in practice broken the bonds of slavery, invented the sanctity of the individual, and warred against tyranny.

As for sex, every society has its codes, with the code of the Taliban and that of Herbert Marcuse, although diametrically opposed, bringing equal measures of misery and death. The judgment of what lies between is fluid and subjective, but in comparing, for example, the Amish to the hip—in terms of functionally orphaned children, neurotic alienated adults, and sexually transmitted diseases leading often to death—some forms of repression take on a certain glow, especially because, sexual drive being biologically constant in every era, its power is determined by its accumulation, focus, and timing, all of which libertines notoriously squander.

And as for war, having argued to Marxists that war can arise from forces other than just economics (such as, for example, religion), I can't deny it. Strangely enough, however, people who think religion the prime cause of war believe that the present war is over oil—which fails to explain why in Afghanistan, where we fight, there is no oil, whereas in Saudi Arabia, the United Arab Emirates, Venezuela, and Norway, where we don't, there is. (Perhaps they attribute the disjunction of their conclusions to the vagaries of geology.) Nor would I ignore the victims of the Crusades, my forbears being among them. The Crusades, however, were a predictable response to the continual expansion of Islam, which had made war from Mecca almost to the gates of Paris. Religious in tone, these were conflicts of nations and people in a recognizable international system.

At times religion has indeed been the cause of much of what its accusers state, but to what extent are these failings caused by religion rather than by the human nature of the religious and/or the character of the political systems in which religions must exist? Although this could be the subject of a vast historical work, as Gibbon would have it, "To a mind capable of reflection . . . leading facts

convey more instruction than a tedious detail of subordinate circumstances,"[1] and the leading fact is that the atrocities of religion
have been far exceeded by those of the fervently secular societies
from which religion has been extirpated.

Jealous tyrannies hostile to the slightest notion of transcendence—
from the "reason" of the French Revolution to Soviet scientific
socialism to North Korean *Juche*—have generated catastrophe on a
scale that dwarfs that of the wars of religion. Casualties attributable
to the purely secular and savagely anticlerical regimes of, inter alia,
Nazi Germany, Soviet Russia, Maoist China, Stalinist North Korea,
and Khmer Rouge Cambodia number 150 million dead and many
times that number condemned to lives of horror and oppression,
the gift of governance in which religion is replaced by worship of
the state and/or militant atheism. In the unprecedented wars and
genocides of modern times, religion cannot have been either a necessary or sufficient cause. And whether or not it is coincidence, in
abandoning revealed principles of morality in favor of those created
on the instant and in service to power, the effect is unvarying. Even
if it is a fiction, divine commandment immune to human revision
is a bulwark against the havoc that follows upon man deciding that
right and wrong are whatever is convenient to the moment.

Less dramatic but insidiously destructive is the atrophy and disappearance of religion in much of the West, entirely uncoerced, falling of its own weight and defects. The dominant narrative of the
modernism that replaces faith is the gray and bloodless portrait that
must arise from a conviction that everything is themeless accident
and to believe otherwise is merely self-deception. Though the arid,
reductionist art and philosophy of the modern West offers a suicidal
indictment of itself, and will not last, it will take a great deal of
human happiness with it as it sinks into the darkness it congratulates itself for having discovered upon the occasion of making itself
blind.

A Venn diagram correlating Americans who worry about theocracy
with those who fear a military coup would probably look like an

only slightly imperfect circle, even though the history of the United States has been entirely free of coups and theocracy and rich in opposition to them, not least among professional soldiers and the clergy. The left enjoys imagining that the fundamentalist Christians it so abhors will install a Jimmy Swaggart–like pope at the head of the government it views as the center of existence—not because of the faintest possibility that this might happen but rather as the rallying point for its objection to political positions and participation informed by principles common to or derived from religion.

Those who offer this objection believe it is sustained by the Constitution. That is, if church and state are to be separate, and the church is what the church believes, beliefs common to the church must be excluded from the law, whereas, with no constitutional separation of, for example, university and state, beliefs common to the university have free run of the law. Such reasoning takes no account of the difference between exclusively religious doctrines, such as the divinity of Jesus, and those that are not solely religious, such as the prohibition of murder. On both sides of the question it is only the primitives who fail to make the distinction, and in this regard one finds among the religious a lesser proportion of primitives who believe that if something is consonant with theology it must be written into law, than the proportion among the supposedly enlightened of primitives who believe that if something is consonant with theology it must not be written into law. They are alike only in that both are wrong, and to justify a flawed position each cites the flawed position of the other. This Mexican standoff was long ago made unnecessary by the Constitution.

How so? First, consider Napoleon's question to the Jews of France upon their emancipation. It was, more or less, are you Frenchmen, or are you Jews? Were such a question asked now in the United States (as it is at times in accusation of dual loyalties), the answer might be, "First tell me if you are an American or a Christian." End of story. But not in France at the time, as the French Revolution *had* asked that question of Christians, the church having been an integral part of the state. Soon after the proposal of the Bill of Rights, the heads of French priests began to roll into baskets. Here, however, the First Amendment, in making questions such as Napoleon's immaterial, protects freedom of conscience from the compulsion, direction, or vengeance of the state. To be an American, one does not need to suppress religion within oneself.

Those who believe that despite the language and legislative history of Article I its purpose is to protect the state from religion, rather than vice versa, have descended to posing Napoleon's question for the first time in American history. Though the Constitution was structured so that such an inquiry need never be made, they have brought it to life in their attempt to delegitimize the religious content of political positions in regard to various questions—as if the First Amendment bars outcomes friendly to the tenets of religion, which it does not, and as if religion is incompatible with democracy, which it is not.

Belief has been attacked of late with a fervor that suggests the desire not merely to disprove but to annihilate it. Throughout history, organized religions have variously been guilty of imagined superiority; aggressive proselytizing; and suppression or conversion by law, economic exclusion, or the sword. In view of the fact that materialism is itself a faith and will act like one, retaliation should not be surprising, but what principle does it promote, protect, or prove? The bitterness of the debate comes not just from fixing the world's troubles upon religion or from behaviors typical of a new (in this case, counter-) faith, or from aggravating cultural differences (Chelsea vs. Corpus Christi, enough said), but from the genuine conviction that God is a needful creation of man, unproven, unprovable, absurd, and, to a reasonable sensibility, even offensive.

This point of view strips religion of its subtlety and complexity while at the same time investing in the power of reason more than it can return (I have always thought that the story of Babel is not about man's pride so much as his overinvestment in his own powers, as illustrated by the stupidity of thinking that he could penetrate the mysteries of the universe by elevating himself a few hundred feet off a plain that lay in the shadow of answerless mountains several miles high). Faith is not hostile to reason, but reason is insulted when its careless practitioners fail to recognize its limitations. Some believe quite religiously that, its past achievements being a guide, science will explain creation, infinity, time, consciousness, art, and love.

Past returns, however, are no guide in a terrain of infinite false summits. Mapping the genome does not explain life or prove that we are only mechanisms any more than do the discoveries that we are composed of cells, that the blood circulates, or that muscle lies under the skin. Nonetheless, with each miracle of science—the electrified bottle, powered flight, the Bluetooth—fools declare that mystery will soon cease to exist. But love, for example, cannot be explained scientifically. That upon seeing one's beloved various molecules embrace various others is an effect, not an explanation, of love, or you would have the same reaction upon seeing a stop sign. Why will a man readily sacrifice himself for his child? Evolutionary biologists say it is to continue his line, but why would he stake his line on one vulnerable being and forgo the potential of tens of thousands of descendants flowing from his own far more survivable body, if not for love, which in essence is unfathomable and often contradictory to reason?

The result of scientific inquiry, a description of process, is not explanation, which is why all the genius of science comes to a halt at the "singularity" perfectly described in the first sentence of Genesis. Science, which—like the senses, art, and theology—apprehends the choreography of the universe, attributes the reference force, the prime enabler of every process, the explanation for both organization and disorganization, accretion and dissolution, to accident. Would a Rolls Royce come into being purely by accident, absent volition, assembled by accidentally created machines, in a factory that appeared by accident, according to immutable laws that arose by accident? Not very likely, and yet a Rolls Royce is almost infinitely less complex than man, much less than the universe. To wit, why is it less respectable to believe in God than to believe in accident?

Whereas by proof, evidence, and replication, reason and science build slowly and solidly within their own realms and would sabotage themselves were they to abandon precision, art and theology are different. I referred to the boy who said, "Don't give me none a dat college stuff!" because I believe that although—like science—art and theology are imperfect enough to have no claim to suppress other means of perception, they are superior in refinement and power because they dare admit the ineffable, which according to its nature science must deny and to which therefore it must be blind.

The ineffable, being ineffable, makes itself known in flashes too transient to contain and without the confines of reason. Art exists, however, to fix imprecisely the quickly fading after-images. Like theology, it deals with uncertainties. Though Voltaire said of God that *"Toute la nature crie qu'il existe"* (All nature cries out that he exists), the proof he cites is too immense to be comprehended systematically. And yet there are other things that, though we know they exist, cannot be captured in the nets of reason. Mozart's aria "Ah, perdona" can be reduced to the frequencies of musical instruments and the human voice, the proportions and patterns made by its notes, their timing, or other physical measures or critical speculations. But neither metrics nor theories of aesthetics can explain the beauty of the piece, just as similar reductions cannot explain the beauty of a face, of self-sacrifice, or of language magisterially deployed. As is much or perhaps all of intellectualized "art," art pressed from theory, even if flawlessly designed and bursting with complexity, will be dead beneath the heart. For to the extent that beauty is immobilized by definition, it, like God, will vanish from sight. For some it never appears at all. Though a chicken that listens to the "Ah, perdona" hears exactly what you do, you hear more. Science is able to identify the difference between you and the chicken, but it cannot isolate what you hear and the chicken doesn't, which, nonetheless, clearly exists. All creation is a kind of music to be read at various levels. Those of a certain capacity or self-imposed limitation are fated to believe that there is nothing legible in the universe beyond a labored, if virtuous, analysis of its elements and relations. Supposing the chicken could talk, he might challenge you to explain your higher apprehensions. Except in the language of beauty, to which he is deaf, you could not. Thus believing he had won the argument, he would crow.

My object is not to plead for the existence of God, who does not need an advocate at court, but, touching upon only the surface of a deep and tranquil lake of argument, to counter the arrogant notion that the faith and astonishment of billions across cultures and time is an absurdity to be addressed with exasperated contempt.

The founders constructed the constitutional system so as to carry forward what they themselves knew as a gracious balance of faith and reason, both of which they took to be indispensable. Now, however, the balance has tipped toward the constriction of freedom of conscience in religion. Broadly speaking, this consists of establishing and enforcing the orthodoxy of rational materialism in government, schools, and the culture at large, and driving out even the suspicion that it is inadequate both to eschatological questions and the soul of man. In a technique as old as politics, even while exerting continuous pressure upon those whose views are supposedly retrograde, its agents deny it. It is, they might say, simply imagined. If this is so, then what has been their position and what have they been arguing?

What is at stake is more than a matter of civil liberties. One of the greatest gifts to man and among the most beautiful and comforting things in life is the occasional glimpse of an insubstantial light beyond the dark clouds of mortality. To catch sight of it demands apprehension beyond reason, and a facility exercised in the appreciation of beauty and what we imprecisely call the education of the spirit. An aggressive minority of some who cannot replicate this in themselves has come forward to attack what for others is the most luminous and self-evident of all truths, even as it is expressed in a variety of ways. They deny that this light can exist and demand agreement by force of negative reasoning. But no matter what their success in appropriating politics and governance to their purposes, belief that is self-evident to heart and mind cannot be extinguished any more readily than the sun. And they shall not, not because they will not, but because they cannot, penetrate to the heart of the natural order or dictate to the universe that it is an accident.

Note

1. Edward Gibbon, *The Decline and Fall of the Roman Empire*, vol. 1, ed. Hans-Friedrich Mueller (New York: Modern Library Edition, 2003), 192.

11

Multiculturalism and the Threat of Conformity

Christopher Hitchens

THE INTERPENETRATION of opposites, or the law of the attraction of same, used to be a reliable standby of the late-night session aimed at solving the world's problems. There was also the unfulfilled but ever-seductive promise of the dialectic: the thesis, antithesis, and synthesis. At its highest, or so some people used to think, this process could transform ideas themselves to the point where they became material forces. However, what was less well understood was the way in which certain propositions, once advanced to their full extent, would turn into their own negations.

For example, if once it was decided that the individual was of relatively little significance when contrasted to the imperatives of the collective, people would awake one day to discover that their own individuality was indeed of small account but, strangely enough, that they were also somehow compelled to exalt and worship, nay even to deify, a single isolated and enthroned person. It might be a human god produced by a history of self-abnegation like the Emperor Hirohito or it might be the product of a massified and aggressive populism like Stalin or Mao, but the pattern would be more or less the same: the less the idea of the individual was esteemed, the more likely that one individual would become promiscuously or even monstrously prominent.

If this "works" in one direction, then there is every reason to suspect that it will work in the opposite one. Let me give an illustration. The late Arthur Schlesinger Jr., who was in his way quite a competent social historian—even if he was to become more celebrated as the historian not to say the hagiographer of a single man—toward the end of his career delivered some lectures, later bound together as a book, in which he expressed criticism of the increasing tendency of the United States to stress "diversity" over the notion of common citizenship. More and more, as he pointed out, people would introduce themselves, or make claims on behalf of themselves, as members of some interest group or "identity" faction. The gay campaigner Andrew Sullivan—actually, that is to say the very least by way of stating who he is, but anyway the Tory, Catholic, literary, political, homosexual polemicist Andrew Sullivan—was at about the same time to make the same sort of point in a slightly different way. How boring it was, wrote Andrew, to attend a meeting and to hear someone stand up and grab the microphone, and to begin by uttering the dreaded words: "Speaking as a . . ." There could then follow an assertion of sexuality, ethnicity, nationality, disability, pigmentation, gender, or indeed any combination of the above. Never mind what you have *done*: it suddenly matters much more who or what you *are*. Who cares what you *think*, or even whether you think at all: what counts is how you *feel*.

The way that Arthur Schlesinger tried to summarize this rash of Balkanizing self-regard was to suggest that it inverted the American national motto—e pluribus unum—and instead threatened to celebrate the risky, destabilizing idea of many being subtracted or derived (or do I mean multiplied?) out of one.

This, of course, was a clever enough wordplay, but it was only a glimpse of what has more recently become the real danger and the real contradiction. Since Schlesinger went public with his forebodings (of which I can remember Edward Said, for example, speaking with approval at least in private), the pendulum has taken or undergone another backswing so that now we are forced to confront the idea that it is precisely plurality and multiplicity that result in—uniformity!

This phenomenon has its origin on the "left": a "left" the best traditions of which, in my own opinion, it has done much to help destroy. Indeed, in my memory the new style began to emerge at a time when the socialist idea of mass movement for social change was undergoing something of an eclipse. It was when the large and generous wave of the 1960s began to recede, whether out of exhaustion or defeat or both, that one started to hear the ominous slogan, "The personal is political." As soon as I first heard it myself, I had a visceral and also a cranial instinct that it boded no good.

At first, I suppose, when I thought about this at all, I thought of it as "self-indulgent" or "individualist" or some other version of the petit bourgeois. I didn't foresee it becoming the way in which almost everybody would be able to adopt a heroic political position for themselves without doing any further work. And I could not have foreseen that it would multiply and replicate the number of subjects, academic and cultural and political, that could be declared as out of bounds or "off limits."

Just to give a very slight instance of what I mean: at least you can say of students of "the sixties" that they—we—defended the right to speak freely, even obscenely, and if anything rejoiced when an epithet however crude or cruel could be seen as having a measurable or palpable effect. It is said, and believed by some in Washington I have interviewed, that the apparently thick-skinned and bullnecked President Lyndon Baines Johnson was so hurt by the taunts of the demonstrators against the Vietnam War that he determined to retire from the fray. In those days, the very idea that the university administration could act as if in loco parentis was a laugh in itself: we had come to college exactly to outgrow our parents, not to seek replacements for them. Nowadays when I turn up to speak at a college, there is a panoply of groups ready to solicit the protection of the dean or even the campus police if anybody should hurt their tender feelings. I have been to classes where the simple, boring words "I find that to be really offensive" are considered to constitute an argument in themselves.

The effect of all this in retarding the grown-upness of the rising generation needs to be cogitated. More important still is the way in which quite important areas of the culture are already beginning to operate under a version of "one size fits all," which—while its advocates may think of it as voluntary and in compliance with certain imperatives of politeness—is in fact quite strictly policed, and is reinforced in the last instance by the credible threat of violence.

Even as I was writing this, I learned of the following sequence of events in Great Britain. Sebastian Faulks is a distinguished novelist, probably best known for his *Birdsong* but also for *Charlotte Gray*. His newest novel, *A Week in December*, concerns life in contemporary London and includes the depiction of a Muslim family. With characteristic scrupulousness, Mr. Faulks, in the course of "researching" his narrative, set himself to read the whole of the Qur'an in translation. When he was asked in a prepublication interview for his opinions, he spoke with characteristic honesty. He said that he had found the Qur'an to be "a depressing book," not to say a "very one-dimensional" work. He contrasted it unfavorably to the New Testament and the teachings of Christianity and said that it had "no plan for life."

Anybody reading this will be about to make my own point for me by being able to guess with absolute confidence what happened next. Mr. Faulks was subjected to death threats and issued a long and heartfelt apology for having hurt the feelings of true believers. Wrong. Mr. Faulks did indeed write a long (and to me, painful to read) apologia in which he sought to soothe any hurt feelings, gave much space to the views of Muslims who had contacted him, and offered to meet them on their own terms. And *then* he was made the subject of a long and extremely menacing manifesto, issued by a British Muslim group with the name Al-Muhajiroun. This organization barely bothers even to nod at the laws of England that govern incitement to the crime of murder.

The Faulks case, therefore, has a slightly old-fashioned ring to it. More and more in the West, the threats of violence are anticipated well before they are even uttered, and the required adjustments or abridgements are made, as it were, in advance of publication. Such was very conspicuously the case in the summer of 2008, when Yale University Press decided to bowdlerize its own edition of a book it had commissioned on the controversy about "the Danish cartoons."

These, you remember, were published in a Danish newspaper and took the form of caricatures of the Prophet Mohammed. As you may have forgotten, the newspaper commissioned the caricatures only because a Danish publisher of children's books had nervously withdrawn an illustrated book for infants about Islam, lest that in turn cause any "offense." The cartoons themselves were thus intended as a satire on those who could be frightened by cartoons. Woe, even to the mildly satirical, in the time of the literal-minded. For weeks afterward, Danish property and Danish citizens were at risk all across the Middle East, and the ambassadors of "Islamic" states in Copenhagen had the temerity to demand that the government censor the Danish press. Not a single major American paper or network—and this in the age that is above all that of "the image"—would show the public the actual pictures, and when a very small magazine for which I write did decide to do so, we were promptly removed from the shelves by a major book chain.

Things were not even allowed to get that far in New Haven. Rather, it was announced that a book about the cartoon controversy, written by a lady Danish professor of some standing, would not after all include a reprinting of the cartoons themselves. The authoress protested at this destruction of the very point and core of her book, but the publisher of the university press overruled her, saying that publication of the offending illustrations would "instigate" violence. To "instigate" is knowingly to try and bring about a certain outcome: how depressing that senior staff at the press of a great university do not appear to understand the meaning of a plain word. Even more depressing is the realization that such people have internalized outside pressure, to the stage where they take responsibility on themselves for acts of criminal violence that might, at some future date, be committed by other people. This is cultural masochism.

The softening up for this capitulation has been going on for some time. And the supposed desire to avoid violence is only a part of it. The fact is that the majority of the world's Muslims, and 100 percent of the Muslim immigrants who have migrated north and west, have black and brown skins. This has led, in Europe already and in the

United States incipiently, to the inclusion of many of its demands under the heading of "multiculturalism." There is even a handy word—"Islamophobia"—that has been coined in an attempt to compromise or even to criminalize any resistance to political Islam: this near-meaningless term[1] is on its way to acquiring the moral equivalence of the word "racism," and thus to expose those who can be accused of harboring it to every kind of contempt and reprisal.

The difference is rather marked, however, for those who are willing to notice it. The antiracist civil rights movement demanded the integration of public facilities like pools and parks: Islamist activists, where they are strong enough to do so, demand separate and segregated facilities, especially where women are concerned. The civil rights movement also made it morally impossible for citizens to make a political point by concealing their faces and wearing hoods. Perhaps the Klan should have sought protection by saying that it was (what it actually is) namely a militant Protestant Christian "identity" movement. Nowadays, those who want to veil and hood themselves or—very probably it seems—to veil and hood others against their will and on the basis of gender discrimination have been defended by the first black President of the United States as asserting their own "rights." So it goes.

Islamist propaganda also, often, makes insulting and threatening remarks about Jews, Christians, Hindus (perhaps most especially Hindus, who are not even monotheists), members of the Baha'i faith, and—depending on the Sunni or Shia faction embraced by the speaker—other Muslims as well. This might seem at first glimpse to be an assault on the principles of the multicultural society, but this is not at all how the multicultural activists see things. On the contrary, they have rushed to make Muslims part of the "gorgeous mosaic," and have frequently undercut the "moderates" among them by recognizing the hard-liners as the true interlocutors and representatives of "the community."[2]

The definition of what constitutes an "out" group is significant, as is the implied corollary that an "out" or "other" group is one that is therefore and thereby entitled to the legal protection of its own right to self-esteem. The definitions alter over time. I once made a documentary film highly critical of Agnes Bojaxhiu, known in the media as "Mother Teresa." The film had some success when shown on British TV, and the *New York Times* critic asked why it was that no American network would ever screen it. Stung by this, NBC in New York invited me to a meeting to discuss an airing, but ended up giving me this explanation for why such a transmission would not take place. It was well known, they said rather guilelessly, that many Jews were employed at the networks. Relations between Catholics and Jews in New York were relatively good, but there had been a time when this was not so. Broadcasting my little effort might have the effect of making Catholics say that it was the Jews who were behind it. This would not be a good thing. Therefore, and with regret . . . Thus, or by this logic, the more "diversity" there was, then the more uniformity would be needed to protect and shield it, and the more "multi" that things became, the greater the number of factions who would be able to insist that censorship, or better still prior restraint, was justified in their own case. Indeed, as you can see from the above, the principle could even be invoked retrospectively, as it were, so as to avoid even the danger of "instigating" animosities of the distant past.

I do not select my religious examples merely to underline my own likes or dislikes. I do so, rather, to point out the absurdity and potential risk—the threat to freedom—of confusing group rights with civil rights. Adherents to Islam in, say, the United States may constitute a small minority, but their mosques are sometimes funded by the Saudi Arabian royal family, which is hardly an oppressed group and which, where it has the power to do so, sternly limits and represses the minority rights of others. Recently in Minneapolis, Somali cabdrivers at the airport announced that they would refuse to carry passengers from international flights who arrived bearing duty-free bags, lest this lead to them being tainted by the unholy distribution of alcohol. (Before you laugh, remember that some Muslim drivers in Europe have now begun to refuse customers with seeing-eye dogs, because of the belief that canines are also "unclean.")

I ask you to picture what the reaction might be if these drivers had been white Presbyterians who favored the return of Prohibition. I think we can be sure that ridicule would have been the least of it. And Somalis are conspicuous in Minnesota not so much by reason of their religion as of their color. But why should either thing permit them to advocate, let alone to practice, prejudicial discrimination? (Aaah, "discrimination." What a useful word to have lost. It once meant the ability to make choices with discernment, as in "discriminating palate." Only when allied to something *non*discriminate, such as the lump-together word "racial," did it become pejorative. The mutation and eventual inversion of the meaning of this valuable word is as good an example as I can suggest for the way in which multiculturalism can become uniculturalism.)

Saul Bellow used to refer to a famous outfit of his own invention: "The Good Intentions Paving Company." I have borne the fortunes of this notorious business in mind while writing this essay, in the course of the composition of which no animals were harmed. Of course I understand that behind the rhetoric and practice of multiculturalism there often stands the admirable idea of an etiquette of good manners for a various and plural society, and the no-less-noble ambition for the redress of many past wrongs. But in a way, it is precisely this slightly surreptitious aspect of the argument that has become the most objectionable to me. Since when has it *not* been the case that censorship is justified because it protects minors, or the innocent? Since when has authority *not* claimed, when imposing trammels and curbs on liberty, that it does so for a wider good and a greater happiness? And since when have such soothing, admonitory, morally superior policies *not* been reinforced by the threat that, if they are not observed voluntarily, they will be backed up by the ruthless use of force? I suppose that I might have a little more respect for the latest advocates of benevolent authoritarianism if they laid less emphasis on the way in which they do all this for my own good, and became more ready to admit their kinship with their predecessors.

Notes

1. I call it "near-meaningless" because the word "phobia" means irrational or unreasoning fear, whereas, as my friend Martin Amis pointed out after he had been subjected to a Niagara of abuse for what he had written about Muslim terrorism, there is nothing at all irrational about the fear of religious extremism. It is, however, not as void of meaning as the term "homophobia," which can only mean "irrational fear of the same" and thus amounts as nearly as possible to the polar opposite of what it intends.

2. See, for an incisive analysis of the alarmingly rapid way this has occurred in practice in the United Kingdom, Kenan Malik's book *The Rushdie Affair*.

12

The Tyranny of the News Cycle

Robert D. Kaplan

OF ALL TYRANNIES, that of the mob may be the worst. Once inside a mob, normally sane people will willingly give up the qualities that make them human and become instead creatures of a carnivorous pack, hunting defenseless prey without a whit of compassion. And what makes the mob so dangerous is its terrible present-mindedness, its total immersion in the transitory passions of the moment. The sense of a past and future separates us from the apes: the mob erases this distinction.

Elias Canetti, a Spanish Jew who went on to win a Nobel Prize in literature, became so transfixed and terrified at the mob violence over inflation that seized Frankfurt and Vienna between the two world wars that he devoted much of his life to the study of the human herd in all its manifestations. The signal insight of his book, *Crowds and Power* (1960), was that we all yearn to be inside some sort of crowd, for in a crowd there is shelter from danger and loneliness.

George Orwell discerned this, too. "Always yell with the crowd, that's what I say. It's the only way to be safe," one character declares in Orwell's novel *1984* (1949). Indeed, Orwell's depiction of tyranny rests to a significant degree on the human proclivity, however much it may be denied, to trade individual freedom for the enfolding protection of the group. Happiness—to be accepted by one's fellows—is, for most people, preferable to freedom.

Canetti and Orwell are traveling along parallel lines in their worries, for a crowd, even if it be fascist, protects you as long as you are part of it. And as any writer or analyst quickly learns, it is better to be wrong along with everyone else than wrong all by yourself; that way there is no penalty for your mistake. Go with the flow. Join the crowd. Better to sleep at night. The crowd, by stripping away individuality in favor of the mass, is the ultimate enemy of freedom.

Of course, even as the mob is the worst manifestation of the crowd, many other sorts of crowds are not dangerous at all. Canetti notes that nations and ethnic groups each constitute a virtual crowd, with particular characteristics that he defines as crowd symbols. The crowd symbol for the Germans is the "marching forest"; for the Dutch it is the "dikes" that protect them from the encroaching sea; for the Jews it is the "multitude" wandering "year after year through the desert." Each symbol captures something permanent about the psychology of these groups. (The Germans, for example, march in unison, first as Nazis, decades later in far more benevolent form as environmental quasi-pacifists.)

What then constitutes the crowd symbol of the Americans? A benign insight would say it is our *mass democracy* that certifies us as a free people, the freest in history. But what if, over time, technology has given us another crowd symbol? What if our real crowd symbol, which has supplanted our democracy and, indeed, surreptitiously governs it, is our *mass media*? Such a crowd symbol, I would argue, is not always so benign.

The media constitute several controling mechanisms. As I have argued elsewhere, the media can never theoretically be wrong, as their cause is always that of the weak and the oppressed. Whether in Darfur, Bosnia, or Palestine, places of real human rights catastrophes to be sure, the media, even so, tend in their well-meaning exposes toward sanctimony, and therein lies the instrument of their subtle oppression: a bleating, lecturing voice, like that of the medieval clergy, that is prone to disregard the sad and sometimes tragic realities of power politics.[1]

But alas, there is a larger, more encompassing instrument of media influence. That is the tyranny of *presentness*: of the present moment, enhanced by repetition and by technology, and rendered pleasurable thanks, occasionally, to the cruelest aspects of human nature—the glee in seeing someone else destroyed—that it obliterates the past and any conception of the future. For we take pleasure in hatred, just as we take pleasure in love or compassion for others. Remember that to live entirely—I mean entirely—in the present affords no historical perspective, and therefore no human emotion except for complete sensory pleasure, or rage. In such a circumstance, each passing moment becomes disconnected from the one before and after it. The whole sense of a narrative is lost. As Orwell showed in *1984*, true tyranny is the abolition of the past.

The world is so much simpler without a past. Everything—especially one's opinions of an hour, day, or year ago—can be discarded, as if it had never existed. As with many a commentator and politician, you can be for a war, then be against it, as if forgetting that you were once for it. And if that is the case, then no mental discipline or integrity is required. Government officials are held accountable for their previous actions; so, too, are military leaders and corporate officials. They have to justify what they intoned in the past; not so pundits and anchorpersons. The media operates without any sense of a past. Pace Orwell, that is the root of its tyranny.

Clearly, what I am talking about is the news cycle, which, as the very term suggests, constitutes a circular narrative, divorced from previous and future ones. It is the news cycle that, as we know, forces political campaigns to descend often into infantilism. Of course, sometimes the issues raised in campaign news cycles are not so trivial at all. To wit, there was the news cycle about presidential candidate John McCain not knowing how many houses he owned. We were told at the time that the mini-scandal might seriously undermine McCain's campaign. But it was forgotten in an instant, for the news cycle is a claustrophobic world all its own. It is like a heated conversation at a dinner party that, weeks later, because of the onrush of events and other dinner parties, no one can recall.

The news cycle drives the media—and by extension, all of us—in a single direction of thought, dislocated from all others. There is little dissent, as in a mob or crowd pack. In one minute in early 2009 we are consumed by piracy, even though it has been a scourge of the Asian and African coasts for hundreds of years during eras of booming trade. In the next minute, it is swine flu that terrifies us, even though more people may be dying of ordinary flu and other diseases worldwide. Yet swine flu, as serious as it is, like piracy, instantly disappears as an obsession to be replaced by others, which few will remember. The democratic uprising in Iran, a truly historic event, still lay several news cycles in the future.

Ours is an era of disjointedness, without a sustained story line. Instead of Thucydides' *The Peloponnesian War*, with its rich moral realism—complete with disquisitions on the arrogance of power and the cruelty of fate, and how the bleak forces of human nature lie just beneath the veneer of civilization—we are treated to war correspondents on television, gasping with out-of-context revelations that are defined as "news." The correspondents are being truthful, but there is little "before" and "after" to their reports, whereas the power of Thucydides rests on a fleshed-out magisterial narrative. Of course, we have our own books that do provide a tragic narrative to wars like the one in Iraq, but for too many of us, they don't define our lives and our waking consciousness as television does. The late French anthropologist Germaine Tillion wrote that "events must run their course before becoming history, so that *all* true history exists only by virtue of its conclusion." But there is no conclusion or closure in the news cycle.

Consider: in recent years we have been terrified and titillated by an all-consuming anthrax scare, a sex scandal involving congressional page boys, a southern governor's marital infidelity, a former White House press official who suddenly turned on his boss with a tell-all book, a tax evasion by a prospective treasury secretary during a time of epic economic calamity, Sarah Palin's memoir. It is in the very nature of many news cycles that they are trivial. And often the more trivial and personal, the more intense the media scrutiny, and the more stirred by them we become. The news cycle also relativizes events, making the trivial seem important and the important seem trivial because they receive the same treatment.

The mainstream media, as we are now aware, have gone tabloid. And the media dominate our conversation, and, therefore, to varying extents, our mental lives, making them poorer and more sterile as a consequence. Although we remain individuals, we nevertheless think en masse. And like the "telescreen" in *1984*, as anyone who has visited an airport knows, you can't turn it off. This, too, is a form of tyranny, one that can only grow as technology makes the moment—makes *presentness*—ever more vivid. Thus, the financial crisis of late 2008 was defined in many media circles as another Great Depression even as the facts ultimately revealed it as a Great Recession, something measurably less severe. It was the vividness of the news cycle that was a factor in stirring panic. Such vividness can lead to analogies that are a little far-fetched: the Great Recession as the new Great Depression, with Barack Obama as the new Franklin Delano Roosevelt, even before Obama began his presidency.

The news cycle is most intense when an individual is being exposed, for many of us are secretly made happy by the tragedies of others, and the media are expert at exploiting this most unsavory of human emotions. Someone may deserve to be exposed. They may have done wrong. Or they have been in a position of authority and got something very wrong, indeed. But it is also the case that the media, which are too often the voice of our worst inner selves, delight in personal destruction, and thus frequently takes things quite far.

Take the case of former Deputy Secretary of Defense Paul Wolfowitz. Wolfowitz was blamed as a chief architect of the Iraq War. He deserved scrutiny and criticism for a war that had gone awry. But the levels of hatred directed at him sometimes became so intense that it was the equivalent of an electronic lynching. Columns and blogs, too many of them, were written about him that had no policy substance at all, or any point to make actually. Their only intent was to humiliate. Wolfowitz, a highly successful former ambassador to Indonesia, the largest Muslim country in the world, was nevertheless depicted as a bumbling, clueless intellectual who knew nothing about Muslim culture, and sent our young men and women in uniform to their deaths. Eventually, the news cycle moved on, rumbling over Wolfowitz's live corpse. Years later, when Iran experienced a democratic uprising that Wolfowitz had vaguely intuited, just as he had rightly predicted Indonesia's successful experiment in democracy, I noticed that some purveyors of the conventional wisdom were now quoting Wolfowitz. The news cycle, because it has no memory, contains the power to rehabilitate.

Observing the Wolfowitz auto-da-fé, I thought of the "Two Minutes Hate" against Emmanuel Goldstein, the "lonely, derided heretic" in Orwell's book about the ultimate tyrannical state. Everyone had to join ceremonially in the destruction of Goldstein's character via the telescreen.

It is not just public figures who come in for this treatment; it can happen to anyone. Consider the Duke University lacrosse players convicted by the media of rape before they were acquitted by the legal process, their lives wantonly destroyed before being tossed aside like broken dolls, as the Orwellian news cycle moves on.

Of course, Wolf Blitzer is not Big Brother. And the very fact that CNN, Fox, Al Jazeera/English, and other networks have dissimilar worldviews helps to prevent the tyranny of virtual mobs unleashed by the news cycle. What worries me is that technology is dynamic, even as it greatly favors the present over the past and future. It carries within it the potential to make reality ever more vivid and tactile, so that every thought other than what you are seeing or hearing via a blogger or anchorperson is obliterated. Technology can favor brave dissent, as we have seen in the streets of Tehran, as well as on the Internet in general. But it can also stifle dissent by the way in which it encourages obsessions that we all share at the same time.

Alas, it is our fear of loneliness that ultimately leads us away from freedom. Loneliness is not altogether a bad thing; indeed, it is a crucial component of our individuality. If we can deal with it, we are less likely to join the crowd, and thereby lose our freedom. Yet because so many of us desperately want to be part of a group, any group, we will adopt whatever crazy and cruel idea the group comes up with, even when it represents the lowest common denominator of the moral values of everyone physically—or virtually—assembled. Think of the taunts against the outsider in the schoolyard. That is the beginning of tyranny.

Imagine a Wolf Blitzer far more powerful than he is today because of the advancement of digital technology. Imagine the television being on constantly, as part of an interactive mother lode in the homes of the future. Then imagine the fate of one who gets on the wrong side of a scandal or major policy decision. Have some compassion for the victim, however deserving of punishment he or she may be. Compassion is one individual caring for another across the daunting, impersonal chasm of the crowd. In the instantaneous mobs of the future, it is only such compassion that will allow us to preserve our freedom.

Freedom is often the very definition of the individual against the masses. The masses cannot ultimately be free: only the individual can be. And the news cycle, because it is intrinsically attractive to the masses, is, like any populist dictatorship, the determined enemy of freedom.

Note

1. Robert D. Kaplan, "The Media and Medievalism," *Policy Review*, no. 128 (December 2004/January 2005).

13

Transnational Progressivism

James Kirchick

IT HAS BECOME fashionable of late to bemoan the American "empire." Such terminology, almost always used as an imprecation, is both a slander and a historical delusion. Having fought for our independence from a genuine imperial power (one that ruled over people without their consent and exploited them economically), Americans have historically been suspicious of colonialism. The United States has never been an imperial power in the sense that European nations once were. If we are an empire at all, then it is a consensual one, an "Empire of Trust," in the words of historian Thomas F. Madden. That is, America's global preeminence has not come about by coercion or the subjugation of foreigners, but rather with their acquiescence, and often against our own desires. We do not invade lands to plunder and rape. According to Josef Joffee, America is the "default power" in the world today because most countries ultimately trust us more than any potential rival, like China or Russia.

As beneficent as American hegemony may be, many seek to undermine it. This campaign consists of odd bedfellows. The first are Islamists who denounce the United States as "The Great Satan." In their worldview, we are the embodiment of secular decadence and the oppressor of the world's Muslim community, or *Ummah*. That women have equal rights, that we don't stone homosexuals, that we allow people to speak their minds—all of these things offend the Islamic supremacists who seek to impose their will on others by force.

Second are authoritarian powers, large ones such as Russia and China and smaller ones such as Iran and Venezuela, that oppose

American preeminence not only out of an ideological fixation of hating America per se, but for reasons of *realpolitik* as well: the ideals for which America stands—national self-determination, the advancement of political liberty, and the free exchange of ideas— threaten their grip on power.

Joining these two reactionary forces are what Hudson Institute scholar John Fonte terms "transnational progressives," who seek to undermine American hegemony not out of a desire to see the rise of other superpowers but due to a misplaced idealism about the functioning of a multipolar world order. During the Cold War, American "fellow travelers" attacked America and its allies because they sympathized with the Soviet Union and wished for an international workers' revolution. Transnational progressives, for the most part, are not as pernicious, for they sincerely believe they are acting in the best interests of their country. They hold that unless American power is "tamed," it will do damage not only to the world, but unto itself.

Transnational progressivism finds its roots in the Wilsonian idealism of the early twentieth-century progressives. Reeling from the catastrophe that was the First World War, they sought to incorporate the United States into a League of Nations that would prevent any and all future warfare. Through agreements like the Kellogg-Briand Pact (which actually outlawed war as "an instrument of national policy") and the Washington Naval Treaty (which sought to limit the size of signatory nations' armadas), the early transnationalists believed that circumscribing American power and overseas commitments would lead other nations, even authoritarian ones, to behave like responsible international citizens. These treaties, of course, and the mind-set that led to them, did nothing to prevent the rise of a belligerent Germany and Japan, and actually discouraged the sort of preemptive action that might have prevented the carnage of the Second World War.

What emerged from the ashes of two utterly destructive continental conflicts was the belief, accepted by the leading lights of Western European politics and intellectual life, that nationalism was the root problem of interstate relations. This worldview made little room for the acceptance of even liberal nationalism—hence the widespread hatred in Europe for Zionism. Rather than swear allegiance to a nation-state, transnational progressives denigrated the traditional notion of the political community, expanding it so as to encompass the nebulous constituency of "humanity" itself, whereby all of the differences of the past, easily attributable to race, blood, and soil, would be forever erased.

The obvious first step in this campaign was to erode, as much as possible, the national sovereignty of states in favor of transnational institutions like the United Nations and the European Union (EU). The EU, whose pretensions to subsume the powers of European national governments have been widely rejected by the actual populace whenever and wherever they have been put to a vote, is the manifestation of the transnationalist dream, not merely for the statist policies it promulgates, but primarily for its potential as a pacifist counterweight to the American superpower.

Transnational progressives claim that the Iraq War was "illegal" because the United Nations did not sanction it (nor, however, did the world body proscribe it), even though Saddam Hussein was in violation of sixteen U.N. Security Council resolutions. In 2004, Democratic presidential candidate John Kerry articulated the transnationalist view when he stated that any proposed American military action must meet a "global test" before it could be deemed acceptable. Like the current American president, who views himself as a "citizen of the world," transnational progressives believe that their loyalties should extend far beyond the shores of the United States.

This is not to say that they are disloyal Americans; indeed, they see themselves as fundamentally patriotic. They simply believe that the interests of the United States are inextricably bound to those of the "international community," an abstract entity that is itself a figment of their imaginations. After all, for a group (whether of people, businesses, or countries) to be a "community," it must possess shared interests, values, and norms of behavior. The United States may have interests and values in common with other democracies, though their interests may also at times conflict. But what does the United States have in common with the theocratic regime in Tehran or the criminals who run the North Korean slave state?

Ironically, though the European transnationalists will never admit it, European social democracy was only able to develop under a security umbrella provided and paid for by the American hegemon they so roundly despise. It was the $13 billion Marshall Plan, which reconstructed the western part of the continent, and it was American defense spending and nuclear armaments that allowed European governments to spend so lavishly on their domestic social programs. Living in postmartial societies, protected by a new superpower uneasy with the burdens of policing the world, it is all too easy to forget that the world does in fact need policing. This realization is even harder to accept when one's own country has failed so miserably in the task.

The transnational progressives speak of their cause in the dulcet tones of social justice and equality. Well-versed in the discourse of American politics, they are aware that the natural impulse of the American people is toward fairness, and they take advantage of that laudable inclination. But fairness in the context of domestic American life is not the same thing as "fairness" in the context of global politics. We can all agree that citizens should be equal before the law. The same logic does not obtain in international relations, where the "citizens" of the world "community" are states, many of them run by thugs or terrorists.

The transnational progressives who seek to undermine American hegemony are all around us. *Newsweek International* editor and ubiquitous television personality Fareed Zakaria has written an internationally best-selling book, *The Post-American World*, which heralds America's decline and celebrates the rise of authoritarian China as a model of effective capitalist development. In 2002, Georgetown professor Charles Kupchan prophesied "The End of the American Era." Former French foreign minister Hubert Védrine, expressing the sentiments of the European political elite, has complained of the United States as a "hyperpower."

But the leading transnational progressive in the world today is the current American president. When asked if he believed in the notion of American exceptionalism, the idea that due to its revolutionary founding on principles of equality, freedom, and justice, the United States is a nation imbued with a unique global role, Barack Obama replied, "I believe in American exceptionalism, just as I suspect that the Brits believe in British exceptionalism and the Greeks believe in Greek exceptionalism." In other words, America is not exceptional, and ought not to have the power and freedom of action historically accorded to it. In a similar vein, in a speech before the U.N. General Assembly, Obama spoke of a world order in which "No one nation can or should try to dominate another nation" and that "No balance of power among nations will hold."

The very notion that the United States could safely inhabit such a global system, or that it is desirable or even realistic, is a dangerous delusion. Throughout human history, the world has experienced two types of international order: unipolar hegemony or violent conflict among nations to achieve it. Take the twentieth century as an example of this dictum. It opened with a catastrophic war between the great world powers in which millions died. As a result, the Ottoman Empire collapsed, and a revisionist Nazi Germany and a Stalinist Russia rose with aspirations to worldwide dominance. What followed was another war bloodier than the one that preceded it.

The rest of the century played out as a superpower competition pitting the United States and its allies against the Soviet Union. It was only after Communism's collapse that the world entered a period of unipolarity, with the United States standing as global hegemon. This, and not some starry-eyed scenario in which all nations work together in an effort to solve international problems, is the best possible world order that we can realistically expect to achieve.

Yet rather than embrace America's benevolent hegemony, transnational progressives seek to weaken it. They do this by demanding that the United States sign a variety of treaties aimed at subordinating its sovereignty to an array of supranational bodies and by insisting that the United Nations be the arbiter of American power

(though why the Chinese Communist politburo or French government ought to be afforded a veto over American action is something
that transnational progressives never fully explain). "The U.S. is
often a delinquent international citizen," complains the prominent
intellectual Tony Judt, citing its status as one of only two countries
(the other being Somalia) not to sign the 1989 Convention on Children's Rights as an example of this misbehavior. That the treaty was
signed by every other country in the world, many of whose delegates
probably never read the document and which clearly have no intention of following its provisions, is a consideration utterly lost on the
likes of Judt and his fellow transnational progressives, for whom the
signing of worthless agreements and deference to the wishes of an
abstract "international community" are signs of enlightenment and
good global citizenship. Last year, in a move widely applauded by
those seeking to hamper America's ability to fight wars, the International Criminal Court claimed jurisdiction over American soldiers
in Afghanistan.

Global power is a zero-sum game; it always has been and always
will be. Any diminishment of American power will therefore be to
the benefit of rival powers, whether regional hegemons like Iran,
which would gain greater influence at the expense of American
decline in the Middle East, or would-be global hegemons like China.
Vice President Joe Biden could not have been more clear in articulat-
ing the transnational progressive mind-set when he said last year in
Ukraine, "We are trying to build a multipolar world." That certainly
pleased the diplomatic mandarins in the courts of Western Europe,
but it probably irked his Ukrainian audience, who must deal with an
ever-more aggressive Russia on their eastern border.

The transnational progressives do not see the world in the same
way that generations of American policy makers—Democrats and
Republicans—have perceived it. Last June, Obama delivered an
"Address to the Muslim World" in Cairo. "Any world order," he
said, "that elevates one nation or group of people over another will
inevitably fail." There is nothing objectionable about the latter part
of this admonition; of course, no "group of people" should be "ele-

vated" above another. Those who have tried to bring about such a vision have murdered millions in its pursuit. Americans have fought and died both within our own country and around the world to prevent such horrors.

But with his suggestion that no "one nation" should occupy a higher plane than others, Obama enunciated a radically revisionist conception of America's place in the world. That's because a world order in which one nation is "elevated" above all others is essentially what we have been living with since the end of the Cold War. And the "one nation" which has enjoyed global preeminence is the United States. Why would he, or any other person who calls himself a "progressive," have it any other way? The alternative would be a global free-for-all in which authoritarian states such as Russia and China vie for superpower status and rogue regimes like Iran and Venezuela terrorize their neighbors with impunity. Without American global leadership there would be no "saving" of Darfur, or massive aid to the victims of typhoons halfway around the world, or protection offered to Kosovar Muslims, or the fulfillment of any other liberal goal.

President Obama has repeatedly assured his foreign audiences that America will stop throwing its weight around. This is just what the trifecta of Islamists, authoritarians, and transnational progressives wants to hear, but they probably never expected that an American president would articulate it. "I understand those who protest that some countries have weapons that others do not," he said in his speech before the General Assembly, an obvious reference to the nuclear weapons–seeking regime in Tehran, and an appeal to the supposed commitment to fairness that a hegemonic America has hitherto been unwilling to demonstrate. "No single nation should pick and choose which nation holds nuclear weapons." The Mullahs, who have long complained about the hypocrisy of a system that allows the United States and Israel to have nuclear weapons but not a theocratic dictatorship that murders its own citizens in the streets, could not have said it better themselves.

In a purely hypothetical world in which every nation's system of government is democratic and thus externally benign, perhaps Obama's rosy statement about nuclear weapons would make sense. But we don't live in a Kantian world of perpetual peace. That the president of the United States would reorient America's role in accordance with a theoretical (and fantastical) ideal indicates that he actually believes in such moral equivalencies or that mouthing them will somehow earn his country international goodwill.

What are the tangible political goals of transnational progressives? Domestically, one aspect of their agenda is the campaign to criminalize political differences by prosecuting former Bush administration officials and Central Intelligence Agency (CIA) operatives who used enhanced interrogation techniques on captured terrorist detainees, techniques they stigmatize as "torture." If these critics showed anywhere near the same level of revulsion for the barbaric tactics of our enemies, their complaints might merit serious consideration. But if their goal is to discredit the United States as a benign hegemon, then they have largely succeeded with their campaign to portray the deplorable incident of Abu Ghraib as some sort of routine occurrence and consequence of American hubris. They have sought to undermine our intelligence gathering in other ways as well, setting their sights on a CIA terrorist assassination program, as if the CIA *shouldn't* be killing terrorists wherever and whenever it can.

The transnational progressives also act in concert—though not intentionally—with Islamists and authoritarians when they call for American surrender in the theaters of the war on Islamic supremacism, whether in Iraq, Afghanistan, or any of the other remote locales where our enemies plot attacks on American soil. When the insurgency in Iraq picked up force in 2005, congressional Democrats backed calls for a retreat, which would undoubtedly have led to even more bloodshed and a victory for Jihadism. As focus has shifted back to Afghanistan due to bettering conditions in Iraq (no thanks, of course, is due to American liberals for that development), they are calling for withdrawal there as well.

But the most dangerous objective of the transnational progressive agenda, at least in the long term, is to chip away at American sovereignty in favor of supranational institutions like the United Nations. Transnational progressives promote a vision of international law whose sole purpose seems to be constraining American power. The goal of the European Union, aside from increasing regulation over the internal affairs of its member states, is to consolidate the foreign policies and economic clout of its over two dozen European constituent states and thus serve as a pacifistic counterweight in world affairs to the United States.

In 2006, a poll of British citizens found that more believed George W. Bush to be a danger to world peace than North Korean dictator Kim Jong Il. Many polls over the past ten years had similar findings; in 2007, a poll found that 32 percent of respondents in five European countries considered the United States the biggest threat in the world, more so than any other state. In the mind of the progressive transnationalists, it is American power—and not Pakistani nukes, an aggressive Russia that invades its neighbors, an authoritarian China, or a fundamentalist Iran—that is the greatest cause of concern. Transnational progressivism is at root a unique response to American power, and is based less on idealism than fear. It is actually Hobbesianism dressed up in the garb of Wilsonian idealism. But it is a perverse sort of Hobbesianism, portraying as it does the nation best suited to serve as policeman for a dangerous world as its principal criminal.

While transnational progressivism finds its intellectual ballast in the American and international left, it is hardly limited to that political disposition. The goals of some "realists" also fit neatly within the agenda. Take, for instance, the preeminent realist thinker Stephen Walt. In 2005, he wrote a book titled *Taming American Power*, the title of which spoke to a view of the United States as a dangerous and unwieldy meddler, a bull in the china shop of international relations that requires humbling not only for its own good but for that of the world. Fareed Zakaria, who, for most of his career, has been of indeterminate ideology but has finally settled upon a fashionably coldhearted realism, looks excitedly upon the rise of China and the gradual decline of America. This equanimity about the world's largest authoritarian power emanates from Zakaria's deep suspicion of democracy, which he considers messy and ineffective, a view he explained in his first best seller, *The Future of Freedom*. Zakaria seems mesmerized by China's economic expansion to the exclusion of all other considerations (the utter lack of political freedom, the existence of gulags known as Laogai, support for tyranny in places as far-flung as Burma, Sudan, and Zimbabwe, etc.). In the estimation of the "realists," a world ruled by China, in much the same way that it is "ruled" by the United States and American norms, would not be all that bad.

But a world in which the United States has less freedom of action (whether political, economic, or military) would be objectively much worse. Indeed, due to the U.N. Security Council veto power wielded by China and Russia—nations that act with no moral compunction whatever in their international dealings—the United Nations has largely been useless in dealing with rogue regimes and other international problems. Both powers view "sovereignty" as an excuse by which to oppress their own people and are loath to support robust international actions that would create a precedent for scrutinizing their own behavior. Thus, the United Nations has been powerless in the face of real human rights atrocities in Bosnia, Rwanda, and Darfur, and thus spends most of its time condemning Israel and the United States. The great crime of George W. Bush and the "neocons," in the estimate of transnational progressives, was that they did not put up with the long-running charade of trusting international institutions to confront real threats and real evil. Of course, if you're a "realist," then these considerations don't really matter.

In one of his iconic fireside chats, Franklin Delano Roosevelt spoke of the United States as the "arsenal of democracy." Today, rather than regard our continued military supremacy as a good thing, transnational progressives see it as wasteful, belligerent, and ultimately unnecessary. There are fair criticisms to be made about whether this or that fighter jet or missile system is worth scarce tax dollars. But the transnational progressives do not believe in unchallenged American military supremacy; what they seek in their attacks on the "military industrial complex" is a dramatic scaledown of our power in the hopes that with a smaller military, the United States will be less prone to use it.

How would the loss of American hegemony abroad represent a threat to freedom at home? Any threat to American global predominance—which would inevitably accrue to the benefit of nondemocratic, territorially expansionist powers—is in and of itself a threat to freedom, not only to our own, but especially to those people living in dark places from Afghanistan to Zimbabwe. How strange that our president, the self-proclaimed "citizen of the world," does not appear to understand this.

14

Students against Liberty?

Greg Lukianoff

CHRIS LEE was afraid for his life. An angry mob of forty of his fellow students had showed up to raise hell at his musical comedy, and the mood was ugly. The students began by standing up in their seats and yelling, "I'm offended," but quickly escalated to slurs and threats of violence and death. The surly crowd succeeded in stopping the play several times and threatened to turn the production into a full-scale riot.

Chris knew that his university promised to protect students who faced threats of violence—especially African American students like himself—but his repeated appeals to campus police did little to discourage the mob. After all, why would his university help him—especially when it had trained, funded, and supported the angry protestors in the first place?

Chris, a student at Washington State University, was the author and director of *The Passion of the Musical*, a student production written in the spirit of *South Park* and specifically intended both to amuse and offend as many different people and groups as possible. He could not have been clearer about his musical's content, warning students that the play was "offensive or inflammatory to all audiences." Chris's warnings were included in ads, printed on the tickets themselves, and posted on the doors of the theater. For good measure, he stood up before the show and told the audience that those who were easily offended should leave. In Chris's words, the goal of the play "was to show people we're not that different, we all have issues that can be made fun of."

While his play did poke fun at a wide variety of groups, particularly religious ones, it was his parody of the Meatloaf ballad "I'd Do Anything for Love (But I Won't Do That)" that caused the most virulent protest. Chris's version replaced the line "but I won't do that" with "I won't act black." Under pressure from the campus police, Chris edited the word "black" out of this performance. Nonetheless, *The Passion of the Musical* earned him the nickname "black Hitler" on campus.

Even so, the threat that Chris's musical posed to the political sensibilities of Washington State administrators was evidently too grave to ignore. Rather than simply allow the play to go on, administrators actually organized a group of students who were angry about the play, instructed them on how to disrupt the performance, and even purchased tickets for them. To top it off, the university president applauded these students the next day for the "very responsible" exercise of their free speech rights. In a turn that truly deserves the label "Orwellian," a violent act of censorship was labeled "free speech."

This is not an isolated incident. Lee's case is just one among many in a general trend in American higher education. Students are learning both from the campus environment and from administrators themselves that it is not only acceptable to silence opinions they deem offensive, but that *doing so is a noble and appropriate act*. This dangerous lesson is taught to students through powerful examples coupled with a systemic campaign of inculcation and outright misinformation led primarily by college administrators. While the worst offenders are often lower-level student services officials, including residence assistants (RAs) and disciplinary officers, they often act with the approval and even support of the university counsel and president's office.

Few Americans are aware of the scale of violations of student and faculty rights occurring on campuses today. Those who are often view it as simply a symptom of America's larger culture war—and it is true that students and faculty are far more likely to be punished if they hold the conservative or Christian point of view on various issues. But the problem is deeper and more insidious than political correctness run amok. Politically correct censorship is just one part of a profound process of miseducation that has potentially dire long-term consequences for our democratic republic.

This miseducation doesn't just occur in the classroom. It is part of the very fabric of American higher education. What follows is a brief overview of the many ways in which students today are instructed in the methods and morals of totalitarian censorship.

Teaching Censorship by Example

In its ten-year history, the Foundation for Individual Rights in Education (FIRE), where I serve as president, has documented hundreds of brazen violations of freedom of speech on campus. In one episode in late 2007, a public university in Indiana found a student-employee guilty of racial harassment—without so much as a hearing—for reading Todd Tucker's *Notre Dame Versus the Klan*, a book that celebrated the defeat of the Klan by Irish students in a 1924 street fight. But the actual content didn't matter: the book had "offensive" pictures of Klansmen on the cover.

The same fall, at Brandeis, a professor was found guilty of racial harassment for using the word "wetback" in order to *criticize* the slur in his Latin American politics class. Meanwhile, a public college student in Georgia was deemed a "clear and present danger" for publishing a collage on Facebook that mocked his university's president for referring to a proposed parking garage as his "legacy." The university expelled the student and required him to undergo psychological counseling.

These are just a few recent examples among hundreds of similar cases. And there are undoubtedly many more that have gone unreported. Indeed, it is safe to assume that the thousands of case submissions FIRE has received over the years represent only a tiny proportion of the actual number of abuses of rights on campus. And whether reported or not, every incident of this kind in which basic rights are disregarded by a university is a forceful and formative lesson to students.

The Lessons of Campus Speech Codes

Casual observers can be forgiven for assuming that campus speech codes no longer exist; after all, a string of court cases dating back to 1989 have ruled them unconstitutional. Speech codes have also been condemned by the national media, Congress, state legislatures, even the president of the United States. Yet despite at least eighteen additional lawsuits since 2003, all of which resulted in the repeal or invalidation of such codes, they remain in place at over two-thirds of public colleges.[1]

The impact of these codes goes far beyond what is known as the "chilling effect." Students are not simply unsure whether they have the right to speak their minds on certain issues. Modern speech codes provide genuine, consistent, and repeated assurance that offensive speech is, will be, and *should be* punished. Students are faced with an environment that constantly reinforces the idea that they cannot open their mouths freely. Moreover, because language restricting free expression is often embedded in university "diversity" and "harassment" policies, students are being systemically taught that such suppression is not just okay; it is a moral and legal imperative.

"Student rights and obligations" policies like Texas A&M's prohibit students from violating others' rights to "respect for personal feelings" and "freedom from indignity of any type"; the University of Cincinnati limits free speech to one designated area of campus, requires advance scheduling, and threatens criminal punishment for violating the policy. Johns Hopkins prohibits "rude, disrespectful behavior," while Fordham forbids using any e-mail message to "insult" or "embarrass."

The most common form of speech codes remain wildly vague and broad about racial or sexual harassment: New York University bans "insulting, teasing, mocking, degrading, or ridiculing another person or group," as well as "inappropriate . . . comments, questions . . . [and] jokes." The University of Iowa defines sexual harassment as something that "occurs when somebody says or does something sexually related that you don't want them to say or do, regardless of who it is." Davidson College's Sexual Harassment Policy prohibits the use of "patronizing remarks" (including referring to an adult as "girl," "boy," "hunk," "doll," "honey," or "sweetie") and explicitly prohibits "comments or inquiries about dating."

Not coincidentally, such vague and broad harassment codes are generally the weapon of choice for punishing controversial, dissenting, or un-PC speech. While colleges should and must protect students from actual harassment, warping the meaning of "harassment" not only violates the law, it trivializes real harassment by recasting it as an amorphous catch-all for expression that offends some individuals. Often the "offended" individuals are not even students, but campus administrators themselves. I have seen administrators goad students into filing harassment complaints despite the fact that the speech in question came nowhere near the legal definition of harassment.

Perhaps the most pernicious development involving speech codes is how comfortable students have become with them. One striking example is a campus debate in which students clearly accepted the school's imposition of a tiny "free speech zone," but then proceeded to debate what kind of speech should be allowed within that zone. The idea that there was something profoundly wrong with having their freedom of expression quarantined to a tiny area in the first place never seems to have occurred to them. To the contrary, they carried the school's zealotry a step further by proposing a speech code even within the speech zone. Nothing better illustrates the thoroughness with which today's undergraduates have imbibed the new sensitivity.

Outright Indoctrination and Thought Reform

The most disturbing violations of rights go beyond censoring or miseducating students about the law and philosophy of free speech. Some university programs aim for nothing less than the total transformation of a student's personal philosophy and beliefs on issues as wide-ranging as moral philosophy, science, and even religion to a set of narrow, preapproved beliefs.

One of the most troubling recent examples was the residence life "curriculum" at the University of Delaware. Delaware's "treatment" (the university's word) program for all seven thousand students in the dormitory system was so far-reaching and expansive that no brief mention can adequately capture it. Not only were students required to fill out invasive questionnaires about their sexual identity, they were gathered together and made to reveal where they stood on given political issues with the goal of publicly shaming those who had the "wrong" opinions. The policy further deemed insensitive speech a crime worthy of the same attention from campus police as murder and rape.

A lesser-known case at Michigan State University involved a program designed as an "early intervention" against students who showed mildly aggressive behavior. Based on a domestic violence model, students—including a young woman caught slamming the door during an argument with her boyfriend—were sentenced to four sessions of pseudo-psychological counseling that they had to pay for themselves. During these sessions, students were required to identify on a "power and control wheel" how they had abused their "white privilege" or other forms of emotional "abuse." Despite multiple constitutional infirmities, the program remained at MSU for years, doubtless teaching many students that such invasive tactics are justifiable if one is engaged in the noble pursuit of rooting out unconscious societal evil.

One might suppose that these illiberal lessons are being balanced, at least in part, by some education about the First Amendment and the importance of free speech in the Western democratic tradition. On the contrary, evidence suggests that by the time they graduate from high school, American students already harbor powerfully negative attitudes about free speech. According to a 2005 survey, 73 percent of high school students either felt ambivalent about the First Amendment or took it for granted. High school students were also more likely than adults to think that citizens should not be allowed to express unpopular opinions and that the government should have a role in approving newspaper stories.

It seems unlikely that such attitudes would improve in a collegiate environment saturated with bad examples of how one deals with differing opinions and misinformation about what is and is not protected speech. Indeed, today's college environment more often provides philosophical and semi-legalistic support (such as "hate speech" theory) for the selective censorship students have seen, condoned, or even engaged in themselves.

The concern that students are learning dangerous lessons about free speech is not merely theoretical; it is demonstrated year after year by students' "grassroots censorship."

Over the years the Student Press Law Center and FIRE have received dozens of reports of student newspapers being destroyed by other students who do not like a given paper's content. One of the funnier examples involved a sorority that destroyed a run of a student newspaper after the paper ran an article documenting mold in the sorority's house. But the trend of vigilante censorship isn't funny at all. The most disturbing examples include incidents where newspapers are actually burned. Perhaps the most famous incident occurred in 1997, when students at Cornell burned hundreds of copies of the conservative *Cornell Review* at a rally because African American students were unhappy with an un-PC cartoon. Students have burned newspapers at Boston College in 2005, Dartmouth in 2006, and the University of Wisconsin in 2007. These modern-day book burnings should terrify any American who is at all concerned about the prospect of maintaining a free society. Amazingly enough, the national media, which styles itself the defender of free speech, has largely ignored these insidious acts.

Nowhere is this intolerance clearer than when it comes to abortion. In 2008, a pro-life group at Missouri State drew attention to its message by setting up four thousand popsicle-stick crosses on a campus lawn, with the permission of the university. That night, students came and destroyed the tiny crosses, even riding their bikes over them. The vandalism was filmed and posted online. In one video someone from the pro-life group asked a young woman why she had stepped on the crosses, to which she replied, "I feel like I have the right to walk across campus without seeing that."

Earlier the same year at the University of Wisconsin–Stevens Point, a member of the student government tore crosses for a similar pro-life display out of the ground while angrily shouting, "Since [abortion] is a right, you don't have the right to challenge it."

Even professors have gotten into the act. In 2006, Sally Jacobsen, a professor at Northern Kentucky University, invited students in one of her classes "to express their freedom-of-speech rights to destroy [an antiabortion] display if they wished to." The antiabortion display had been erected by an NKU student group with permission from university officials. Professor Jacobsen was actually photographed helping destroy it. While this is especially disturbing behavior from a professor, it is likely that the continued and systemic miseducation of students about the meaning and importance of free speech do more to encourage such behavior than the words of one professor ever could.

The idea that there is a serious problem on college campuses is often met with skepticism, trivialization, and outright denial. The last is the easiest to overcome—at least for those willing to listen—because FIRE has documented hundreds of outrageous and absurd cases of censorship and has posted thousands of pages of evidence on its website. However, even when people begin to accept that these incidents are really happening, a tendency exists to downplay their significance, as if four years of being subjected to an environment that approves of and even glorifies the "well-intentioned censor" does not have serious consequences.

What most Americans fail to understand is that our current constitutional interpretation in which free speech is strongly protected is a fairly recent innovation, even in the United States. Far from being unchanging and inviolable, constitutional interpretations shift over time and are powerfully affected by public attitudes. That is why the sea change in attitudes toward free speech among college students today has worrisome implications for the rest of us.

In recent years, our colleges and universities—which once represented the vanguard of the movement for free speech, free minds, and free expression—have become openly and moralistically hostile to genuine individual liberty. The value of free expression is perceived to be at odds with goals that were considered "more important," like inclusiveness, diversity, nondiscrimination, and tolerance. As a result, well-intentioned policies meant to advance these worthy goals have transmogrified into all-purpose tools that allow administrators to punish speech they dislike, including criticism of the administrators themselves.

The new censorship is also producing a generation which believes that a severe tension exists between civil rights (such as the newly manufactured right not to be offended) and civil liberties (most notably, freedom of speech). In this environment, a culture of tacit and sometimes open approval of ideologically based censorship has blossomed. Students in today's colleges live in an atmosphere where free speech is appreciated only for approved ideas and sentiments, and in which efforts to suppress that freedom are considered at best understandable and at worst as noble or romantic efforts to protect the community from offense or discomfort.

Without an understanding of why free speech is actually a necessary element of a pluralistic multicultural society, I fear that this generation's commitment to free speech will become too anemic to resist such ideological encroachments. Further, if genuine freedom of speech ceases to be a popularly held value, if it instead comes to be morally stigmatized, then on a practical everyday level the protections of the First Amendment will mean less and less as time goes by. As FIRE cofounder Alan Charles Kors has put it, "A nation that does not educate in liberty will not long preserve it, and will not even know when it is lost."

Note

1. Public colleges, as state institutions, are bound by the free-speech protections of the First Amendment. Private colleges are not directly bound by constitutional

guarantees of free speech. However, the overwhelming majority make extensive promises of freedom of speech in their policies, student handbooks, and promotional materials. Several courts have found these policies to be binding contracts, and they do create the reasonable assumption that students will enjoy at least as many freedoms as their peers at public colleges. This article therefore treats most public and private colleges as having roughly the same obligations to protect free speech. The exceptions—like devout religious schools, military academies, or schools bound by state laws that provide free speech at private universities—are an excellent topic for another article.

15

Belief in False Gods

Barry C. Lynn

IN RECENT YEARS, I've given dozens of talks across America on the structures of our international political economy. Early on I noticed an odd phenomenon. Merely to speak the word "globalization" often evoked a physical effect in people. Many in the audience would look down, hunch over, begin to fidget.

It was only after long discussions with my listeners that I began to understand why. Americans, I realized, had been taught to associate globalization with the image of a billion Chinese and another billion Indians all working really hard to make the things we used to make. More daunting yet, we had been taught that there is nothing we can do to change this, because globalization is not a human-controlled process at all, but an immensely powerful natural force that directs how we interact with these other peoples, in ways we can barely grasp.

In other words, many Americans had been taught to believe in a metaphysical explanation of how our society functions. Rather than view ourselves as the masters of our own destinies, many of us see ourselves and our society as subject to the decrees of natural powers that have all but determined our future.

Globalization is by no means the only such force we perceive acting on or within our society. Americans today believe in a myriad of mechanistic processes directing us toward certain ends. For some, the dominant forces are technological. For others, biological. Many believe in forces produced by some dynamic in capitalism, or in free markets. Whatever the source, the practical result is the same: to evoke any of these awe-inspiring forces in a conversation about our political economy has much the same effect as to speak of "God's will."

And so, even when we believe our most vital political liberties are endangered, we increasingly do not view ourselves as free to do anything about it. Rather than sally out to protect our liberties, we sit, we wonder, we fidget, we fear.

One of the more striking characteristics of the writings of the founders, and of the men who dominated American politics in the first half of the nineteenth century, is how starkly conscious they were of the tenuousness of our existence as independent citizens in an independent nation. The Declaration of Independence may begin with the statement that the "laws of nature and of nature's God *entitle*" all people to be equal. But it's clear these Americans believed it was up to them to erect and then protect a government whose powers they could wield to enforce such common claims against other groups of people with different interests.

To the extent this attitude reflected a philosophy, it was that of the empiricists. A generation before the American Revolution, David Hume wrote of the dangers of basing political decisions on any belief that society is directed by either "brute unconscious matter" or a "rational intelligent" supernatural being. Practically, this meant the founders, even if they believed privately that God determined the fall of each leaf, understood that in public they had to act *as if* they were completely free to shape the world around them. And most did seem to believe it was entirely in their power to shape the relations of the United States with any other nation-state, as well as between the individual citizen and our domestic corporate estates.

Perhaps the easiest way to understand why so many modern Americans feel so powerless is to flip through the works of a few of today's most influential doctors of philosophy. In my own travels I spent a lot of time asking audience members what books lay on their nightstands, and which ones, back in college, created the deepest impressions. Hume was rarely among them. Instead I discovered that a great many Americans today devote their attention to writers who promise to educate them about the workings and whims of some natural force operating upon or within our society.

On the subject of globalization, the single most energetic and influential modern metaphysician is Thomas Friedman. In his book *The World Is Flat*, Friedman devotes entire chapters to detailing the nonhuman, suprapolitical forces that, he contends, are refashioning relationships among nations. Friedman even conjures a full-blown theory about how industrial interdependence is leading inevitably to global peace and prosperity, and declares his theory proven. Friedman also, helpfully, identifies himself openly as a "determinist."

When it comes to technology, Americans can choose among a wide array of books that explain how various new media exert effects on us far greater than the actions of any mere government or private corporation. One of the more representative such works is *An Army of Davids*, in which libertarian blogger Glenn Reynolds argues that, if we just sit back and relax, technology will slay all the corporate goliaths for us.

Belief in the market as a mechanistic device able to sort, in an entirely neutral fashion, the wheatier ideas and businesses and entrepreneurs among us from the chaff, traces almost directly to the economist Milton Friedman, especially his 1962 volume *Capitalism and Freedom*. In that slim work, which has now been assigned to two generations of college students, Friedman coined a whole new language in which wealth was created and freedom preserved not by human beings operating tools, making laws, and wielding arms, but by an abstraction he called the "free market."

The idea that capitalism is infused with some deterministic force was expressed most elegantly by the Austrian economist Joseph Schumpeter. Although few of us, back in college, actually got all the way through *Capitalism, Socialism, and Democracy*, most did study the famous passage in which Schumpeter coined the term "creative destruction." In the process, we were also instructed that capitalism is a "process of industrial *mutation*—if I [Schumpeter] may use the *biological* term—that incessantly revolutionizes the economic structure *from within*."

And for those among us who, for whatever reason, remain unconvinced by these various metaphysics of the twentieth century, we can always turn to those writers who purvey the reductionist theories of the nineteenth. Take neo-Darwinist Robert Wright, author of such books as *The Moral Animal* and *The Evolution of God*. In his 2000 work, *NonZero: The Logic of Human Destiny*, Wright claims to have discovered "a direction in human history, or in biological evolution, or both."

In recent years, it has become fashionable among members of America's educated elite to recoil in horror at the theories of "creationists" and "religious fundamentalists" who, they believe, subvert the self-evident truths of science. Yet to the extent that any member of our educated elite views the world through the metaphysical prisms fashioned by today's best-selling doctors of philosophy, their beliefs are just as theological in nature.

Of course, the gods of our educated elite don't have faces. And unlike those of the religious "fundamentalists," these mechanical gods appear to leave a lot less room for the exercise of what used to be called free will.

I will be the first to defend the right of any American to believe whatever he or she wishes about first causes. What concerns me is how such mechanistic explanations for political-economic events affect how my fellow citizens view themselves as political actors.

Consider a few of the potential effects of allowing such beliefs to shape how we perceive the world around us.

To understand globalization as a force that automatically weaves the nations of the world into a single economic system may make it harder to see the immense trading companies, like Wal-Mart and General Electric, which are the actual powers that nowadays determine the division of labor among nations. Such a belief may also make it harder to perceive how the ruling classes of mercantilist states like China increasingly use these same "American" companies to serve their particular interests, say by moving more of our machines and our technologies from our hands into theirs.

Similarly, to view the market as an all-embracing apparatus that determines, in a neutral fashion, the outcomes of our political economy may make it harder to spot the monopolists who use immensely powerful corporate governments to enclose our marketplaces, to seize the properties of our independent entrepreneurs, and to determine how much we pay for the basic stuff of our lives.

And to perceive technology as some sort of natural force that influences equally the actions of all the various individuals and groups in society may make it harder to understand when one group of people, like those who control AT&T or Google, uses concentrated capital to consolidate control over some technological activity within our society—and hence to consolidate various forms of political power.

One way to understand how effective these metaphysical interpretations can be in disguising the concentration by real human beings of real political power is to look at how America's relationship with China was revolutionized over the last fifteen years.

In the quarter century after Richard Nixon traveled to Beijing, American leaders of both parties worked to integrate that Communist-run country into the world system we had established after the Second World War, and did so with great care, great skepticism, and until the Tiananmen Massacre, great success. During these years, our leaders assumed the relationship between our nations was entirely political in nature, and that all aspects of it were subject to conscious political control.

Then, in October 1997, Bill Clinton laid out an entirely new "strategy" for managing America's relationship with the authoritarian regime in Beijing—which was to get the government in Washington out of the way. From now on, Clinton said, the job of integrating China into the world system would be handled not by our elected leaders but by the impersonal forces of technology and globalization. The "Internet" and the "modem," Clinton assured us, along with China's growing economic "interdependence" with the rest of the world, would have a "liberalizing effect." The all but inevitable result, he said, would be the opening of that "closed political system."

Clinton was not alone in expressing such beliefs. Two years later,

George W. Bush's future secretary of state Condoleezza Rice declared that "economic liberalization in China is ultimately going to lead to political liberalization. That's an iron law."

We can interpret these statements in one of two ways. Either Clinton and Rice were consciously using metaphysical constructs to justify policies favored by people who intended to use their control of our China trade to empower themselves. Or they really believed that suprapolitical forces would somehow mechanically transform the Maoist state into a quasi-liberal democracy.

Either way, it is now starkly clear that as we lolled around waiting for globalization and technology to manage our relationship with China, the leaders of the regime in Beijing were toiling diligently to lay their hands on as many human institutions and systems as possible in order to make them better serve their interests. And so, rather than a flourishing of democratic capitalism, we have seen the elite consolidate power over that nation as a whole. Far worse for American citizens, we have seen that same Chinese elite manipulate many of our banks and our corporations in ways that have enabled them to consolidate direct control over many of our most important economic systems.

When President Clinton announced his intention to turn the management of our nation's relationship with Communist China over to globalization and technology, America was an immensely rich and independent nation. Today, those who lift their eyes from the pages of our modern Panglosses will see that in less than a generation America has been made to depend directly on Chinese sources for most, in some cases all, of our most vital drugs, food additives, electronics, machines, and clothes, as well as the cash we borrow to pay for it all.

One way to read the history of liberty in America is to focus on how successful the American people have been in resisting the use—by conscious political actors or the social "scientists" and other pretend theologians in their pay—of such metaphysical frames to justify the consolidation of power.

In the early days of our republic we kept ourselves almost entirely free from such reductionist theories. Even as European elites employed various newfangled metaphysics to bring their scientifically "enlightened" populations under control, Americans continued to believe that we could change our political relations at will, so long as we were able to consolidate sufficient political power.

And in fact we did use our powers, directed through our state and federal governments, to protect ourselves from all would-be rulers, whether they wielded nation-states abroad or corporate estates at home. The result was a wider distribution of power among the citizens of the early United States than in any modern nation before or since.

Our greatest expression of faith in our power to remake our world according to republican principles came in the Civil War, when we organized ourselves into great armies finally to destroy those last and most awful vestiges of feudalism—the slave plantations. Yet it was also during this cataclysmic event that the political balances of the old republic were at last upset. Soon after the end of the war we discovered that while the citizen soldiers were at war, a new class of Wall Street operator had empowered itself with great piles of capital and the corporate governments we had so carefully husbanded up to that time.

Overnight, it seemed, we saw our markets corrupted, our properties seized, and private governments erected over us by men like Jay Gould and John D. Rockefeller and J. P. Morgan.

It is no coincidence that this was also when metaphysical theories began to play a big role in political debate in America. Herbert Spencer's theory of "survival of the fittest" came first. For newly minted lords seeking ways to justify their use of brute political power to capture control over entire industrial activities, the idea that they were merely following a natural "law" of "progress" was very attractive. Which is why the steel monopolist Andrew Carnegie personally arranged to import Spencer himself to America in 1882 for a speaking tour.

Various versions of Marx came next, most importantly the "light" socialism of the Teddy Roosevelt wing of the Progressive movement. For the newly professionalized bureaucrats and corporate managers and systems engineers and sociologists and economists seeking to justify their use of the central state to get their hands on the powers already concentrated by private monopolists, the idea that the natural "progress" of history had determined that the "professional" would one day reign supreme was a highly useful story.

This is not to say that all these classical progressives were in on some vast conspiracy. As with Clinton and Rice, most appear to have truly believed in their mechanical gods. And as with China today, the practical problem then was that while the true believers waited for these supranatural forces to deliver us to some promised Utopia, old-fashioned human nature got in the way, especially the element that leads one man or a few to seek to impose their will on all the rest.

And so, in America, from J. P. Morgan's capture of the railroads, to Teddy Roosevelt's Bureau of Corporations and New Nationalism, to Henry Ford's private state at River Rouge, to Herbert Hoover's Associationalism, to the almost militarized National Recovery Administration (NRA) of the first New Deal, we saw ever more confusing concentrations and combinations of power that blurred the line between public and private. To understand how dangerous these corporatist embraces were, we need only recall that Mussolini, Stalin, and Hitler were avid students of American progressive arrangements and practiced preachers of progressive metaphysics.

Salvation came from below. Throughout the dark decades after the Civil War, those who believed not in the new metaphysics but in the old republican principles of Madison and Jefferson had organized themselves into new political groupings, like the Granger and Populist movements. In 1896 these small-R republicans finally recaptured control of a party, the Democratic. In 1912 they even captured the White House, and in their first year and a half in power managed to push through a number of acts that restricted the power of the financiers. Yet almost as soon as war broke out in Europe in 1914, the lords and their professionals used the resulting financial and military crises as an excuse to push aside the republicans within the Wilson administration and to reassert their control over the state.

Not until after the collapse of the economy in the Great Depression did the heirs to Madison and Jefferson consolidate sufficient power to refashion America's political economy. The single most important date in this second American revolution was May 27, 1935, when the Supreme Court overthrew the NRA in a 9-0 decision.

Although we now tend to view this decision in a purely political light—the throwing of a wrench into the New Deal by "conservatives"—the decision in fact marked the culmination of an intellectual revolution effected largely by the republican jurist Louis Brandeis. Eight years earlier, Brandeis had written in a dissent that "the doctrine of the separation of powers was adopted by the convention of 1787 not to promote efficiency but to preclude the exercise of arbitrary power. The purpose was not to avoid friction, but, by means of the inevitable friction incident to the distribution of the government powers among three departments, to save the people from autocracy."

In getting the Court to expressly reject the doctrine of efficiency so favored by the progressives, Brandeis also stage-managed an implicit rejection of materialist metaphysics in favor of a political philosophy based on nothing more than an honest, empirical, appreciation of human fallibility.

The decision changed the course of American politics. For the next two generations, real power shifted from the high financiers and their "professional" priests to the legislator and lawyer—who used common law and common politics to restructure the political economy from the ground up. And the results, which included the harnessing of the giant industrial powers and the establishment of clear protections in the form of open markets and antimonopoly laws for the liberties of the small proprietor, while imperfect, bore a surprisingly good resemblance to the republic of Madison and Jefferson.

In the 1960s and 1970s a new generation of would-be lords began to promote an updated version of Spencerism—mainly in the form of free-market fundamentalism. Following the election of Ronald

Reagan in 1981, they moved swiftly to destroy the antimonopoly laws that formed the basis of the system put into place during the second New Deal.

Also in the 1960s and 1970s, a new generation of professionals, especially among the economists—who had spent the intervening years huddled over the old teleologies of progress—sallied out to take a share of the power the new lords intended to concentrate and promptly set about providing cover for the predations of the new monopolists.

And so the American people once again saw our factories and stores and farms, even our industrial skills, stripped away in the name of "efficiency." And we saw our great manufacturing corporations transformed into trading companies designed to import what we ourselves had invented, and for generations had made, in a process that rendered us dependent on a foreign authoritarian power. And we saw the powers of government, which we so carefully separated in 1787 and again in 1935, unified again in a brand-new corporatist embrace.

All is not lost. We can make ourselves free again. We can rebuild our communities, restore our open market systems, restore our industrial systems to our own control, and restore our system of checks and balances. We need only dust off the various antimonopoly laws that served us so well in the past—including those we used to regulate our trade with other nations—and update them to serve us again in the twenty-first century.

However, we will be able to do so only after we emancipate ourselves from the belief that we are in any way directed by globalization, technology, capitalism, the free market, Darwinian biology, or any other metaphysical force.

The concentration of power in America in the hands of a few financiers, and their sale of that power to the authoritarian regime in China, was not decreed by any god. The power to stop these human actions lies right in our own traditions, our own minds, our own hands.

Liberty is ours to make, again.

16

The Fairness Doctrine

David Mamet

IN THE 1970S I was walking in New York's Central Park and saw a very well-dressed gentleman. He wore an obviously bespoke hacking jacket, perfectly cut pants, and a beautiful custom-made shirt, and he carried a walking stick.

I have never seen a fellow so conflicted. There he was in the middle of Central Park, stuck looking a fool and he very well knew it. The stick had a nice silver head and could not pass as, say, an umbrella with its fabric gone astray. It was a walking stick, and he was carrying it just one hundred years too late, and short of throwing it in the lake, he was going to have to *wear* it. And that is how we Americans feel about the term "the Homeland." It is ugly and false, but we're stuck with it; it retains some marginal utility, as it means "our country"—and we'll use the term as little as possible, and we'll all get through it somehow.

But I have never heard anyone use the term "politically correct" without verbal or gestural quotes. We, to our credit, *just don't like it.* We understand the term consciously or unconsciously as an imposition, and it goes against the American grain.

We'll take "the Homeland" shrugging, as even the fact of its imposition hides a deeper truth: that we love our country. But "politically correct" will just not wash, for, at the bottom, we know that it means "totalitarian." How can any politics be "correct"? A person's politics may be acceptable or unacceptable; we may find such reasonable or foolish, loathsome or enchanting. But to deem it "correct" implies that it adheres to one true form, which, of course, can only take place in a dictatorship. We just don't like that term, and when it can be said without wincing and without quotes, it will mean the country has veered toward dictatorship.[1]

If there is an official or semiofficial imposition—or even review— of language, the ability to recognize an occurrence, an event, or a race independently corrodes. Not just our ability to speak, but our ability to see diminishes. In popular idiom, give a dog a bad name and you see a bad dog. If peace is "good," and war is "bad," per se, if any peace is superior to any war, moveon.org feels it acceptable to make an ad-hominem jibe about the name of an American hero, calling him General Betrayus.

Our country—not our government, but our country, our *society*— has been stringently involved in expunging from our speech racial and sexual epithets. But to the extent that such becomes official, we are not allowing but inviting government to police our language, and one aspect of government of which we are aware is that once it begins anything it does not stop. Government cannot police itself, which is why we have periodic elections.

The most important part of our American Constitution is the First Amendment: "There shall be no law limiting freedom of speech." As long as we can communicate, as long as one no doubt well-meaning group cannot seize high ground and control our speech, we have the capacity to alter any circumstance for the common good, which is to say, to bring about a situation wherein only a portion of the populace is unhappy.

Laws against "hate speech" seem like a good idea, but the question is and always will be, "Who decides?" Why is someone who kills his fellow better than someone who kills his fellow while shouting, "You dirty kike"? I confess, it escapes me.

Speech may be used to foster hate, but once the government becomes involved, it is a certainty that if not those originally empowered to decide, their descendants will limit speech for their own particular political and personal reasons. And a stepchild of the concept of "hate speech" is the Fairness Doctrine, a political measure pushed by Democrats to require broadcasters to "balance" political content, thereby diluting the power of conservative talk radio.

The Constitution could be reduced, if necessary, to its First Amendment: "There shall be no law limiting freedom of speech." *No* law. That amendment means that both the acceptability of speech and the worth of ideas must be adjudicated between citizens, and that freedom will never be usurped by government.

For the First Amendment ensures not that speech will be fair, but that it will be *free*. It cannot be both. It may be free and onerous, indeed hateful and obscene, or it may be fair, which is to say adjudicated, in which case the power to limit speech is given to a judge. And who among us is wise enough to so rule? *None of us*, which is why the founders wrote the First Amendment. For none of us can "create" language. We can *suggest*, but language is formed by the interaction of multitudes in the purpose of the culture as a whole. The culture will choose between Beta and VHS, between "blog" and "bodywash," between "the homeland" and "politically correct." And it is the culture that has censured racial and sexual epithets, the harsh penalty being exclusion from the group.

With the enforcement of a doctrine that any broadcast medium voicing one political opinion must voice another, dissenting opinion will be the beginning of the end of free speech. Here's why.

First, who is to say what is political opinion? The line between political opinion and reportage is so blurred now as to be almost indistinct. Should such a pernicious doctrine become widespread, energy will inevitably be devoted to convincing, persuading, and suborning those authorities who are to rule on whether or not any utterance is an expression of political opinion.

Further, such a doctrine, rather than fostering open discourse, will tend to limit it, because those media organs with a limited budget will, of necessity, shy away from political speech. The Fairness Doctrine may cause the government to insist on a media outlet airing the contrary view, thus causing the station to offend its particular listenership and, thus, limit its attractiveness to those advertisers who have invested to appeal to the station's prime listenership.

Last, such a so-called Fairness Doctrine will, if it has not already, clog the courts.

And what of the offhand comment, utterance, or quip that the individual and the broadcast medium will have to self-censor rather than risk not offense but prosecution for lack of fairness? The Fairness Doctrine *must* limit spontaneity and discourse, and increase self-censorship. The fewer things we can *say*, the fewer things we can *see*. The great danger here, as in all government, is rule not of the law but of the administrative committee, acting, whether "good-willed" or not, in reference only to its own wisdom in the supposed service of a law that itself cannot *be* fair—as it is subjective. This is the beginning of the tyranny of the police state.

This doctrine of "fairness" will affect the left only marginally, but it will silence dissent on the right. The few but powerful right-wing outlets will be forced, over time, to dilute their listenership, while the left, the instigator of the doctrine, will be secure from its implementation behind its traditional stance of "neutrality"; further, its contemporary control of the legislative process will ensure that claims for impartiality are enforced only to the benefit of the side in power. The effect of the so-called Fairness Doctrine will eventually be the end of freedom of speech.

Or those wishing freedom from government intervention will shy away from any view that might possibly be considered political, and the vast, unfettered forum between right and left—the traditional possession of the American public—will become mired in the courts, which will be called upon to rule over every utterance and assess its political content. Anyone, right or left, seeing an opportunity or feeling a grievance, will possess the right to petition government for a ruling; government will grow even stronger, and, being made not of the all-wise, but the put-upon, harried, or indeed suborned bureaucrats, will rule only to the limit of its interest and capacity, which rule never will be "fair," which always is subject to partisanship or crime, and which, at best, will be arbitrary.

So, in the name of "fairness" we will have created an ongoing inquisition—much as we have on the subject of race—and given to government—which is to say, to the bureaucrats in power—the right to stifle speech.

Thomas Jefferson wrote that given the choice between government without newspapers or newspapers without government he would unhesitatingly vote for the latter. We are on the verge of experiencing the former, or, indeed, the close conjunction of the state and the press, which amounts to the same thing.

Note

1. Note the new concept of the nonword "s/he." How is it pronounced? When one comes across it printed all thought stops, as one "reads to oneself," and the meaning and intention of the page are forgotten, replaced by a blunt intrusion announcing itself as superior to the matter's content.

17

The War on Negative Liberty

Katherine Mangu-Ward

IN EARLY 2001, near Jalalabad, Afghanistan, a group of women gathered to eat ice cream in secret. Since agents of the Taliban's Department for the Promotion of Virtue and Prevention of Vice often attacked Afghan women caught enjoying a scoop in public, the group took the precaution of ducking into a neglected restaurant in the back of a bazaar and settled within a protective wall of hanging sheets. Once inside, they carefully lifted their burqas and spooned up forbidden bowls of vanilla ice cream. American playwright and activist Eve Ensler, who described this scene in her book, *The Good Body*, recounts the warning of her guide, Sunita: "If we get caught, it could mean a flogging or even an execution. It depends on what kind of mood the Taliban are in today." Rumors that Taliban men were circling the bazaar in pickup trucks soon set the women to flight, their ice cream barely finished.

Ice Cream in Brooklyn

Now imagine a place as far from Taliban-controlled Afghanistan as possible. It's August 2009, and the ice cream man is jingling through Brooklyn's Prospect Park. An idyllic American scene, yet parents are on edge. Vicki Sell, mother of three-year-old Katherine, told the *New York Times* she considers the behavior of the bell-ringing vendors "predatory." The jingle, say the Brooklyn parents, turns children into whining beggars. The sugar and additives in the ice cream make them hyperactive monsters. And the ice cream peddler lurks in the area long after his line of initial customers is gone, forcing parents to rebuff a new barrage of pleas every few minutes. Sell says she has repeatedly called the city's 311 complaint line in an effort to evict the unlicensed vendors, and would like to see them banned from the park.

At first glance, any comparison between the gentle beeping of a Brooklyn mom dialing 311 on her iPhone and the roar of the Taliban pickup truck seems absurd. But it remains true that both want the same thing—a targeted ban on ice cream.

The Taliban forbids ice cream to women for symbolic reasons. It is decadent, Western, and hard to eat gracefully in a burqa. In Afghanistan, the state seeks not just political control, not just personal obedience, but dominion over the souls of the men and women who live under the watchful eyes of the virtue police. To ban ice cream consumption in public is to proclaim that the sphere of individual liberty does not extend even to the inner folds of the women's voluminous burqas. For those women, any freedom that can be found must be minuscule, fleeting, and necessarily illusory, collapsed into a few furtive bites of ice cream.

By contrast, the Brooklyn moms support bans for purely practical reasons. Dealing with the ice cream truck is inconvenient, and they would rather not bother. Whether or not they succeed in banning the jingle of the ice cream man, as Americans they will continue to operate within a vast sphere of liberty. Their children scamper around in a world of free association, free speech, and free movement. They have robust expectations that they will enjoy a large degree of privacy in their own homes and move largely unmolested in public.

Yet there is a strange kinship between the Taliban and the Brooklyn parents. Both worry about what is lost in the pursuit of corporeal pleasures. They sense the oppressiveness of unhealthy desires. They are daunted by the prospect of taking responsibility for setting their own limits. The Taliban might brandish the language of virtue and vice in pursuit of total control, but their alarm at the prospect of helplessness in the face of temptation is just as real as that of the

Brooklyn parents. And so the response is the same: A call for the state to set limits for them on their own seemingly inconsequential behaviors—and for everyone else around them.

The Brooklyn parents undoubtedly consider themselves to be freedom-loving Americans. But how could people who cherish freedom clamor for the state to take away their choices? Isaiah Berlin's now-familiar distinction between the two types of liberty helps clear up the confusion. Negative liberty, or "freedom from," hinges on the idea of noninterference. True liberty, say John Stuart Mill, Benjamin Constant, Friedrich Hayek, and others who champion this view, consists in carving out the largest possible area where individuals will be left alone to do as they please.

The Brooklyn moms have an entirely different concept of liberty, one that Berlin calls positive liberty: the freedom to fulfill your potential. The liberty of Jean-Jacques Rousseau, Karl Marx, and John Rawls senses threats not only from an encroaching state or violent individuals, but from circumstances like poverty or ignorance as well. Under this conception of liberty—often used to support causes such as universal health insurance and unemployment benefits—freedom can be threatened by someone's own bad inclinations or unhealthy habits.

"Once I take this view" that even one's own desires can threaten liberty, writes Berlin, "I am in a position to ignore the actual wishes of men or societies, to bully, oppress, torture in the name, and on behalf, of their 'real' selves, in the secure knowledge that whatever is the true goal of man (happiness, performance of duty, wisdom, a just society, self-fulfillment) must be identical with his freedom—the free choice of his 'true,' albeit often submerged and inarticulate, self."

This is why the Taliban and the Brooklyn moms can come to the same conclusion about ice cream bans. While they disagree on the parts of the self that need to be checked or limited—and the Brooklyn moms prefer democracy to determine those limits—they agree that state intervention to limit highly personal choices will make people better, and even freer.

Cigarettes in New York

Positive liberty has been ascendant in the United States since the early twentieth century. All around us, dings and dents appear in the surface of the sphere of negative liberty, disfiguring it, perhaps beyond recognition.

Consider the case of smoking bans. Setting aside health concerns about secondhand smoke, much of the discussion about restricting smokers rests on the desirability of discouraging them from harming themselves with their irresponsible behavior. When New York's ban on smoking in bars or restaurants sends smokers out into the cold and rainy streets, that's a feature, not a bug. As the list of places where smoking is not permitted grows longer, smoking becomes less appealing. Choice remains, but unhealthy impulses are circumscribed by increasingly restrictive rules. The same arguments are made for increasing taxes on cigarettes—to extract additional tax money from smokers is to do them a favor. After all, they shouldn't be spending that money on cigarettes in the first place. Supporters of smoking bans nearly always present their view, at least in part, as altruism. And the smokers themselves often buy into the argument. In his 1998 book on smoking regulation, *For Your Own Good*, Jacob Sullum quotes a Kentucky smoker on a cigarette tax increase in 1990: "I hope they price them out of my range, because I am really wanting to stop."

Those who lobby for and approve of smoking bans and ice cream–free zones don't see the ever-growing list of banned behaviors as an infringement of liberty. Instead, restrictions like these are a convenient and practical solution to the problem of what Berlin called "the divided self." All people have both good and bad impulses. The bad impulses can be powerful, stopping us from making good choices just as surely as a law might. This is why mothers want the ice cream truck's jingle taken away—to minimize the chance of bad choices not only in their children, but also in themselves. After all, holding firm against the onslaught of whining is a tough task. Those who propose nanny-state bans and taxes often see themselves simply as removing temptations, reshaping desires, or otherwise limiting the availability of "bad options." They seek to realize a form of positive liberty.

Three years after the smoking ban, the New York City Board of Health voted to ban the use of trans fats in food served in restaurants. The logic behind the ban was identical to the justification of smoking bans. Although the science is clear on the harmfulness of these particular fats, people will not spontaneously give them up—trans fats are just too delicious in donuts, fried chicken, and pie crusts. Regulation requiring calorie counts on menus continues down this road, albeit more subtly. These mandates deprive people of the choice to remain ignorant. What was a punch line just a few years back ("What are they going to do next, ban donuts?") becomes a reality before the joke, or the donuts, have time to get stale. The trans fat ban was accomplished under the supervision of New York City Health Commissioner Thomas Frieden, now the head of the national Centers for Disease Control and Prevention. Fully assuming the role of parent, Frieden told the *Financial Times* that he felt "when anyone dies at an early age from a preventable cause in New York City, it's my fault."

A softer form of the same view has recently come on the scene under the name "libertarian paternalism." As described by legal scholar Cass Sunstein, now the head of the U.S. Office of Information and Regulatory Affairs, and University of Chicago economist Richard Thaler in their 2008 book *Nudge*, the state should expand its practice of deciding which inclinations are good and which are bad, and then nudging citizens in the direction of the good (while not explicitly outlawing the bad). Call it positive liberty light.

Foie Gras in Chicago

A new tax on Twinkies or hot dogs, both bêtes noires of antiobesity crusaders, takes only a small chunk out of the sphere of negative liberty. The general population won't take much notice one way or the other, and those who do will be divided between the negative-

and positive-liberty view. But any limit on Twinkie consumption is a hard blow to the competitive eater. There's always something else delicious on the menu if foie gras is banned, as it was briefly in Chicago from 2006 to 2008, but it's a sad loss for the chef who has been striving to perfect his searing technique for decades—and for his customers.

The Taliban doesn't care if it's a hot day, or if you have a sweet tooth, or if you've been looking forward to ice cream all week. In free societies where a philosophy of positive liberty is ascendant, the dynamic plays out differently, but the idea is the same. A handful of people may be disappointed when they don't find foie gras on the menu. But if their culinary whims interfere with the larger goals of maximizing the chances of self-actualization, the Chicago City Council couldn't care less.

"The smaller is the domain where choices among alternatives are made collectively," Anthony de Jasay wrote in 1997, "the smaller will be the probability that any individual's preference gets overruled." Yet people leap in eagerly to assist the state in overruling choices of which they disapprove. The Energy Policy Act of 1992 limited American showerheads to 2.5 gallons per minute. Recently, *Consumer Reports* went looking for the best showerhead. They found one from a British manufacturer that was stellar. Too good to be legal, in fact, since the fixture's multiple heads cause it to exceed water-use limits. The product reviewers at the magazine took it upon themselves to "contact" the Environmental Protection Agency. Rather than enjoying a bit of essentially harmless duck-and-weave around the law, citizens report on each other for violations—even while acknowledging that those violations have offered a far better product.

In a similar sad tale, European Parliament Directive 2005/32/EG banned the sale and importation of one-hundred-watt incandescent bulbs starting September 1, 2009, with lower wattages phasing out over time. Getting caught selling wasteful old-style bulbs brings a whopping seventy-thousand-dollar fine. A functionally identical ban goes into effect in the United States in 2012, justified by the need to reduce energy use in the face of global warming.

Compact fluorescents do use much less energy than their old-fashioned incandescent cousins. Never mind that the flickery blue of fluorescents in America's (cost-conscious) office buildings have become synecdoche for the soul-crushing aspects of life as part of a large bureaucratic organization. They manage to illuminate things, anyway. Plus, they reduce electricity bills for most people. We should be happy! In the face of such scientific urgency and budgetary practicality, a 1783 reply from British Prime Minister William Pitt's pronouncement might sound old-fashioned and out of date: "Necessity is the plea for every infringement of human freedom. It is the argument of tyrants. It is the creed of slaves." After all, if there is only one kind of lightbulb in the stores, that is the kind of bulbs that people will buy. As the memory of the old choices fade, people often do not feel like slaves at all. Certainly, they do not experience freedom differently than they did before environmentally friendly compact fluorescent bulbs were invented, and they could only choose incandescents for their table lamps. The average person who prefers the old bulbs can even stockpile enough bulbs to light their houses for a good while. Sales of incandescent bulbs were up 150 percent in the European Union in August 2009, but stashes of the bulbs won't last forever.

Once again, however, individuals with preferences slightly outside the ordinary lose out in the pursuit of positive liberty. The EU ban makes no exception for artists or museums. Yet to substitute long-lasting, environmentally friendly compact fluorescent bulbs into exhibits like Felix Gonzalez-Torres's 1993 installation *Untitled (Strange Music)*—a stark jumble of old-fashioned incandescent blubs intended to burn out and be replaced—would change the piece beyond recognition.

By and large, citizens will remain unmoved by the plight of the work of Gonzalez-Torres, or the bulb-intensive creations of artists like Laszlo Moholy-Nagy, Olafur Eliasson, Carsten Höller, or Jorge Pardo. Given the steady stream of bans "for your own good," and the still-absent squads of jackbooted thugs breaking into our homes, most of the time Americans (and this goes double for Europeans) acquiesce—after all, there's a kid in the background whining for ice cream, and it's distracting.

This is why advocates of negative liberty must add a caveat. Not only must I be free from interference with what I would like to do today, I must have a reasonable expectation I will be free to do what I like within my sphere of liberty tomorrow as well. Perhaps I, too, will want to become a modern lightbulb artist. Surely this should be one of the choices available to a free person. The incursions associated with positive liberty make no promises about where they draw the line on interference in the name of freeing the good self from the tyranny of the bad self. As Edmund Burke put it, "The great inlet by which a colour for oppression has entered into the world is by one man's pretending to determine concerning the happiness of another."

A Cup of Tea in Boston

Positive liberty is ascendant in part because it is so easy to let the fights over daily inconveniences or restrictions slide. Larger infringements, when long-established, go uncontested as well. Extract thousands of dollars from their paychecks each month, and the American people will collectively shrug. But every now and then, the people will leap to the defense of liberty. Catch them at the right moment, and people can get exercised about the most unexpected things.

Sometimes the smallest, seemingly silliest infringements on personal liberty can be the most effective recruitment tools for the cause of liberty. The greatest example in history of a people fighting tooth-and-claw for negative liberties, of course, started with a tax on tea. A small tax on a luxury good should have been irrelevant to the American colonists in the face of larger concerns about the conduct of their distant government. Most of the colonists were drinking smuggled tea anyway. But the refusal of Boston's Royal Governor Thomas Hutchinson to give in to public pressure, as other officials had, and send the taxed tea back to Britain, was a small act weighted with symbolism. The British didn't want to lift the tax on Americans largely because it wanted to symbolically assert that it *could* tax Americans. The colonists responded to this symbolism with some of their own, and hoisted the tea into the harbor.

One might be forgiven for wondering if modern Americans would have the gumption to follow the steps of the Boston tea party patriots. But while it's not quite the same magnitude, Americans—New Yorkers, to be specific—did recently show a little of the old inclination to bang a few dents out of the sphere of negative liberty. This chapter may have started with ice cream. But in the end, all discussions about Americans and liberty must come back to caffeinated beverages.

Tone deaf and cash strapped, newly minted New York governor David Paterson looked around for things to tax at the end of 2008. Unlike the tax that inspired the Boston tea party, Paterson's proposal to tax full-sugar soda at an additional 15 percent wasn't a power grab. It was just more of same. Paterson saw a great opportunity for a little more positive liberty—people want to be thin, yet they drink soda—plus a chance to make some money. The rebellion was nothing much: a few bloggers got angry, a couple of newspapers published editorials, a poll or two was taken, and that was enough to signal a little electoral discontent. So the already insecure new governor let the tax go. He took recourse instead in a public-service ad campaign showing goopy fat pouring out of a soda bottle, with a reminder to "cut back on soda and other sugary beverages" lest you "drink yourself fat." A great triumph for the negative conception of liberty? Hardly. But it's something, a reminder that as much as negative liberty may be out of fashion these days, for each American begging the government to take away their cigarettes and ice cream, there are still some folks who will occasionally throw an elbow when government tries to infringe on their personal decisions.

18

The Abandonment
of Democracy Promotion

Tara McKelvey

ONE OF THE newest models in a Vargashi car factory is called the Avalanche-Hurricane or, as it is known among the Siberian workers, an antidemocracy truck. It is encased in steel armor and thick window grilles and comes with accessories such as a water cannon and pepper spray canister, and each vehicle costs approximately five hundred thousand dollars. The factory director told a *New York Times* reporter, who wrote about the trucks in an April 2009 article, that he hopes to sell two or three of the vehicles over the course of a year.

So far the trucks have not done much to thwart democracy, or to generate revenue either, since none have actually been sold, but the fact that they are being manufactured captures a growing sentiment in Russia that democracy has become unruly, and in this sense the new line of trucks is a disturbing sign of things to come. After nearly two decades of democracy, some officials in Moscow believe that freedom and liberty have gotten out of hand, and they are looking for methods to tamp it down. Part of the officials' discomfort seems to stem from the fact that tens of thousands of Russians have been expressing unhappiness with the corrupt leaders who are in charge of their country and are demanding change at the top.

Russia is not an isolated case. Democracy has been taking some serious knocks in countries around the world. According to Freedom House, a New York–based organization that promotes democracy and liberty, it has been on the decline over the past three years. Yet despite the threat to political freedom in Russia, Pakistan, Egypt,

Ethiopia, and other countries around the world, Americans have begun to show considerably less interest in helping to promote democracy as part of the nation's foreign policy. These trends will reinforce each other in the coming years and make things considerably bleaker for those who are fighting for freedom around the globe.

Americans have turned away from the principles of democracy promotion largely in response to President George W. Bush's disastrous efforts in this arena. It may seem natural to scale back on this aspect of foreign policy after the excessive zeal of the Bush administration. Yet this shortsighted view will diminish the positive influence the United States has on the rest of the world. Even worse, pulling back on democracy promotion could harm people in other countries who are most vulnerable to autocratic leaders. With the election of Barack Obama, democracy advocates in Cairo, Addis Ababa, and other cities around the world are rightfully concerned about whether they will continue to have American support in their dangerous work.

In some cases, Obama administration officials have been placing more emphasis on protecting the relationship between the United States and other countries than on supporting the work of local democracy activists. People who work for Freedom House say they have "met with several U.S. Embassy officials who have sought to distance themselves from civil society and human rights leaders who were not favored by the host government," according to a July 2009 report. If the efforts of local democracy activists are stymied, then the autocratic leaders of the nations they live in will be emboldened to take away even more liberties.

Yet despite the threat to freedom in countries around the world and the potential danger to democracy advocates abroad, President Obama has demonstrated that he is significantly less interested in democracy promotion than his predecessor; moreover, top members of his cabinet share his views. Secretary of State Hillary Clinton, appearing before the Senate Appropriations Committee in April 2009, said, "The foreign policy of the United States is built on the three Ds: defense, diplomacy, and development." Democracy was not included. Meanwhile, the Joint Chiefs of Staff have sent a national-security memo to President Obama, urging him to abandon democracy promotion in Afghanistan, and in the president's proposed 2010 foreign operations budget, funding for democracy projects in the Middle East and North Africa has gone down.

When President Obama gave his speech about Afghanistan at West Point in late 2009, he talked about defeating Al-Qaeda and reducing the threat of terrorism, but said nothing about helping to build democracy. He has been trying to tamp down expectations for the future of that country, and some U.S. officials seem almost disdainful of the attempts at building a democratic society that are currently under way. To be sure, the Afghan government has a long way to go. The 2009 election of President Hamid Karzai was widely considered a sham, and his government has been rife with corruption. One official who oversaw the elections in Logar Province was forced to hide out in a barricaded office for three months because he had received death threats from the Taliban. He and other officials put their lives on the line in an attempt to build a democratic society; thousands of Afghan people risked their lives in an attempt to make sure the polls would be open, yet many of them felt their efforts were not fully acknowledged or appreciated.

President Obama's attempt to scale back expectations for Afghanistan and overall for democracy promotion abroad has caused little stir among liberals. Democrats in general are less likely than Republicans to support the notion of democracy promotion, with only 54 percent saying that it should be featured in foreign policy, according to a 2007 Pew survey; 74 percent of Republicans believe U.S. foreign policy should embrace it, and are more likely to say that the United States should "help establish democracies in other countries." This means few liberals will be willing to take on the issue of democracy promotion or try to ensure that it becomes a top priority.

The twenty-first century dawned as the age of democracy promotion. Then-President Bush made it clear to tyrannical leaders that he intended to tear down their regimes and to allow for the blossoming of democracy around the world. Rather than kowtowing to dictators because Americans wanted oil, gas, and natural resources or access to air bases within their borders, like former U.S. presidents, Bush made it clear that he would take a hard line against dictators and would support the efforts of those fighting for democracy.

These principles were the bedrock of the Bush Freedom Agenda, but that was not the way things turned out in the real world. Bush was tough on dictators in places like Zimbabwe, where Americans had few or no interests, and was considerably less strict with autocratic leaders in countries such as Uzbekistan, which was the home of the strategically important Karshi-Khanabad air base. Moreover, the war that was waged in Iraq to make that country safe for democracy descended into chaos while he was in the White House. To be sure, a fragile form of democracy gradually emerged in Iraq, but it has come at a terrible cost and has nearly discredited the undertaking of democracy promotion altogether.

The cost of the Freedom Agenda was staggeringly high, causing worldwide opinion of the United States to plunge to its lowest point in decades. Yet there was some merit in putting despots on notice. The current U.S. president is no longer making hyperbolic and inflammatory statements about democracy; instead, President Obama is circumspect in his efforts to assist activists who are working toward greater freedom and liberty in other countries. His approach to democracy promotion is cool and low-key—so much so that he appears to be overly cavalier about it. In fact, Obama's ambivalence about democracy promotion represents a sharp break with the past, and his approach to the issue has disturbing implications.

Democracy itself, of course, is wildly popular and is often cited by people on the left and the right in support of a broad array of programs. Democracy *promotion*, however, is a controversial part of U.S. foreign policy, based in a network of Washington-based institutions and rooted in bureaucratic flowcharts and line items in the State Department budget. Moreover, a common understanding of the term has been elusive, since it seems to encompass everything from broadcasting jazz programs to Poland in the 1980s to deploying troops to Iraq in the 2000s.

President Ronald Reagan extolled freedom and democracy around the world and reached out to dissidents in Central and Eastern Europe through Radio Free Europe/Radio Liberty, which provided news programs as well as a message of hope to those who lived under repressive regimes. In Cuba, people tuned in to Radio Martí, which broadcast programs produced in the United States and provided a balance for the anti-American propaganda put out by the Cuban stations.

The U.S. information strategy worked, at least to some extent, since it provided news, as well as moral support, for Central European dissidents and Cuban activists. In 1990, Americans watched joyously as Lech Walesa, the leader of Solidarity, was elected to office in Poland, and then cheered as the Soviet Union began to crumble.

From the outside, the shift from Communism to democracy seemed quick and easy. Back then, however, it was not at all clear how things would turn out. In July 1989, after meeting with a group of dissidents in Eastern Europe, President George H. W. Bush wrote in his diary that he was afraid the situation was spinning out of control. He and his advisors also worried about what would happen if Germany were reunited. Nevertheless, he kept his cool and maintained cordial relations with President Mikhail Gorbachev. By the end of the following year, Bush and other world leaders had helped bring about not only the relatively peaceful revolutions across Eastern Europe but also "a unified Germany, a transformed EU," wrote historian Philip Zelikow in *Foreign Affairs* (November/December 2009), and "a preserved and extended Atlantic alliance." It was an impressive string of successes.

The second President Bush was much more aggressive about democracy promotion, and yet in contrast to his father's efforts the countries of the Middle East have not made a smooth transition to democracy, despite tremendous investment in the region. This has caused many people in the United States, particularly liberals, to

swear off democracy promotion altogether. Even its most ardent supporters have trouble with the fact that democratic elections sometimes produce undesirable results. George W. Bush's historic push
for Palestinian democracy turned out far differently than expected
when Hamas, the Islamic resistance movement, won a majority in
the Gaza elections in 2006.

In previous decades, Americans sometimes responded in a brutal manner to election outcomes they did not like. After a socialist
candidate, Salvador Allende, was elected in Chile in 1970, Henry
Kissinger famously said, "I don't see why we need to stand by and
watch a country go Communist because of the irresponsibility of
its own people." Three years later, Allende was deposed in a U.S.-
backed coup. No policy maker today would advocate such extreme
actions. Nevertheless, legions of people have spoken out strongly
against incorporating democracy promotion into U.S. foreign policy;
the enemies of such an approach have multiplied at an alarming rate
and can be found on both ends of the political spectrum.

On the far left, where the work of Noam Chomsky is admired,
many people believe democracy promotion is a diabolical plot to
expand U.S. hegemony around the world. According to these critics, American-style democracy promotion conflates democracy with
free-market capitalism, and actually places a higher value on the
latter. American officials attempt to remake the world in their own
image and graft their views about democracy onto other societies.
Human rights advocates and some progressives are also opposed to
democracy promotion, but for a different reason. They argue that
human rights, not democracy, should be the focus of U.S. foreign
policy.

Meanwhile, on the far right, isolationist conservatives like former presidential candidate Pat Buchanan maintain that Americans
should not get involved in difficult, messy projects abroad, regardless of how well-intentioned they might be.

So should we simply give up on democracy promotion altogether?
That is clearly not the answer. Previous mismanagement of democracy promotion, however egregious, does not mean that all future
efforts are doomed.

Promoting·democracy in other countries is messy and hard, but abandoning these efforts constitutes a threat to freedom on a global scale. The United States should not ignore people in other countries who are risking their lives on behalf of democracy simply because the Bush administration failed in its efforts. A Kabul-born psychologist who lives in Washington says that if Americans turn their backs on the Afghan women who have been marching in the streets in order to secure more freedom, "They will be lost." Yet, despite the fact that Afghan women, Egyptian lawyers, Chinese students, and many others are counting on American support in their struggle for freedom, there are signs that President Obama will not be there for them.

When Egyptian President Hosni Mubarak said in 2009 that he planned to reinstitute restrictions on U.S. funds for democracy projects, Obama did not protest. Instead, the State Department accepted the changes, apparently because the president believed it was more important to maintain good relations with Mubarak; as a result, American money will be distributed only to groups that have been approved by the Egyptian government. As the president's critics point out, Mubarak can now determine how American taxpayer dollars are spent. The incident reveals how President Obama views democracy promotion. His attitude seems to be: it is a good idea, but don't go overboard with it.

Obama and his top officials apparently believe that it is better to get along with tyrants like Mubarak than to confront them, and to eschew symbols in favor of achieving pragmatic goals on the ground. This was the clear impression made by Obama's failure to speak up for Iranian students protesting the repressive Islamic regime in 2009. When administration officials favor a form of democracy promotion that values pragmatism above all else, however, they are missing something important. To put it simply, despotic leaders do not always listen to reasoned arguments. "I can't remember any text of mine where it said one should fight Hitler without violence," said Adam Michnik, who was one of the leading dissidents in Poland in the 1980s. "I'm not an idiot. In the state of Saddam, the opposition could find a place only in cemeteries."

Maintaining a tough stance against tyrants and being vigilant about encroachments on democracy in other countries is crucial. In Lebanon, for example, where democracy is fragile at best (the nation currently ranks as only "partly free," according to Freedom House) and ill prepared to defend itself against the determined opposition of religious fanatics, America has a clear and vital (if limited) role to play, particularly since the international community has been weak and indecisive. Indeed, democracy experts have applauded President Obama's decision to increase its support in this area. The administration's proposed funding for democracy promotion in Lebanon was raised 50 percent, from $18 million in fiscal 2009 to $27 million for fiscal 2010.

For many Americans, the success of democracy in faraway countries such as Lebanon may seem unimportant, but the United States benefits in a variety of ways from free and open societies in other parts of the world: Democracies are more likely to be economically advanced and, at least in theory, buy American goods and provide additional markets for the United States; democracies are also less likely to wage war on each other.

To be sure, the United States needs a finely tuned, culturally adept approach to promoting democracy, rather than the gunslinger one that was used in the past, and it should moreover be based on an understanding that simply granting people the right to vote does not guarantee a truly democratic result.

One cannot measure with precision the relationship between investments to support democracy in a particular country and its transformation into a free and open society, but some methods have been successful. People in Central Europe benefited from listening to Radio Free Europe, and these kinds of efforts should be continued. The United States should also support freedom of expression through online media and fund efforts to help prevent authoritarian governments from using the Internet to crack down on activists. (Iranian police have recently created a twelve-person unit to track activity on the Internet, and are stepping up efforts to collect information on activists from online sources.)

Financial support should be provided to reformers and democrats in Iran and other countries around the world in a more equitable fashion, rather than devoting resources almost exclusively to the places where the United States is engaged in armed conflict; currently, Iraq, Afghanistan, and Pakistan receive roughly three-fourths of the funding that is allocated for democracy promotion. In addition, the United States should work harder to present itself as a model of democracy, since its image as a beacon of freedom and justice suffered a blow in recent years because of the Abu Ghraib prison scandal and Guantanamo. (In Iraq, the Abu Ghraib picture of the hooded man is known as the Statue of Liberty, and insurgents have used it as a recruiting tool.)

Moreover, President Obama should say explicitly what he intends to do in the area of democracy promotion in the Middle East and elsewhere, since democracy advocates in these countries need to know that they have friends in the United States and that the funding will continue under the current administration. Over the past year, administration officials have been trying to make progress on global issues such as climate change, nuclear weapons, and financial reform, and have placed less of an emphasis on democracy promotion when dealing with leaders of other nations. At first glance, this seems like a realistic and wise approach, but it is a mistake. Idealism plays an important role in American foreign policy, and Obama should provide strong rhetorical support for the efforts of democracy activists abroad so that the leaders of authoritarian nations hear the message.

By and large it is easier to promote democracy through development aid rather than to save or repair a democracy that is floundering. However, when things fall apart in other countries, the United States may have to intervene, whether through diplomatic or military means.

Just as a factory director in Siberia is counting the cash that he will earn from selling armored trucks, leaders in other countries are banking on the fact that they can smash their opponents into the ground when there is no resistance from the United States. The

Egyptian Ministry of Interior has recently requested an additional $27 million from their government "for added 'street control' in anticipation of 'expected' demonstrations and strikes,'" or roughly the same amount that the U.S. State Department reduced for democracy assistance, according to Jennifer L. Windor, the executive director of Freedom House.

Despite the flawed history of democracy promotion, it belongs high on the U.S. foreign-policy agenda and should be supported by substantial resources. The threat to freedom is strong in many countries around the world, and abandoning the people who live in those autocratic regimes would be a travesty.

19

Ingratitude and the Death
of Freedom

Mark T. Mitchell

I THINK it is fair to say that gratitude is a somewhat neglected notion, one consigned to the realm of good manners but rarely uttered in discussions of politics. But this oversight comes with a price, for as I will argue, gratitude is one of the necessary, though easily neglected, bulwarks of a sustainable freedom.

Any serious discussion of gratitude must at the same time consider its opposite, ingratitude, for—and I am not the first to observe this—we tend to be an ungrateful lot. In 1930 the Spanish philosopher Jose Ortega y Gasset observed that modern people are, among other things, characterized by their "radical ingratitude." This claim does, of course, need defending, and I can imagine the objections from a variety of quarters.

When we speak of gratitude, there will be those who think primarily of etiquette: "I taught my children to say 'please' and 'thank you,' and they usually do." There will be those who think in personal terms: "I have a nice house, a new car, and a boat. Sure, I'm grateful." Or there will be those who think in terms of the nation: "We live in the greatest nation on earth! Darn right, I'm grateful." But, although the language of gratitude is not dead—far from it—something is amiss. Our modern, affluent, technological, well-fed society seems to oscillate between smug self-satisfaction and hand-wringing despair, the latter coming on the wave of each new economic, political, social, or natural disaster.

Gratitude though means more than good manners; it means more than the pleasure associated with possessing plenty of nice things;

and it surely means more than mere relief that we've managed to escape, or at least survive, the latest crisis. These are perhaps shadowy reminders of gratitude, but they are not the heart of the issue.

Gratitude is a way of inhabiting the world. It is a disposition toward the world that reminds us that we are not alone. We are not solitary creatures owing nothing to no one. Rather, gratitude points to our dependence. It is a fitting attitude in the face of our creatureliness. When our thoughts are characterized by gratitude, they are outward looking. Gratitude breaks us out of the cocoon of self-satisfaction and self-concern that is a constant temptation and impels us to think of the ways our lives are related to others.

But gratitude is not a disposition we can simply choose to exhibit. We can choose to be friendly regardless of how others treat us. We can choose to act justly even if we have been wronged. But gratitude is different. It's a response to goodness. We are grateful when, for example, a stranger helps us find our way in an unfamiliar city, or when a friend presents us with a gift. In both instances we are responding to an act of goodness. Gratitude, then, is different from friendliness or generosity, for they can exist regardless of how another person behaves toward us. They can be initial dispositions. Gratitude, though, is a response. It requires the action of another before it can come into being.

Is there a moral duty to be grateful? Or to put matters in another way, does ingratitude indicate a moral failure? David Hume argued that there are some moral duties "to which men are impelled by a natural instinct or immediate propensity." Hume ranked gratitude to benefactors, along with love of children and pity to the unfortunate, as moral duties to which humans are naturally drawn. Immanuel Kant wrote that gratitude is "the venerating of another on account of a benefit we have received from him." Gratitude, according to Kant, is not merely a duty among others but a "sacred duty," and to violate it would be "to extinguish the moral principles of benevolence, even at their source." Why does Kant place such an emphasis on gratitude? The person who is indebted remains always under obligation to the benefactor. This, Kant believed, is true even if the receiver pays back the benefactor in kind; no matter what the receiver sub-sequently does, it will always be the case that the benefactor acted first when nothing but goodness impelled him. To be ungrateful is to forget or ignore this original act of goodness.

Is it also appropriate to think of gratitude as a virtue, as an excellence of character? Cicero included gratitude among his list of virtues and ingratitude among the vices. As he put it, the virtues (or a good share of the virtues) "proceed from a natural inclination to love and cherish our associates." Nature, itself, ratifies the law that gives birth to and supports the virtues. Without the ratifying power of nature, "what becomes of generosity, patriotism, or friendship? Where should we find the desire of benefiting our neighbors, or the gratitude that acknowledges kindness?" Gratitude is, for Cicero, a virtue rooted in nature itself. Thus, to act ungratefully to a benefactor is to act contrary to nature.

If we see gratitude as a moral duty, ingratitude is a failure to live as duty requires. If, on the other hand, we see it as a moral virtue, ingratitude reveals a flawed character. In either instance, ingratitude is a moral failure that we naturally recognize and condemn.

Furthermore, gratitude requires freedom. It cannot be demanded. It must be freely given. There is, then, an obvious connection between gratitude and freedom of the will. At the same time, there is a connection, perhaps less apparent, between gratitude and political freedom. This connection is best understood when we consider the relationship between gratitude and stewardship.

Gratitude, properly conceived, implies action. To be sure, it is a disposition, but the disposition of gratitude creates a sense of responsibility toward one's benefactor. If one receives a gift, for instance, gratitude would include taking care of that which has been given. If the receiver of a gift carelessly discards it, we would accuse him of ingratitude. To be a steward is to be a caretaker of that which has been entrusted to us. This may be a piece of property, an idea or a concept, or a way of life. Stewards hold something "in trust," and to be a good steward is to faithfully fulfill that trust.

If gratitude, properly conceived, entails stewardship of that which has been entrusted, then ingratitude implies a failure to steward the gifts one has received. How is ingratitude manifested today? Let's consider four objects of gratitude that have steadily eroded in our modern world, leaving four debts of gratitude unattended, four aspects of reality unstewarded.

First is the loss of God along with an acknowledgment of a moral law that exists prior to human will. One feature of the modern world, as opposed to that of the medieval world, is the ascendancy of skepticism. While religion has not yet faded into oblivion, the West is increasingly characterized by its secularism. Even in societies where religion remains strong, there is mounting pressure to domesticate religious belief in a purely private sphere so that political and social engagement is, for all intents and purposes, bereft of religious content. God has perhaps not been killed, as Nietzsche gloated, but he has, in many quarters, been reduced to a mere placeholder or at best a subjective reflection of our best opinions about ourselves. Debts of gratitude to such a contentless being are not obvious or pressing. Nor are moral limits recognized as meaningful in a world where the moral law has been tossed aside.

Second, we have lost contact with the natural world. In an age where we are increasingly insulated and isolated from nature, we can become blind to the gifts all around us. When we come to think of our milk, meat, and vegetables as products of the grocery store, we have lost sight of reality. We have lost sight of the simple fact that we are sustained physically by animals, by the grass that feeds them, and by the dirt that nourishes the grass, all of which in turn are nourished by the sun. This is no small oversight, for when we fail to recognize our debts of gratitude to the natural world, we will readily, even cheerfully, neglect our duties. The result will invariably be characterized by carelessness, exploitation, and greed.

Third, we have too often lost a sense of place. Ours is a highly mobile society. We can travel with ease, and we can leave home and begin anew someplace else. Even if we stay put, the possibility of leaving can remain forever a live option in our world of infinite choices. But when the places we inhabit are seen as merely stepping-

stones to the next job, the next opportunity, or the next means to
stave off our boredom, commitment to a particular place wanes. We
content ourselves with being residents though not citizens. Such
attenuated commitments are inadequate to generate the love and
affection for a particular place and people that is necessary for long-
term stewardship. Stewards—so necessary for the health of a place—
are replaced by individuals who see themselves not as caretakers
but as consumers, extracting what they can from a community and
leaving it when it no longer satisfies.

Finally, we have experienced a loss of the past. America has always
been a place of the future. But in embracing the promise of tomorrow, it is all too easy to forget or at least neglect our debts to the past.
To be bereft of a coherent and meaningful attachment to the past is
to be unaware of what we have inherited. When we are ignorant of
the mores, practices, customs, and institutions that constitute our
collective past, we will readily neglect them in our headlong pursuit
of the future. We will easily cast them aside if short-term advantage
appears to necessitate their removal. Cultural and political stability
therefore require awareness of the past. We bear the burden of those
who have gone before. We owe a debt of gratitude that can never
be fully repaid. When we are properly grateful, we seek to preserve
what has been entrusted to us, tending it for a time—and if we raise
our sons and daughters well, if they have seen us bear our burden
faithfully and with care, they may assume their own burden of gratitude when our time is past. In this way—and no other—culture is
transmitted.

At the end of the long winter at Valley Forge, George Washington
praised the steadfastness of the American soldiers in such difficult
circumstances. These soldiers, he wrote, "will despise the meanness
of repining at such trifling strokes of Adversity, trifling indeed when
compared to the transcendent Prize which will undoubtedly crown
their Patience and Perseverance, Glory and Freedom, Peace and
Plenty to themselves and the Community; The Admiration of the
World, the Love of Country and the Gratitude of Posterity!" Yes, the
world would admire them, and their country would love them, but

generations yet unborn would rise to thank them, for their sacrifice lasted only a few months, but the debt of gratitude would extend down through the generations as free men and women reaped the bounty of the sacrifices made in that frozen place. In other words, gratitude directed at the past ultimately implies a sense of duty to the future. Washington thought in those terms. His rhetoric suggests he believed his men thought the same.

The fact that today, one of the most significant things we are passing on to our children is a national debt of breathtaking size, a debt that will necessarily truncate their freedom, suggests that we have lost the extra sense of gratitude and the corresponding sense of stewardship that the general and his men shared.

Gratitude, properly conceived, gives birth to ongoing acts of stewardship. From God we have been given life. We have knowledge of the moral law that provides the basis of order for human relations. Gratitude leads to respect for the dignity of human life and a willingness to live within the limits imposed by the moral law. The natural world provides us with that which sustains our physical existence. We should care for it with wisdom and gentleness. We have inherited from our collective parents a way of life in a particular place, a way of organizing ourselves politically and socially, a way of governing ourselves. These goods, practices, and institutions cannot survive much less thrive if they are treated casually or neglected. They require careful tending, constant nourishment, and loving care.

The freedoms we enjoy require not only vigilance but also fidelity, so that even when alterations in our social and political institutions are introduced, an underlying continuity remains. The alternative is perpetual innovation, which is to say perpetual revolution. Freedom cannot thrive in such a volatile atmosphere. When we are tempted to take our freedom for granted we are in serious danger, for freedom is only sustainable when carefully preserved and wisely protected. When it is treated merely as an item to be consumed or as a right to be demanded, freedom is in jeopardy.

Ironically, freedom itself can foster the mental habits that undermine freedom. Chief among these is ingratitude. The affluence we enjoy is, in large part, a product of our freedom. Yet affluence can actually distract us from a proper sense of gratitude. In ages of marginal or even scanty provisions, it is perhaps easier to think in terms of gratitude, for nothing is taken for granted. A person might even pray earnestly for daily bread and then thank God when it arrives. In an age of plenty, comforts are easily taken for granted, and how much more the daily bread by which we live? Could it be that gratitude is more difficult precisely because we have so much for which to be thankful?

Affluence and the headlong pursuit thereof can induce in us the belief that consuming is our proper end and that freedom is the natural state of human affairs. Neither is true. A life given over to mere consumption is not befitting creatures capable of noble acts, and freedom is a tender plant that requires jealous protection against its natural foes. If we are not attentive, the heady wine of freedom can induce us to forget or neglect the debts of gratitude we owe. Like spoiled children we demand the benefits of freedom while ignoring the fact that these fruits are the product of generations of struggle, sacrifice, and hard work. The debt goes unpaid, and the capital is recklessly spent.

Gratitude, ultimately, is born of humility, for it acknowledges that both the creation and our civilization are gifts. This recognition gives birth to acts marked by attention and responsibility. Ingratitude, on the other hand, is marked by hubris, which denies the gift, and this always leads to inattention, irresponsibility, and abuse. In political terms, the hubris of ingratitude is a caustic acid that reduces all in its wake to the fetid condition of servitude, for a spoiled child needs nothing so much as a master.

Thus, if gratitude is the mother of stewardship, ingratitude strips away the ground for an adequate account of stewardship and leaves nothing behind but a narrow concern for the self. Forgotten is our collective debt to God, the natural world, to a place, and to the past, all of which are necessary for an adequate understanding of our debts to both the past and the future. When duties are neglected, all that remains is the pursuit of pleasure or power. Neither pursuit sustains freedom. In fact, as these become increasingly the focus of our individual and corporate lives, freedom is correspondingly diminished. Freedom, to be durable, must exist within the context of responsibilities that limit freedom, yet in the process heighten its meaning by orienting it according to ideals of self-sacrifice, love of community, and care for others.

If freedom produces conditions that induce ingratitude, and ingratitude represents a threat to freedom, then it seems we have reached the ironic position where we extol the virtues of freedom yet discover that the very thing we champion is a danger to itself. What can be done? Clearly we must attempt to cultivate the disposition of gratitude. This will give birth to acts of stewardship, which are necessary to sustain an orderly and mature freedom. Unconstrained by stewardship and gratitude, freedom will invariably descend into license, and license will eventually decline into lawlessness. In such an atmosphere, tyranny is nurtured even as freedom suffocates and eventually dies.

20

The Anticapitalists

Michael C. Moynihan

IT DIDN'T HAVE the impact of Susan Sontag's famous Cold War apostasy, when in 1982 she confused an audience of New York liberals with her eminently reasonable observation that the truth about communism was more often found in the pages of *Readers Digest* than in the *Nation*, but economist Robert Heilbroner's verdict shocked many of his comrades on the left.

In a March 1989 essay for the *New Yorker*, six months before the collapse of the Berlin Wall, Heilbroner, a lifelong socialist, conceded that the Marxian experiments of the twentieth century had collapsed in ignominy. "Less than seventy-five years after it officially began," he wrote, "the contest between capitalism and socialism is over: capitalism has won. The Soviet Union, China, and Eastern Europe have given us the clearest possible proof that capitalism organizes the material affairs of humankind more satisfactorily than socialism."

A few years later, writing in the socialist magazine *Dissent*, Heilbroner concluded ruefully, "The farther to the right one looks, the more prescient has been the historical foresight; the farther to the left, the less so."

And so it was. After twelve years of Republican rule, almost fifty years of cold war with the Soviet Union and its proxy states, the American left was adrift, sitting on the sidelines, humbled, as a Democratic president promised to "end welfare as we know it." A generation after the New Left presaged the end of capitalism, the rhetoric of Marxism—the patient explanations of dialectical materialism, the Stalinist diagnoses of false consciousness—seemed a bizarre historical anachronism. As one Harvard economist told me in 2007, though there were notable holdouts still enchanted by "scientific socialism," most academic economists agreed that the days of central planning were finished.

Historical prognostication is an unrewarding—and usually unwise—enterprise. Those whose predictions have been vindicated are rarely recognized for their prescience, while the naïve and optimistic—think of the incessant invocation of Francis Fukuyama's essay "The End of History" in the months after September 11, 2001—are forever associated with a single misjudgment. And as long as there is a significant number of academics, journalists, and pop-culture figures hostile to the free market, convinced of the internal contradictions of capitalism, any significant rupture in America's economic order will allow them to climb back on the soapbox and declare ideological exoneration.

Only a handful of economists foresaw the various financial crises of 2008, but when the housing market collapsed and credit markets froze, when the government-sponsored mortgage giants Fannie Mae and Freddie Mac flamed out and the financial services firm Lehman Brothers disappeared overnight, the free-market skeptics pounced.

Browse the stacks at your local bookstore and you will find them lined with books by those academics and pundits once identified by William F. Buckley as those who "stay on their toes waiting eagerly for capitalism to fail." In his 2008 book *The Predator State: How Conservatives Have Abandoned Free Markets and How Liberals Should Too*, James Galbraith, son of the famous progressive economist John Kenneth Galbraith, argues that free markets don't work, free trade is a "myth," and the very concept of economic freedom is "palpably absurd." Evoking the classic collection of essays of intellectual disillusionment with communism, British financial journalists Larry Elliot and Dan Atkinson bequeathed to American readers *The Gods That Failed: How Blind Faith in Markets Has Cost Us Our Future*, a book celebrating "the collapse of the free market model and the validation of state intervention." If the title wasn't sufficiently evocative, the authors draw an oblique moral equivalence between competing Cold War ideologies when lamenting that "The collapse of communism marked the dawn of market fundamentalism." Meet the new boss, same as the old boss.

One cannot begrudge the American left a measure of excitement when it considers the political possibilities presented by the current crisis. After the post–Cold War wilderness years, a movement of the activist left, ensconced in universities and waging a low-intensity culture war against all perceived manifestations of racism and sexism, briefly coalesced around the so-called antiglobalization movement.

Antiglobalism was anticapitalism by another name, but the political conditions at the time—unprecedented prosperity, low unemployment, a Democratic administration—demanded activism by euphemism. Left-wing radicalism was being supplanted by Clintonian centrism. In Europe, too, countries that held fast to generous social policies and often absurdly generous safety nets, nevertheless significantly liberalized their economies. It is now unsurprising that Sweden has a significantly lower corporate tax rate than the United States, the Netherlands is a tax shelter utilized by millionaire rock bands like the Rolling Stones and U2, and a handful of countries in Central and Eastern Europe long ago realized Steve Forbes's dream of a flat income tax.

As a result, the late 1990s antiglobalization movement was a mélange of radical causes, lacking in leadership and without a clearly defined set of political goals. During the violent anticapitalist riots that gripped Seattle in 1999, a *Wall Street Journal* reporter asked a protester, identified as a member of a lesbian rights organization, what motivated her opposition to the World Trade Organization (WTO). "It's a general question of oppression," she answered. "The WTO doesn't care about women's rights." Indeed, when the reporter pressed for specific complaints, the activist drew a merciful blank.

But before the movement could find a leader and draft a Port Huron Statement of its own, jihadism interceded. After the terror attacks of September 11, the antiglobalization militants reemerged on the more radical fringes of the antiwar movement, now arguing that while a vague economic imperialism was most certainly a component in America's wars in Afghanistan and Iraq—filmmaker Michael Moore argued that the bombing in Afghanistan was a ruse to clear the way for an oil pipeline—it was American empire that was the "root cause" of the current conflict. Corporate villains would make appearances, notably Halliburton and the Carlyle Group, but "neoliberalism" would take a backseat to neoconservatism.

In the Obama era, those niggling wars in Iraq and Afghanistan are still being waged, but the interest of the erstwhile antiwar protesters has waned, sapped by both the financial crisis and the change in presidential leadership. After the imperialism interregnum, an issue now of insignificant interest to those politically invested in the Obama administration, the movement left lurched back toward the debate over economics, forgoing the small wars against globalization and launching a blitzkrieg on capitalism.

Barbara Ehrenreich, author of the *New York Times* best seller *Nickel and Dimed*, was once content with bemoaning the rise of big-box stores like Wal-Mart and the "futile pursuit of the American dream." But now, in the current financial mess, she sees the "fall of capitalism." In previous crises, she argues, capitalism's death was greatly exaggerated, though this time "the patient may not get up from the table."

Writing on the *Huffington Post*, novelist Jane Smiley too presaged the end of capitalism: "There can never be such a thing as a free market, because it is human nature to cheat, monopolize, and buy off others so as to corner the market." Those who believe in the primacy of markets, Smiley averred, "must be spouting this junk just to suck up to tyrants."

In a fawning interview with CNN septuagenarian Larry King, filmmaker Michael Moore gleefully deduced that, with banks collapsing and Washington tinkering with the economy, "We're seeing the end of capitalism . . . and I say good riddance." His new film, *Capitalism: A Love Story*, concludes that "capitalism is an evil, and you cannot regulate evil. You have to eliminate it and replace it with something that is good for all people and that something is democracy." Replacing a financial system (capitalism) with a political system (democracy) is nonsensical, but the line brought audience members at its Venice Film Festival premiere to their feet.

Of course, previous crises have provoked similar utopian excitement. During the darkest hours of the Great Depression, novelist Upton Sinclair thundered, "Capitalism has served its time and is passing from the face of the earth," to be replaced by an intellectual vanguard that institutes "a new system . . . to take its place." Anti-Semitic radio preacher and New Deal enthusiast Father Charles Coughlin adjudicated that "this plutocratic, capitalistic system must be constitutionally voted out of existence!"

While it is indeed worrying that Oscar-winning filmmakers can declare capitalism an "evil" system that deserves to be uprooted and a Pulitzer Prize–winning novelist believes the free market a delusion, such sentiments are hardly unfamiliar in recent American history.

While popular anticapitalism was in hibernation during the 1990s, it flourished in academia. It is, therefore, worth looking briefly at the leading lights of academic anticapitalism, the more extreme antecedents of today's growing intellectual movement.

The anticapitalist manifesto *Empire*—written by Italian academic Antoni Negri and Duke University professor Michael Hardt, and published by Harvard University Press—became a standard text in university syllabi, was frequently name-checked in the speeches of Venezuelan President Hugo Chavez, and is often cited as the bible of the new New Left. Their follow-up work, *Multitudes*, was twice reviewed in the *New York Times*, and the two contributed an opinion piece to the paper following the anti-WTO riots in Genoa, Italy. They were, the *Times* correctly observed, the two scholars "who took the academic world by storm."

But Negri has a rather different reputation in his home country. Italian President Francesco Cossiga once breathlessly denounced him as having "poisoned the minds of an entire generation of Italy's youth," for he was the rogue intellectual who spent time in prison on terrorism charges, accused of being the intellectual leader of the

Red Brigades, a Marxist-Leninist terror group responsible for the kidnapping and murder of Italian Prime Minister Aldo Moro.

Though the criminal complaints against Negri are thirty years in the past, his politics haven't mellowed. Capitalism is still an alloyed evil, one that needs to be replaced by an aggressive, revolutionary leftism. But just what do they have in mind? According to Negri, Stalinism was a "subtle and modern phenomenon" that was occasionally excessive but "extremely productive"; the Khrushchev regime enjoyed the "almost total support" of ordinary Russians; the suggestion that a system which presided over the "Doctor's plot" was ever tainted by anti-Semitism "is completely absurd." "The Soviet Union didn't survive," argues Negri, "not because its existence was an impossible dream, but because the Western strategy of closure and repression and antihumanist hate won."

According to the Slovenian philosopher Slavoj Zizek, Hardt and Negri have achieved "nothing less than a rewriting of *The Communist Manifesto* for our time." Like the *Empire* authors, Zizek, in the overheated description of the *New York Times*, is a "rock star [greeted] by sold-out crowds" in Europe, a man "anointed 'the Elvis of cultural theory,'" the subject of a fawning art house documentary whose director compares him to Rolling Stones guitarist Keith Richards.

Zizek, a frequent contributor to the *New York Times* opinion page, also grounds his anticapitalism in Soviet totalitarianism. "Better the worst Stalinist terror," he declares, "than the most liberal capitalist democracy." If Stalinism was indeed a negative development, it was because it was too *capitalistic*: "Stalinist 'totalitarianism' was the capitalist logic of self-propelling productivity liberated from its capitalist form, which is why it failed: Stalinism was the symptom of capitalism." On the twentieth anniversary of the fall of the Berlin Wall, the *Times* selected Zizek to deliver its opinion page commemoration, an opportunity he used to denounce the "new anti-Communist scare" in Eastern Europe and to argue, without corroborating evidence, that "the large majority" of those liberated from Soviet tyranny "did not ask for capitalism."

While it is unsurprising that, in the groves of academe, figures like Zizek, Hardt, and Negri are regarded as innovative, challenging thinkers worthy of close study, it would be a mistake to presume that their extremism, their deliberately obfuscatory jargon, disqualifies them from the polite company of mainstream media, that they haven't moved the center of more mainstream criticism significantly to the left. And for all of his collective nonsense, Zizek is doubtless right on one point: that on the political left—as distinct from the mainstream democratic left—"what lies ahead is the next, 'Leninist', step—towards politically organized anticapitalism."

And unlike the period that followed the Seattle riots, there now exists an intellectual leader of the anticapitalist movement.

In the acknowledgments of her best-selling book *The Shock Doctrine*, Canadian author Naomi Klein thanks Negri's coauthor and collaborator Michael Hardt for his guidance in economic theory and provides an effusive blurb for their latest book, *Commonwealth*. (She also tips her hat to the journalist Seamus Milne, who recently wrote that "communism in the Soviet Union, eastern Europe and elsewhere delivered rapid industrialisation, mass education, job security and huge advances in social and gender equality.") According to Klein, liberal economic reforms are universally unpopular; therefore, free-market "fundamentalists" exploit times of civil and political upheaval—shocks—to force capitalism upon reluctant populations. The book's bogeyman, the libertarian economist Milton Friedman, advocated, according to Klein, a "fundamentalist form of capitalism [that] has always needed disasters to advance."

Despite serious academic challenges to her case against Friedman and a deeply tendentious reading of modern economic and social history, Klein's book was a massive success—turned into a film by Hollywood director Michael Winterbottom and broadcast on British television, translated into twenty-seven languages, and greeted with near universal praise in the mainstream media. But while Klein traveled the globe to explain the economic shocks sustained in Chile three decades ago, a new economic crisis was enveloping global financial markets.

Mario Monti, an Italian economist and former antitrust enforcer at the European Commission, views the shocks created by the global financial meltdown as an opportunity to remake global finance: "For opponents of free markets in Europe and elsewhere, this is a wonderful opportunity to invoke the American example." Rahm Emanuel, Obama's hyperkinetic chief of staff, was more forthright: "You never want a serious crisis to go to waste."

This would appear to be the ideological obverse of Klein's "shock doctrine"; the deeply sinister proponents of "disaster capitalism," as Klein calls it, have been pushed aside and replaced by the shock troops of "disaster socialism." Indeed, rather than denounce her comrades on the left for mirror imaging the malevolent strategies of "neoliberalism," Klein, without a hint of irony, recently endorsed a *liberal* exposition of economic shock:

> Do we want to save the pre-crisis system, get it back to where it was last September? Or do we want to use this crisis, and the electoral mandate for change delivered by the last election, to radically transform that system? We need to get clear on our answer now because we haven't had the potent combination of a serious crisis and a clear progressive democratic mandate for change since the 1930s. We use this opportunity or we lose it.

As one critic observed, Klein wasn't concerned with the shock, just the doctrine.

And it is a doctrine that many members of the political class, both in America and abroad, seem willing to entertain. The European right, whose hostility to free markets has long perplexed American conservatives, have weathered the political storm of the current crisis rather well. But they have done so by co-opting the language of social democrats, offering thundering denunciations of "American-style" capitalism—a point too often ignored by disengaged journalists in the United States. The Associated Press reported that, after his victory in the 2007 presidential elections, French President Nicolas Sarkozy was an "uncompromising pro-American conservative."

His triumph at the polls was a "decisive victory for Sarkozy's vision of freer markets."

Not exactly. Like its counterparts in Western Europe, French conservatism zealously protects the country's welfare state and, in the tradition of Charles de Gaulle, reacts swiftly to any perceived excesses of capitalism. Far from advocating "freer markets," as the Associated Press assumed, Sarkozy would later declare, "Financial capitalism is a system of irresponsibility and . . . is amoral." With a wave of the hand, the French president told journalists, "Laissez-faire is finished."

Italian finance minister Giulio Tremonti, an ex-socialist who now serves as a foot soldier in Berlusconi's army of bureaucrats, announced that "globalization had failed." On the other side of the globe, Japan's newly elected prime minister Yukio Hatoyama broke with his pragmatic predecessors when he declared an end to both "the fundamentalist pursuit of capitalism" and "the excesses of the current globalized brand of capitalism," both of which, he neglected to mention, brought an astounding level of wealth to his country.

Whether the allusion is intentional or not, critics calling for the humanization, moralization, and aggressive reform of the free market—the specifics of which will presumably be provided at a later date—echo Alexander Dubček's demand that Eastern Bloc communism be allowed to present a "human face."

But what does all of this mean in an American context? Remember that many—though not all—anticapitalists demand nothing less than a fundamental rewriting of the rules that underpin America's economic system, a new system in which the state guides large swathes of economic policy. If this sounds needlessly alarmist, it shouldn't. While the American market is judged irreparably broken by many mainstream critics, it is instructive to view those societies looked upon as a reasonable alternative.

In his book *Flat Broke in the Free Market: How Globalization Fleeced Working People,* Jon Jeter, former *Washington Post* bureau chief in South America, writes that Hugo Chavez's "socialist government has dramatically improved the living standards of poor and working-class people." And for this, writes Jeter, he is "vilified by elites in the United States and Europe."

In *The Predator State*, James Galbraith says that the "market has a tendency to undermine the law," but he writes that Chavez, who routinely shuts down "counterrevolutionary" media outlets and has distributed lists of thousands of political opponents to government agencies, was "elected in fair and free elections, and ruled according to law." Cuba, a country that has neglected to have a fair and free election in the fifty years of communist occupation, is briefly mentioned as a country "determined to reduce poverty."

These aren't anomalies. Michael Moore cites Cuba's health-care system as a model to be emulated in the United States. A new documentary from the Oscar-winning director Oliver Stone heaps praise on the "revolutionary" governments of Cuba, Venezuela, Bolivia, and Ecuador. Naomi Klein gushes that "Venezuela offers heavily subsidized oil to poorer countries and shares expertise in developing reserves; and Cuba sends thousands of doctors to deliver free health care all over the continent, while training students from other countries at its medical schools."

While there is little worry that Chavez's destructive brand of populist and authoritarian socialism will be exported to the United States anytime soon, it is nevertheless deeply unsettling that mainstream figures like Moore and Klein, who command large audiences on television and in the multiplexes around the world and are well positioned to recklessly stoke post–financial crisis fears, desire to end, not mend, capitalism.

To the anticapitalist, the current climate is the starting point of a Gramscian long march through the economic institutions, a rollback of the liberalization and deregulation of the past half century. For the millions in China, India, and Vietnam who have escaped the grinding poverty induced by central planning—and the countless other societies that have seen great reductions in poverty through free trade and free markets—there is no greater threat to freedom than a return to the failed policies of the twentieth century.

21

The Rise of Mass Dependency

Chris Norwood

IT WAS a dark and stormy night, and some 20 people had gathered for a meeting of the Residents Association of a public housing complex that was officially home to 2,485 adults and children, and unofficially to at least 3,000. The complex happened to be in the South Bronx, but it could have been almost anywhere in the country. The drab, red-brick twenty-story buildings rose like monotonous ghosts behind the well-lit community center.

The association president welcomed the few people taking seats and urged them to bring more people to join the Residents Association. "We used to have big meetings and wonderful events," she related. "We even used to have Christmas parties where we had presents for all the children, but we just don't have the money for that now."

The moment defined what was missing. People were attending not a meeting but the memory of a meeting. The residents who had come expected, literally, nothing—beyond perhaps some vague sense of civic participation.

They did not have to be told that the powers who crucially decided their existence no longer responded to their most basic concerns. That was obvious from the first order of business—the report from the maintenance division. The maintenance report began, as the supervisor said, with "the good news." The division had managed to fix the cracked sewer pipes discovered under the buildings before they split open and flooded the neighborhood.

"We avoided typhoid," he said, joking—or perhaps not. "The bad news is that doing that used up most of the year's maintenance

budget." In sum, the residents faced almost a year of broken eleva-
tors, peeling paint in the hallways, and ongoing deterioration.

As it happened, on this same evening in early 2008, the city's
mayor, Michael Bloomberg, was winging across the nation, with the
most recent proposal in his "unannounced" presidential campaign.
Bloomberg had become an energetic national cheerleader for forming
a national "infrastructure" advocacy group, called Building America's
Future, to push for $1.6 trillion in federal money to repair American
infrastructure. The mayor chided other politicians for their "shortsighted, politically motivated" spending while the nation's roads
and bridges fell apart. The city nevertheless had rejected all pleas to
fix its own crumbled public housing complexes where, overall, five
hundred thousand New Yorkers, some 12 percent of the entire population, lived. The federal government had built this housing, the city
said, and it was their responsibility to fix it.

The announcement that maintenance was over for the year halted
the usual, sad litany of complaints. No one even bothered to bring up
the saddest, most galling complaint—constant failure to replace the
bin handles of the garbage chutes on each floor when they broke. For
lack of a one-dollar handle to open the chute, hallways stank with
the garbage the residents had to pile on the floor.

Large as the public housing population was in numbers, its powerlessness had become so defining that government at every level
could ignore the fundamental sanitary obligation to properly maintain sewer pipes and remove garbage in these complexes.

The condition of this small gathering showed too well the causes of
this defining powerlessness. Most were women and elderly. It wasn't
simply that they were poor, at least within American standards, but
that they were substantially incapacitated. In these buildings, only
43 percent of families had an employed member; the remaining
households were headed by people on disability or welfare and the
elderly. That 22 percent still received public assistance underscored
a high level of chronic illness—a major reason New Yorkers were
excused from the work requirements of welfare reform.

Among the twenty people present, two were in wheelchairs, a

commonplace sight in a neighborhood where diabetes constantly resulted in foot neuropathy and lower-limb amputations. In interviewing one thousand adults in this complex, the neighborhood health organization I ran had recently found that 30 percent already knew they had diabetes and another 31 percent were at high risk for developing it. Yet diabetes is a preventable disease, especially when people exercise.

Until two years ago, residents from these buildings could use a free city exercise center and pool nearby. It was one of New York's last six remaining free public-exercise centers, all located in neighborhoods with extraordinary diabetes rates. But the Parks Department had suddenly imposed a membership fee for their use. It "wasn't fair," the parks commissioner had explained, for some people to have free exercise.

His explanation rang rather hollow, since at the same time the city was pouring free sports money elsewhere into the Bronx—$500 million in tax-free bonds for the Yankees to build a new baseball stadium. In any case, within a few months, the fees drove away half the regular users of the centers—the poorest, of course, with the most pressing risk for diabetes.

Still, for all the government disinterest in and even contempt for the ordinary basics of civic life evident in this brief tour, the problem was hardly that government bureaucracies wouldn't spend money in neighborhoods like the South Bronx. What the federal, state, and local governments refused to support were things that contributed to health, normalcy, and independence, no matter how low the cost might be. By contrast, billions upon billions, without question or restraint, were poured into programs, institutions, and bureaucracies whose result was to make the local citizenry ever more dependent—or controlled.

In the many AIDS residences clustered in the South Bronx, for example, the hundreds of "clients" routinely each had three, four, or five "case managers"—that is, social workers. There would be a case manager at the residence, another at the medical clinic, another at the drug treatment center, and yet another at the city welfare agency; clients were well advised to keep an endless succession of appointments with all of them lest they be found "out of compliance" and have their benefits suspended.

The city's annual cost of diabetes—in disability, amputations, lost work, and overall medical bills—had reached $6.5 billion, the equivalent of 10 percent of the entire city budget. Yet even as it careened under this burden, the disinterest of the city's health establishment in preventing further diabetic disability was so complete that, as the *New York Times* noted in a scathing 2006 front-page article, the Department of Health spent less than $1 million a year on diabetes prevention.

Nevertheless, during the two decades when these waves of disease formed and crashed, an enormous "public health" superstructure was able to keep building itself and consume a greater share of the national wealth, despite its undeniable failure to reduce the escalating toll of chronic disease.

Indeed, virtually everywhere one looked, one saw the same phenomenon of expensive superstructures growing rapidly and at vast expense, whose function was not to solve problems but to define and manage different classes of dependents. The criminal justice system was another sector that steadily acted to increase its "clients," even when its own action, or inaction, led to increased crime. Studies showed that preparing inmates for release with drug treatment and job training would halve re-imprisonments, but most states couldn't be bothered. As a result, two-thirds of former convicts are back inside within three years. California alone sends fifty thousand released inmates a year back to prison, not for new crimes but for parole infractions such as traffic tickets.

The men in these prisons—so obviously and painfully missing from the residents' meeting—are a constant wound and injury to the normal conduct of life in low-income neighborhoods throughout the nation. They are also, certainly, the most controlled and probably expensive American population. At a price of $60 billion a year, the penal system already supervises one in thirty-one American adults.

Other "missing" men have been segregated in the AIDS residences increasingly seen in poorer areas. There were at least ten such residences in the South Bronx alone, mainly a men's world—the last stop for thousands whose lives have been marked by drug abuse. New York City now has thirty thousand AIDS patients in its support programs. The same city that could hardly keep the local sewer pipes from collapsing can regularly pay slumlords two thousand dollars a month for each of the tiny cubicles in the AIDS "hotels" where up to four hundred men are jammed together with nothing to do but watch TV and tend to their medical and social service appointments. Day after day, the occupants dwell in a black hole of boredom and unrelieved idleness that practically guarantees their relapse into drug use.

Meanwhile, unemployed young men hang around in the public housing lobbies and in front of the buildings, blocking the way and creating both annoyance and crime. Patrol cars drive by to disperse them in a futile dance that goes on week after week, and nothing changes except that it costs more. The high school dropout rate is approaching 70 percent for the city's black male teenagers. Stop-and-frisk protocols that disproportionately target black and Hispanic males clog the courts and prisons with juvenile offenders who come out as hardened criminals. Millions upon millions are being spent on these kids in ways that mainly act to create more criminality.

Indeed, far from a failure to spend adequately on "poor" people, it looks increasingly as though the United States is determined to bankrupt itself in a national obsession to enforce, augment, and outrightly create unnecessary dependency, avoidable illness, and disability, along with ever larger systems of control. A seemingly unprecedented reversal has taken place. The historic experience of the powerful over the powerless is to exploit them—a course the United States itself pursued during slavery, segregation, and the various uses of immigrant and cheap labor. But, today, the burgeoning system of controls and "services" for the powerless has become so warping and yet central to how the United States functions that its core economic life is built on the vast and draining sums spent on them.

While these billions benefit the medical industrial complex, the prison industry, and social welfare bureaucracies, the overall spending is as unsustainable as it is corroding to any normal civic life in the neighborhoods where it is concentrated. Even the push to "end welfare as we know it"—the one national success in curbing dependency—is being undermined by the explosion in disability. Perhaps most frightening is the extent to which "health care" has become the new, preferred—and largest—system of control. Yet except in the most conventional partisan terms, this phenomenon has remained fundamentally unexamined and almost undiscussable.

The result we face today—a mass dependency of unprecedented scope—has no real parallel in history. I mean something far beyond ordinary illness or disability. I mean a dependency so accepted and widespread *as policy* that system after system acts in different ways to create ever more dependents—from the repeated jailings that turn once-redeemable young people into hardened criminals to the blatant failures of disease prevention that leave millions chronically ill. Disability payments, Medicaid and Medicare, and Social Security consume 40 percent of the federal budget—and that is without the cost of various auxiliary industries like social services, prisons, and the "public health" structure.

While it's perfectly possible to be poor or unemployed or disabled or old and lead a fulfilled life, the mass dependency we are looking at finally feeds on itself to overwhelm the very notions of fulfillment and happiness. In neighborhoods where this dependency is most concentrated, it defines the tenor of life itself, from what people see in the streets—the many folks in wheelchairs, the many others lounging around with that air of nervous purposelessness—to their very sense of life's possibilities.

Ordinarily, the specter of community after community where half the population is chronically ill would be considered a national emergency. But for largely low-income American communities from Appalachia to the South Bronx, debilitating rates of chronic illness are now accepted as their ordinary—even deserved—condition.

Little is better proven than that the strongest way to confront the national morass of chronic disease is to directly educate the ill and at-risk to improve and control their own health. To implement this well-documented remedy, however, would require a massive shift in attitude and policy; it would require granting all those low-income and minority people, all those welfare recipients and the "case-managed"—even those fat folk eating bad food whom the nation is not so subtly being taught to regard as a despicable underclass—a level of autonomy, independence, and personal responsibility that has become unallowable.

In this respect, health is the rock-bottom issue for the United States. Either the nation will insist that its health establishment concede to strategies that palpably restore health to dependent communities, or the nation has no future.

Strange to say, the horrific AIDS epidemic had one redeeming aspect: it provided the single most powerful American lesson of the success possible when stricken communities learn to fight for their own health.

I first came to the South Bronx twenty years ago to start a women's AIDS prevention project. I'd written the first book about women and the epidemic, and I became convinced that the only way for them to have a chance was to become educators and leaders themselves in fighting the disease that was killing them. Several "experts" assured me that the black and Hispanic women most affected by AIDS—most without high school degrees—would never stick to the intensive training they would need for this role, but they did. The example of these women—many with only an average year to live— still fighting for others deeply impressed the community; within a few years men asked to join us, and our fight widened.

I had no "appropriate" background to start such a program, no social work degree or master's degree in public health, but in this I inadvertently became part of the most instructive contemporary movement in reclaiming the health of distressed American populations, including those with lives marred by drugs, prison, family collapse, and social isolation. In the crisis of the epidemic, others across the nation were also launching community groups with a similar mission.

Through this grassroots strategy, commonly known as "peer education," the United States developed a public health army it had never before seen: an army of the rejected, the paroled, the uneducated, the sick and dying, and composed largely of volunteers. Day after day and year after year this invisible army attended to its mission, going down alleys into crack dens, trudging up stairs to take sick mothers to the hospital, teaching, cajoling, encouraging; it was the main reason the United States, whose own epidemic was so far advanced before anything was done, was able to gain any substantial control over AIDS.

Equally, becoming a peer educator had a profound impact on these women and men; it renewed their lives. Always having been the object of various "services," they now instead had a respected role in their community. When medications finally appeared that enabled those with AIDS to live longer, they began to return to school, get jobs, retrieve their children from foster care and seriously raise them—the ordinary steps to productive adulthood that had eluded them through years of being a case to be "managed."

But the AIDS army had been enabled by a unique circumstance of funding. Through special annual federal AIDS allocations—which eventually reached $2 billion a year—local community groups could reliably obtain health dollars that, for once, empowered those with disease to assume a key role in advancing health. As the great waves of chronic disease started rolling over these same distressed neighborhoods—asthma, diabetes, heart disease—our organization would get an occasional grant that allowed us to show yet again that community education worked. But without steady funding outside the command of the medical industrial complex, these small initiatives ended when their grants ran out.

Not even conclusive research from the most credentialed imprimatur could budge the medical industry into widely helping its captive base of the chronically ill learn to stay well. In 2002, the National Institutes of Health released the stunning results from the largest American diabetes prevention study ever undertaken. The national study had enrolled a diverse group of "prediabetics" from twenty-three states. Some one thousand in a "lifestyle" education group received several sessions of teaching and coaching to lose modest amounts of weight and engage in modest exercise; another thousand were put on standard drugs for blood sugar control, and the rest were handed the usual "information" pamphlets.

After three years, only 14 percent in the "lifestyle education" group developed diabetes, compared with 22 percent of the medication group and 29 percent in the pamphlet/no help patients. Results were the same for all racial and ethnic groups.

A year of good health gained through education costs only one thousand dollars; with drugs, a year's delay in diabetes cost thirty thousand dollars. These outcomes were announced to great acclaim in the *New England Journal of Medicine*. And then . . . nothing happened. In a country with 50 million prediabetics, probably no doctor can still "prescribe" the "lifestyle education" course in preference to a costly and less effective drug regimen because no one will pay for it. This includes Medicare and Medicaid, the public insurance plans bearing the major national cost of diabetes. The NIH could have started training community groups in poor areas to start teaching lifestyle courses locally, but that didn't happen either. The medical industry just continued its own gruesome mission—performing eighty-two thousand diabetes-related lower-limb amputations a year.

But something else did happen. The rise in chronic disease became the excuse for an ever franker coupling of health with social control. This process was most advanced in New York City where Dr. Thomas Frieden, Mayor Bloomberg's health commissioner, had become nationally known for his bans on indoor smoking and trans fats. Whether or not such health-centered regulations "worked"— the smoking ban was quickly followed by a drop in heart attacks in New York and other localities—the clear preference for control spelled death to any alternative. Tellingly, the Department of Health ignored diabetes, even as it exploded to the point that it cost the equivalent of 10 percent of the city budget. For a disease whose prevention so clearly demanded that people be seriously educated to take command of their own health, there was no plan, or even noticeable public discussion, until the department was embarrassed by press coverage.

For the city's large AIDS population, however, there was indeed a new plan. Frieden proposed that the Health Department itself now send "representatives" directly to their homes to prod them into taking their medication properly. Evidently, the city could afford a large, new policing initiative even as it was becoming so broke that Dr. Frieden soon threatened to close children's dental clinics.

The funding for New York's large network of community and AIDS peer programs was federal, but the city controlled its distribution; in 2005, the Health Department started defunding community-based support and care, diverting the money to hospitals. And in 2006, the federal government ordered localities to allocate 75 percent of their AIDS funds to medical facilities and "professionally managed" social services. Community programs largely collapsed.

As the "health" establishment defunded the enthusiastic local AIDS armies, ending the only significant involvement of low-income Americans in fighting disease, the results were predictably disastrous. In the Bronx, in the two years prior, women's AIDS deaths fell by 20 percent, progress widely considered unattainable; after the defunding of community programs, progress halted and deaths decreased by only 6 percent in the next two years. In Brooklyn, women's AIDS deaths actually increased for the first time in years.

Yet the New York City Department of Health was widely considered the best public health department in the land. In 2009, Dr. Frieden was appointed director of the federal Centers for Disease Control and Prevention.

Let's return to the residents' meeting where people are saying their "good nights" and "get home safes." As they trudge—or wheel—into the rainy darkness, they would probably have taken little comfort in learning that a city which couldn't replace a garbage chute handle was even then planning multimillion-dollar initiatives to increase the ranks of the new managerial class, which—unelected and totally removed from any local influence—more and more decided how they would live. The city's university system was preparing to build yet another school of social work, along with a graduate school of public health to produce more "masters" in regulating illnesses that need not have occurred in the first place.

As they approached their buildings, the small band of elderly women looked warily at the young men who had nothing else to do but hang out in the sad fluorescent light of a public housing lobby. There was always the desperate hope that, at least during the summer, these surly youth would be occupied by six weeks of work in the city's youth job program; however the city, state, and federal governments were already planning to cut summer youth slots. Finally locked in their apartments, they could look out the window at something that scared them even more—the AIDS residence across the street.

Although to many Americans, places like this housing complex and its surrounding community may seem like sad exceptions, the portrait of these communities presages a very near future for the United States as a whole. As noted, fewer than half of adults work, but within current trends the same will be true of the nation in short order. The country is so rapidly being overtaken by both historical and emerging forces driving ever larger portions of the population into publicly supported dependency that, already, illness, disability, and old age are, in effect, major products of the nation that is the leader of the free world. In barely twenty years, there will be only two employed adults for every person on Social Security.

The most immediate and powerful route to revival and increased independence for the most stricken neighborhoods is clear: to widely teach and empower their residents to overcome chronic disease. Obviously, where levels of chronic disease—especially diabetes— widely outrank welfare, disease has become the biggest source of poverty as well as the powerlessness, controls, and dependency that so automatically surround American poverty. But even though the public health establishment and industry alike know that this widespread grassroots education could slash disability, death, and despair while renewing millions of lives, the answer so far has been no.

Whether the nation can overcome the institutionalized opposition to allowing all its citizens to seek the health and happiness of being on their own feet is the single domestic issue that will most decide what the United States becomes. At present, with age, unemployment, disability, serial incarceration, and a morass of chronic illness locking whole neighborhoods into unsustainable dependency systems, it is hard to believe that the nation has a future any of us will like.

22

Liberty and Complacency

Glenn Harlan Reynolds

"THE PRICE OF FREEDOM," Thomas Jefferson famously warned, "is eternal vigilance." I've wondered, sometimes, if that price is not too high—or, at least, higher than many are willing to pay. But recent events suggest that I was too pessimistic.

Eternal vigilance, after all, is pretty hard to maintain. It is the natural tendency of human beings to grow complacent, to focus on their own lives, to disregard threats to liberty, and to ignore politics whenever possible. (Jefferson himself wrote, in the Declaration of Independence no less, that "all experience hath shown that mankind are more disposed to suffer, while evils are sufferable, than to right themselves by abolishing the forms to which they are accustomed.") Most of the business of government is, frankly, boring—and government officials are often at pains to make it more so, in order to discourage public involvement. But, of course, to those officials, and to special-interest groups, the boredom is relieved by their direct stakes in the outcome, in the form of increases in wealth and personal power, which ordinary voters do not possess.

But complacency is also bred by good government. To the extent that people think of the government as working for them, and trust it to do so in a fairly honest fashion, they are likely to pay less attention to its doings. Trusting the government, people fail to see it as something dangerous, in need of close watching, as the framers did.

This complacency is, in some ways, a good thing: show me a polity where the masses are closely attentive to politics, and I'll show you a polity that's in some sort of crisis. A polity in which people can ignore politics, on the other hand, is one in which most of the people are happy.

That latter condition has described American politics in recent years. But the complacency seems to be fading, and while that may be a good thing for the future of liberty, it is probably also a bad sign for the state of American governance today. But the shift from complacency to resistance is a natural one in Anglo-American politics. It is also one that we are seeing today, though perhaps in a form inadequate to the threat it faces.

As Pauline Maier writes, "Americans of the Framing era believed that government was dangerous and required close watching. Although wise citizens understood that government officials were prone to human failings, they were warned to be on guard against the very earliest abuses of power, since tyranny was seen as something better prevented than cured."[1]

The Whig thinkers of the era, Maier reports, looked to history for signs of the abuses that justified resistance: corruption, one-sided peace treaties that favored national enemies, the appointment of "worthless and wicked men" to government posts, and the like.[2] And resistance itself took place over a continuum.

In the ordinary course of events, the usual means of restraining power—courts, elections, the right of petition—should be enough. But operations that take place within the machinery of government are at risk from the machinations of those who control that machinery; votes may matter less than the counting thereof, and lawsuits less than the deciding thereof. So where ordinary politics are insufficient to restrain government officials from overreaching, the remedy is to be found first in "resistance"—often including what Gordon Wood calls "out of doors political activity," and then, should that not suffice, in outright revolution. As Wood writes, this sort of action was not much like the anarchic urban riots of the 1960s; it was organized and expressly political.[3] But this resistance, while not strictly lawful, was also not strictly lawless. Unlike revolution, it took place within the existing framework, not in an effort to break and replace that frame: "To the participants such associations of the people outside of the regularly constituted government seemed as necessary under the new republican governments as they did under the British."[4] As Maier also notes, "Eighteenth-century Americans accepted the existence of popular uprisings with remarkable ease. . . . Not that extra-legal uprisings were encouraged. They were not. But in certain circumstances, it was understood, the people would rise up almost as a natural force, much as night follows day, and this phenomenon often contributed to public welfare."[5]

In order not to be merely a mob—and to undercut claims of mobdom by the authorities and their supporters—the resistance process, though in some ways violent, was also focused and restrained. Targets were focused and related to the grievance at hand. Fatalities were rare, and violence was usually aimed at property (revenue cutters, customs offices, and the like) rather than at individuals: "It was authority, rather than the crowd that was conspicuous for its violence to life and limb."[6] The process of resistance was also a measured one, starting out with mobs and minor rioting, and growing strong if the complained-of abuses were continued.

Such self-organized resistance provided a warning to authorities (unheeded in the case of the American Revolution) that they were overstepping their bounds, and also served to familiarize citizens with self-rule and to form bonds that were to prove useful during the next stage. And such risings continued throughout subsequent decades, though by modern times we find only one real example of a mass movement organized in opposition to governmental abuses: the civil rights and antiwar movements of the 1960s. Both, interestingly, received a rather sympathetic treatment from the press.

But there are more recent examples. In my own home state of Tennessee, an effort in the 1990s to install a state income tax yielded a robust grassroots resistance that ultimately prevailed; ten years later, there is still no enthusiasm among the state's political class for another try. This came to a head in a protest rally at the state capitol in 1999, and may provide some guidance as to how such out-of-doors politics may play out at the national level as well.

Just a few days earlier, adoption of an income tax had appeared

all but certain. Tennessee's pro-tax Republican governor, Don Sund-
quist, had used a combination of pork and arm-twisting to bring
many legislators over to his side. Though the Tennessee Supreme
Court had previously ruled that an income tax would violate the
state's constitution, tax proponents believed that the current elected
court, fearing revenge by the powers that be, could be counted on
to uphold a tax. Leading opinion makers, newspaper editorialists,
and academics were firmly on board. The legislature was meeting
in special session, and the main question seemed to be what kind of
income tax would emerge, not whether there would be an income tax.

All of this evaporated overnight in the face of overwhelming
opposition. Thanks to a combination of talk-radio discussion and
an e-mail campaign spearheaded by the state Libertarian Party, the
capitol found itself, almost literally, under siege.

Thousands of cars circled Capitol Hill, bearing down on their
horns and tying up traffic throughout downtown. Hundreds of protesters occupied the Legislative Plaza, with many barging into the
capitol itself, carrying signs and—in one case—a can of tar and a
feather pillow. "Put a stop to this or we'll get you," said one protester in the Senate speaker's office. Phone and e-mail systems were
jammed with complaints and threats.

Despite vows to "do the right thing" notwithstanding popular
opinion, the legislature cracked. One legislator was rushed to a hospital with chest pains; many others complained about the "incivility"
of the public response. The legislature recessed, hoping the protesters would leave. They didn't. Finally, the special session adjourned,
leaving the income tax question to be taken up—if at all—in the
regular session next year. It was never passed.

Ten years later, we are seeing something of a reprise on a national
level, as taxpayers and citizens began to rally in opposition to the
politics of stimulus and ObamaCare. The protests began with bloggers in Seattle, Washington, who organized a demonstration on February 16, 2009. As word of this spread, rallies in Denver and Mesa,
Arizona, were quickly organized for the next day. Then came CNBC
talker Rick Santelli's February 19 "rant heard round the world," in

which he called for a "Chicago tea party" on July 4. The tea-party moniker stuck, but angry taxpayers weren't willing to wait until July. Soon, tea-party protests were appearing in one city after another, drawing at first hundreds, and then thousands, to marches in cities from Orlando to Kansas City to Cincinnati. As word spread, people got interested in picking a common date for nationwide protests, and decided on Tax Day, April 15. Over a million people, by some estimates, showed up at hundreds of rallies nationwide, and the tea-party protests continued without letup into the summer, morphing into the "Town Hall" protests as members of Congress returned to meet their constituents over the summer.

As I write this, it is still too early to tell how things will work out. But one thing is already plain: while the establishment organizations were either ineffectually spinning their wheels (as was the Republican Party) or cutting their own deals in exchange for support (as were the AARP and the pharmaceutical industry), the people themselves, and particularly the senior citizens most likely to be affected by the changes in health care and taxation, were rising to the occasion. And although some groups tried to join the bandwagon once it was in motion, they were clearly followers, not leaders.

If there were leaders in this movement, they were mostly self-appointed. Talk-radio hosts, large and small, played an important role. But so did individuals—like Mike Wilson, organizer of the first Cincinnati Tea Party protest—who had previously never done anything of the sort. And new tools ranging from blogs, to Facebook, to Twitter and Meetup made it easy for people to organize themselves. This is part of a general phenomenon dubbed as "smart mobs" by Howard Rheingold, author of a book by the same title, in which modern communications and social-networking technologies allow quick coordination among large numbers of people who don't know each other. In the old days, organizing large groups of people required, well, an organization: a political party, a labor union, a church, or some other sort of structure. Now people can coordinate themselves. We saw a bit of this in the 2004 and 2008 presidential campaigns, with things like Howard Dean's use of Meetup, and Barack Obama's use of Facebook. But this was still social networking in support of an existing organization or campaign.

What's interesting about the new "tea party" phenomenon is that it happened without an existing organization, or campaign, or even a single spokesperson. And that, it turns out, may answer some of the framers' concerns.

The framers were less concerned with complacency than we are today, but they were very concerned with corruption. By "corruption," they meant not only the bag-of-cash sort of dishonesty— though to modern minds they spend a lot of time worrying about treason, perhaps befitting a generation that was, after all, contemporary with Benedict Arnold—but also what moderns would call institutional corruption. Institutions, in time, inevitably become attuned to the interests of those running them, rather than those they are supposed to serve, something the framers—understanders of "public choice" economics before the term was coined—clearly grasped. And institutions are also vulnerable to subornation. Control the leaders of a traditional, hierarchical organization, and you control the organization itself.

This corruption was dealt with in a variety of ways. Fears of outright bribery certainly played a part. My students in Constitutional Law are often surprised when I point out that Madison didn't want a super-majority requirement for passing legislation, because a super-majority requirement meant that opponents (e.g., foreign nations hostile to a trade bill, the example Madison used) would only have to bribe a minority of Congress. This seems surprising to them. The framers are like gods; how could they be worrying about foreign powers bribing big chunks of Congress, something very much at odds with our view of the elevated character of politics at our nation's birth—but, as I note, they were contemporaries of Benedict Arnold and students of history, in which bribery, even (or perhaps especially) in republics, often played a major role. Additional checks were provided by separation of powers (which divided governmental functions among branches), federalism (which divided most government among the states), and the limitation of federal power to subjects which were few and distinct (limiting the impact of bribery, and making it harder to conceal).

But, of course, where the framers felt the risk of corruption was particularly severe, or the harm from corruption especially great, they went a step further, by relying directly upon the people. In criminal cases, or important civil cases, they relied upon juries. Being drawn from the body of the people, and not being repeat players in the process, juries were harder to suborn in any systematic fashion.

And in the area they feared most, governmental armed force, the framers went still further. Article I of the Constitution is full of references to "the militia," an armed body composed of pretty much the entire populace (in the beginning, free blacks often served along with whites) as the primary means of enforcing laws, repelling invasions, and suppressing insurrection. The framers, instructed by English history, feared a standing army, believing that it could easily become an instrument of tyranny. The militia, on the other hand, dispersed power too widely for subornation. It could not betray the people, because it was the people. Were the government to abuse its powers, it would find the militia unwilling to enforce the law; were it to attempt a military coup, it would find itself opposed by overwhelming numbers.

We have come a long way from the framers' era now, with the standing army they feared becoming a normal part of government, and with the militia system, though not quite defunct, largely moribund. But the logic behind it continues to make some sense. Institutions—political parties, courts, the institutional press—are capable of acting out of self-interest, or of being neutralized by bribery or blackmail, or of simply performing poorly via incompetence. (And, if anything, such tendencies have worsened since the framing era.) When that happens, the people themselves must respond and become active in politics in a way that they are normally too complacent to do.

This modern response is generally tamer than that of the framing era; so far, at least, we've seen no burned revenue cutters, and, with the exception of a symbolic appearance at the Tennessee capitol, no tar and feathers. But the rise of a genuinely popular movement in favor of liberty, self-organized and spontaneous, at a time when all the political branches and traditional-media sources were controlled by those with a different view, and when the minority party was disorganized and ineffectual, is a very good sign indeed for the future of freedom in the United States. Regardless of what happens in the current political debate, the popular response in 2009 indicates that the public can still turn out in large numbers when it sees its interest threatened, even in the absence of any viable organizational leadership.

Complacency, it turns out, can't be counted on. When liberties are threatened, Americans will still "rise up almost as a natural force, much as night follows day," and that's a very good thing—at least for those outside the political class.

But the above analysis is rather cheery, and for a book on new threats to freedom, it is probably worth spending some time on a less sunny view of how things might turn out. I am a noted optimist, after all, but optimism is an attitude, not a predictive strategy.

The notion that the citizenry will turn out and self-organize in response to threats to liberty depends on a number of assumptions. The first is that the citizenry will notice and recognize threats when they occur. The second is that the citizenry will respond. The third is that the response will be effective. All of these are open to doubt.

Recognizing threats to liberty is not to be taken for granted. Modern Americans, for the most part, lack the educational focus on history and tyranny that was common in the framing era. In an Oprah-ized age, people's attentions are directed differently.

Second, responding to threats, even once noticed, requires action. Complaining on the Internet or in calls to talk radio probably doesn't rise to the level of "action." Constructive action requires organization and political behavior, ranging from taking to the streets in protest (and perhaps even out-of-doors activity) to nominating and electing candidates. With all the distractions in American life, and with the increasing disaffection of many Americans from organized politics, that's not to be taken for granted.

Third, the response must be effective: it must be severe enough, focused enough, and persistent enough to force political actors to change their behavior. Brief spasms of unfocused popular rage aren't enough. But as the ongoing flow of information and entertainment promotes a sort of national ADHD, the persistence, in particular, seems more difficult to maintain.

Will the optimistic or the pessimistic view of this sort of political action win out? Now, as in the framing era, that depends on what the public does, and how much, ultimately, the public values freedom. But it has always been so: "A republic, ma'am, if you can keep it."

Notes

1. Pauline Maier, *From Resistance to Revolution* (New York: Norton, 1991), 43.
2. Ibid., 45.
3. Gordon S. Wood, *The Creation of the American Republic* (Chapel Hill: University of North Carolina Press, 1969), 319–26.
4. Ibid.
5. Maier, *From Resistance to Revolution*, 3.
6. Ibid., 13.

23

Threats to Philanthropic Freedom

Naomi Schaefer Riley

THERE WAS "a new face this year" at the Council on Foundations annual meeting in Atlanta, according to a blog entry from Kristin Ivie, a program associate at the Case Foundation who attended the May 2009 event. That new face was "Uncle Sam." "In plenary, on panels, in the audience," Ms. Ivie reported, "members of the federal government are ready to engage in addressing social problems alongside foundations in a new way."

Among those "ready to engage" were Melody Barnes, President Obama's director of domestic policy; Edward DeSeve, special advisor to the president on the implementation of the stimulus package; and Democratic Congressman John Lewis of Georgia. While these officials gave humble-sounding presentations, profusely thanking the audience members (mostly the staffs of philanthropic foundations) for all of their good and hard work, the government also offered a more pointed message.

Representative Lewis, for instance, couched his comments in his own autobiography, recalling his role as a leader in the civil rights movement. "I got in the way, I got in trouble, and we brought about a nonviolent revolution in America," he told a rapt audience. Then, he continued,

> It is time for the nonprofit and foundation community to get in trouble, good trouble. Get in the way. Be creative. Be daring. Speak up. Speak out. You won't get arrested. You won't be beaten. You won't go to jail. But push. . . . Find a way to share your ideas with members of Congress. . . .

We need to know what you're doing to improve the common good. It is important that we all give something back. It is important that we leave America a little greener and a little more peaceful for the next generation. That is our calling, that is our mission.

Mr. Lewis gives an inspiring speech and few would doubt his commitment to doing what's good for this country. But he is helping to perpetuate a fundamental misunderstanding of the role of philanthropy in the United States. Moreover, he is pushing further open the door to government's regulation and restrictions of what donors can do with their own money. And while the tone may sound collaborative—he wants donors to "find a way to share your ideas with members of Congress"—there is a serious threat to freedom in Uncle Sam's newfound interest in philanthropy.

"Leaving America a little greener and a little more peaceful" may be Mr. Lewis's mission, but it is not and need not be the mission of every philanthropic foundation.

Mr. Lewis is part of a growing chorus of activists and government leaders who would like to offer philanthropists some "guidance" about where their dollars should be directed. Perhaps the first voice heard on this subject was that of Greenlining, a Berkeley, California–based activist group whose main claim to fame had been pushing banks to lower lending standards for racial minorities. (The name is a play on the term "redlining," used to describe banks that were allegedly discriminating in their lending.) For whatever reason, the subprime mortgage crisis didn't seem to put much of a damper on Greenlining's spirits.

In 2007, the group put out a report claiming that though "communities of color" made up the majority of Californians, the state's foundations were spending only 5 percent of their dollars on them. Since philanthropies are tax-exempt, Greenlining suggested, they should be held more "accountable" to the public.

What counts as spending on minorities? Greenlining only includes the money that is donated to organizations whose board and staff are more than 50 percent minority. Thus, an inner-city soup kitchen with a mostly white staff or board would not be counted, even if the line snaking out the door was entirely made up of blacks and Hispanics. And nonprofits devoted to curing breast cancer or saving endangered species also wouldn't count unless their leadership and staff were of the right color combinations, too.

Some California legislators were alerted to the Greenlining report, and they saw blood in the water. A few months later, State Representative Joe Coto introduced the Foundation Diversity and Transparency Act, which would have required foundations with more than $250 million in assets to report the racial, gender, and sexual orientation of their board members, staffs, and grantees. The state's foundations and nonprofits rightly saw this as a threat to the privacy of the many people they employ and help. (Why does the public have the right to know whether the people in that soup kitchen are gay or not?) And they recognized it as the first step toward greater government restriction of how they can make charitable contributions.

Still, these realizations came too late. The California nonprofits were blindsided, even as the bill passed through the state assembly. It was stalled in the California state senate for several months while some backroom dealing took place.

Dr. Robert Ross, president and CEO of the California Endowment, a private health foundation that works with underserved populations, attended a hearing for the bill in the Senate. He told the *Wall Street Journal* that the foundations "were roughed up pretty badly." He reported that the legislators and activists supporting the bill told the public that "well-heeled philanthropy is too busy spending money on opera and museums of fine art to make their resources available to minority and low-income communities."

But then Dr. Ross recalled, the head of the Senate's black caucus told him, "If you guys show some problem-solving leadership on this, we'll look to that kindly." And so, in the summer of 2008, the bill's sponsors agreed to drop the issue in return for a "donation" of tens of millions of dollars from the state's largest foundations to the favorite causes of Greenlining.

• The threat to the foundations worked so well in California that Greenlining launched similar campaigns in Florida, New York, and Pennsylvania. Meanwhile, officials at the federal level got wind of it as well. At the Council on Foundations' annual meeting in 2008, Democratic Congressman Xavier Becerra of California complained about the lack of philanthropic grants going to racial minorities. "We're not trying to mandate something," he told the audience, but "we will, if you don't act." When one of his fellow panelists suggested that greater diversity in philanthropic giving could be achieved voluntarily without regulation, Mr. Becerra responded that at one time "South Africa said it would voluntarily change . . . its apartheid regime."

Mr. Becerra is not the only one who speaks in these ominous tones toward the philanthropic community. Al Piña, the chairman of the Florida Minority Community Reinvestment Coalition, has been using a Greenlining report on the Sunshine State to pummel local philanthropies about their own giving records. In particular, he has gone after Publix Supermarket Charities, the largest foundation in the state, for failing, he says, to give enough money to minority-led organizations. "Publix can fight all it wants," Mr. Piña told the *Chronicle of Philanthropy*, "but I can guarantee you, it will come to the table, either kicking and screaming, or in peace."

It would be a mistake to think that the legislators and activists who are trying to create new rules for philanthropy are only concerned about the race of its recipients. Indeed, every aspect of their operations is being scrutinized. Greenlining, for instance, has pushed the idea that foundations should invest more of their endowments with black and Hispanic money managers. Either with legislation or the threat of legislation, these activists hope to press independent, private philanthropic foundations into doing its bidding.

And Greenlining is not alone. The National Center for Responsive Philanthropy (NCRP) came out with a report in 2009 called "Criteria for Philanthropy at Its Best." The report suggests that foundations "provide at least 50 percent of grant dollars to benefit lower-income communities, communities of color, and other marginalized groups, broadly defined." NCRP looked at 809 of the largest foundations in the country and concluded that the majority of foundations are "eschewing the needs of the most vulnerable in our society" by neglecting "marginalized groups."

NCRP's report, which ran to hundreds of pages, went much further into detail than Greenlining has. The committee advised that at least 25 percent of grant dollars be used for "advocacy, organizing and civic engagement to promote equity, opportunity and justice in our society." It advised foundations to give more money to support the operating costs of nonprofits, as opposed to just individual programs. And finally, the committee advised foundations to have boards of trustees that include at least five people. "Diverse groups make better decisions and . . . a minimum of five people are needed for a plurality of perspectives to reflect collective or social preferences."

When NCRP's report came out, it was widely criticized both within the philanthropic world and without. Aaron Dorfman, executive director of NCRP, appeared at a panel at the Hudson Institute, where he tried to defend the contents. "You may hear that NCRP is trying to impose a narrow and arbitrary vision of philanthropy on all foundations. Nothing could be further from the truth. [We are only] opening up a debate and challenging our sector to do better." But at the press conference releasing the report, NCRP chairman David Jones invited Congress to look at the report and judge whether foundations are serving the public interest. Representative Becerra, who was also present at the press conference, thanked the committee "for giving us in Congress something to work with." There is little doubt that the folks at NCRP are fishing for greater government involvement in the philanthropic sector.

A few months later, NCRP reiterated some of their ideas from "Philanthropy at Its Best" in another report following the Bernard Madoff scandal. The 105 foundations that invested more than 30 percent of their assets with Mr. Madoff, NCRP noted, had a median board size of three people. The implication seemed obvious. Small boards make for bad, if not corrupt, decisions.

But, pace NCRP, it is not the job of a foundation board to "reflect collective or social preferences." Rather, it is supposed to reflect the intent of the donor. If, after a lifetime of hard work, a woman decides to give all of her money to an art museum, it is not the role of trustees to suggest that she consider donating instead to inner-city after-school programs. No matter how worthy the cause, and especially after the donor has passed away, the role of the trustees is to adhere to her wishes.

That is why people pick their friends and relatives to sit on the boards of foundations—because those are the people who know and understand their wishes the best. And while the ethicists at NCRP are trying to suggest that something corrupt results when members of a board are too close to each other or to the donor, there are plenty of reasons to think otherwise. British social scientist Digby Anderson has written extensively about friendship. He tells a story about the chairman of one company who sat as a non-executive director on the board of his friend's company. The friend did the same for him. Rather than have a corrupting effect, Mr. Anderson writes that the arrangement was morally beneficial to both men in their jobs. "All of the other board members might try to curry favor by saying what they thought the chairman wanted to hear. Only his friend could be relied on to tell him the truth."

It is true, though, that our close friends and family do not necessarily reflect the views of the whole society. The idea that the people who operate foundations and distribute their wealth must have the interests of the whole society in mind is gaining adherents, particularly on the political left.

Perhaps of greater concern, though, is the suggestion that the tax-exempt status of philanthropies means they must be answerable to government officials, which has received the stamp of approval from some judges. In a recent monograph from the Philanthropy Roundtable, called "How Public Is Private Philanthropy?" John Tyler and Evelyn Brody chronicle the ways in which some recent lawsuits depend on this theory.

For instance, in 2002, the attorney general of Pennsylvania

attempted to stop the Milton Hershey School Trust from diversifying its holdings by selling a controlling amount of stock of the Hershey Foods Corporation. His petition stated, "Any public sale of the controlling interest in Hershey Foods Corporation by the School Trust, *while likely to increase the value of the trust*, could also result in profound negative consequences for the Hershey community and surrounding areas, including, but not limited to, the closing and/ or withdrawal of Hershey Foods Corporation from the local community together with a dramatic loss of the region's employment opportunities, related businesses, and tax base."

The attorney general asserted, "the ultimate beneficiary and real party in interest of all charitable trusts is the general public to whom the social and economic advantages of the trusts accrue," and declared, "Accordingly, the broad interests of the Attorney General necessarily entail protecting the public against any social and economic *disadvantages* which may be occasioned by the activities and functioning of public charities."

This is an incredible assertion—that a state government can exercise control over the actions of an individual philanthropy because its actions may affect the regional tax base. The government's role with regard to philanthropy is not to make sure that every philanthropy is benefiting every member of the public. It is rather to ensure that a philanthropy is engaged in some kind of charitable activity, and that the trustees are performing their fiduciary duties when they make decisions about spending and investing. That the courts ultimately upheld the attorney general's petition sets a horrible precedent. It will only give other public officials dangerous ideas.

Still, the courts have impinged on philanthropic freedom before. In 1970, a plaintiff sued thirteen western New York foundations, alleging that they had discriminated against himself, his family, and his foundation for reasons of race—because those foundations had not given him a job or given his children scholarships. As odd as the claim was, a panel of the Second Circuit did not dismiss the case. Instead it found that in granting tax-exempt status to certain entities and not to others, the government "would appear to be certifying that every foundation on its tax exempt list is laboring in the public interest," and that those foundations are nothing more than state actors. As such, their activities could be seen as discriminatory.

Writing in his dissent, Judge Henry Friendly said that the panel's holding, "unless corrected will be the source of enormous damage to the great edifice of private philanthropy which has been one of this country's most distinctive and admirable features." Further, he noted, tax exemptions have never previously been thought to be sufficient "to convert the recipient into a *de facto* arm of the government."

But from the depths of this Great Recession we're in, it looks as though almost every sector of the American economy will begin to act as a de facto arm of the government. From health care to banking, individuals and private organizations will have less and less flexibility to make their own decisions in the coming years.

In February 2009, President Obama proposed to reduce the charitable deduction for the highest two income-tax brackets by as much as 30 percent. He argued that fairness would dictate that the same contribution by two different people from two different levels of income should amount to the same tax deduction. But regardless of whether this policy is egalitarian, the idea behind it was to raise revenue for government programs by increasing the amount of taxes paid by charity-minded rich folks. Though economists like Harvard's Martin Feldstein warned that such a tax increase would significantly reduce the amount of charity given, the administration seemed unfazed. After all, they would just turn around and give those increased revenues to the people who really deserved it. The government, they would presumably say, is a much more effective and evenhanded distributor of wealth than some eccentric philanthropist.

It is not just the people in government who find American philanthropy too haphazard to be fair. In his recent book, *Millions of Buckets, Billions of Dollars*, Stephen Goldberg argues for a "virtual nonprofit stock market" that would rank nonprofits according to their effectiveness, as judged by the collective wisdom of those familiar with them. Though he doesn't propose that the government accomplish this, Goldberg and other professional nonprofit staff generally prefer a top-down approach to charity.

But that approach is not what has made American philanthropy as successful as it's been. At the end of his dissent in the aforementioned case, Judge Friendly then takes on the notion that it is somehow problematic for a foundation to give to one group over another—and that any one figure can dictate where the money should be best spent. He writes,

> There are hundreds of thousands of foundations ranging from the giants to the pygmies. While most foundations, particularly large ones, give mainly to institutions serving all races and creeds, although hardly in the completely non-discriminatory way required of public institutions, I see nothing offensive, either constitutionally or morally, in a foundation's choosing to give preferentially or even exclusively to Jesuit seminaries, to Yeshivas, to black colleges or to the NAACP. Indeed, I find it something of a misnomer to apply the pejorative term "racial discrimination" to a failure to make a charitable gift.

But that is exactly the claim that the leaders of NCRP and Greenlining, not to mention their local affiliates, are making. The threat to philanthropic freedom began when a few activists cast aspersions on foundations that were doing good work—the work their missions dictated—just not the work that these activists preferred. Such groups are welcome to their opinions. But as these ideas have begun to interest politicians who are hungry in economically difficult times for control over more pots of money, the situation has become more perilous. And if the courts offer their imprimatur to the idea that tax exemption should mean greater government oversight and control, the philanthropic sector could be in trouble.

The problem is not just that current endowments will be diverted to purposes that their funders never intended. If this were to happen, many nonprofits would go under as a result, but America's philanthropic tradition would remain intact. The real crisis would be this: With all of these new rules and regulations to think about, many wealthy Americans might just decide not to spend their money on charity at all. Who needs the hassle when, for the time being anyway, no government bureaucrat will harass them about which Lear jet they'd like to buy instead?

24

The New Behaviorists

Christine Rosen

We have not yet seen what man can make of man.
—B. F. SKINNER

WHEN BARACK OBAMA won the presidential election in November 2008, observers credited the extraordinary effectiveness of his grassroots organizing with helping him to achieve his historic victory. But Obama had another unacknowledged ally on his side: behavioral science. A team of behavioral scientists, including at least one Nobel laureate, advised the campaign on everything from honing his message to fund-raising techniques to voter turnout tactics.

After the election, Obama appointed several members of this behavioral brain trust to prominent positions in his administration. In areas such as health care, environmental regulation, and the economy, Obama is relying on these experts to launch one of the most ambitious behaviorist-style policy projects in American political history. Drawing on the recent findings of behavioral economics, they hope to encourage us to conserve energy at home by using "smart meters," save better for retirement by automatically enrolling us in the company 401(k) plan, and help us make smarter choices about mortgages and credit cards, among other things.

Recent health-care legislation debated in Congress, for example, would give tax credits to employers who offer their workers financial rewards for losing weight or quitting smoking. As one Indiana state senator told the *Economist*, marveling at the detailed requirements for spending included in the federal economic stimulus package, "They're going to control your behavior with specifications and regulations." If he is successful in his role as behaviorist-in-chief, Obama will usher in an era of social reform akin to the Progressive movement of the early twentieth century. And he will do it by getting us to change the way we behave, little by little, every day.

Pavlov's dog. Skinner's box. Some people have heard of these behavioral scientists and their unlikely muses, but few people know the unusual history of the science of behavior. In the early twentieth century, American psychologist John B. Watson, the founder of behaviorism, described his vision simply: "It is the business of behavioristic psychology to be able to predict and to control human activity." Building on Russian physiologist Ivan Pavlov's pioneering work on classical conditioning in dogs, Watson spent years performing animal studies that demonstrated the powerful effects of reward and punishment on learned behavior. By 1913, when he published his groundbreaking essay, "Psychology As the Behaviorist Sees It," Watson was determined to create a new kind of psychology, one that actively applied to the real world knowledge gleaned from laboratory research. To Watson, the behaviorist was not merely a psychologist; he was a social engineer whose expertise would help design a better world.

Of course, long before the rise of behavioral psychology, people used creative techniques to make themselves behave. Odysseus had himself lashed to his ship's mast so he could not succumb to the temptation of the Sirens' song while sailing past their mythic island. The twelfth-century Jewish philosopher Maimonides advised educators to use frequent positive reinforcement, including food, to encourage their youngest students to focus on their studies: "Study and I will give you nuts, figs, or a piece of sugar." And Victor Hugo allegedly developed the habit of writing in the nude to prevent himself from leaving his desk when he was supposed to be working.

The early behaviorists of the twentieth century added the imprimatur of science to these efforts. Theirs was an enterprise based entirely on the observation of behavior in real time. Rejecting introspective psychology of any sort, they did not try to ferret out people's subconscious motives or repressed memories. It was the immediate environment that must be changed, they argued, not the individual id. In this sense the behaviorist message has always been simple yet empowering: change your environment, and you will change your behavior. Retrain yourself to respond to the right incentives, and you will become a better person. "Behavior has a pattern, like bones," one behavioral scientist told the *New Yorker* in 1947. "Bones grow, and so does behavior."

John B. Watson, the founder of behaviorism, left academic psychology in the 1920s after a scandal involving a liaison with one of his research assistants. He fled to Madison Avenue and eventually became an executive at the J. Walter Thompson advertising agency, using his scientific training and the authority it conferred to transform the field. It was Watson who recalled from his research in the laboratory that rats reached for the most readily available objects, so he advised vendors to place candy and magazines within easy reach of people waiting in the checkout line of stores. Drawing on his research on classical conditioning, he told companies that their advertisements must provoke one of three reactions if they were to make an impression: fear, rage, or love.

In addition to his work as an advertising executive in the 1920s, Watson wrote a best-selling child-rearing manual that applied behaviorist principles to the proper care and rearing of children. Many of these techniques are still in use, such as "time-out," the temporary purgatory to which modern parents banish their misbehaving children. Everyone from Dr. Spock to the legion of crypto-Mary Poppins–style nannies that star in reality television series like *Nanny 911* use time-out to change children's behavior, and they have behaviorism to thank for its creation.

By the mid-twentieth century, Watson's Madison Avenue–style behaviorism had given way to the "radical behaviorism" of Harvard psychologist B. F. Skinner, whose theories and applied behavioral technologies continue to impact therapy, self-help, education, and community design. Skinner was the quintessential popular scientist; his book *Beyond Freedom and Dignity* was on the *New York Times'* best-seller list for twenty-six weeks, and he was featured on the cover of *Time* in 1971.

Like Watson, Skinner insisted that the science of behavior—and particularly the knowledge he had gleaned from his animal experiments in operant conditioning—had everyday applications. Consistent, repetitive punishment and reward administered in a perfectly controlled setting nearly always yielded positive results—results that could be achieved in people as easily it could in the pigeons Skinner trained in his laboratory. An inveterate tinkerer, Skinner created a "baby box," a climate-controlled crib where children could loll around in perfect safety and comfort, freeing their mothers from the burden of constant surveillance. Skinner's youngest daughter spent the first two years of her life in an "air crib," where, Skinner reported in an interview with the *New Yorker* in 1947, she was always "naked and happy."

During the cultural upheaval of the 1960s, a dedicated army of behavioral psychologists applied Skinner's vision of behaviorism to juvenile delinquents, prisoners, preschool children, and "back-ward" mental patients such as schizophrenics. Their techniques quickly spread to mainstream patients, particularly autistic children, many of whom have responded well to a form of early, intense therapy called Applied Behavior Analysis. Skinner's behaviorism had a strong utopian streak; he wrote a novel, *Walden II*, that described a community based on behaviorist principles, which his disciples used as a model for real-world experiments in communal living in Virginia and Mexico that still exist today.

But Skinner's lasting impact was in the arena of self-help. Articles advising readers how to get "Thinner with Skinner" promised weight loss through behaviorism; other popularizers offered self-help manuals for quitting smoking and becoming more assertive. One of the most popular diet books in the 1970s was published by behavioral psychologist Richard Stuart and Barbara Davis. *Slim Chance in a Fat World: Behavioral Control of Obesity*, argued that "the environment rather than the man is the agent of control of human behavior," and placed little emphasis on personal responsibility or willpower to tame one's desire to overeat.

Today, Skinner's legacy can be seen in contemporary "commitment devices" such as the website StickK.com, whose motto, "Put a contract out on yourself!" uses behaviorist principles to let you devise a personalized self-help regimen, complete with built-in punishments (like automatically sending unflattering pictures of your fleshy self to your friends if you fail to lose weight, or donating money to a cause you loathe if you fail to meet your particular personal goal).

More seriously, a new, crusading progressivism is emerging among regulators and legislators eager to use science to justify policies that would encourage individual self-control. Forty states now levy taxes on soda and junk food, and crusaders against obesity are calling for the federal government to regulate soda as strictly as it does tobacco products. Across the country, private companies have enacted wellness initiatives that aren't as anodyne as their names imply: the Cleveland Clinic's Wellness Initiative includes a ban on hiring anyone who smokes, and its director recently told the *New York Times Magazine* that he would like to stop hiring obese people as well.

Who are the new behaviorists, and where are they taking our society?

Like Watson and Skinner, the new behaviorists argue that it is the system, not the individual, that must change. Behavioral economists such as Richard Thaler and Cass Sunstein, authors of the book *Nudge,* champion the benefits of what they call "choice architecture" and advocate a form of "libertarian paternalism" in social policy that values the "nudge" over the traditional coercive shove. Like earlier behaviorists, they place their faith in science (in this case a hybrid of psychology and economics that in recent years has challenged neoclassical economic theory) and the wisdom of a technocratic elite to reshape behavior. But they are especially concerned with the broad negative social effects and costs of irrational, impulsive behavior. As Thaler told National Public Radio recently, "People are economically unsophisticated and often can't resist temptation." The "choice architects" whom he wants to entrust with the design of policy, he argues, are simply deciding "what people would choose if they had the time to think about it."

What behavioral economists and libertarian paternalists want to do is reconcile political theory with the scientific study of human behavior since, they argue, the old categories of political theory no longer apply. Virtue? Behavioral economists view it as unobservable, value-laden, and mushy; you might as well ask if social policy has a soul. Personal responsibility? Impossible in a complicated world governed by complex "systems" and limitless choices. The result is a kind of stimulus-response politics that promises to liberate citizens from having to make complicated choices in exchange for limiting their freedom.

In some cases the changes suggested by choice architects are benign, such as a proposal to arrange food in school cafeterias so that the healthier options look more appealing—and thus are more likely to be eaten. As well, they urge employers to craft retirement savings plans that require employees to opt *out* of saving part of their paychecks rather than opting *in*, in an effort to combat the incredibly powerful force of human inertia.

The new behaviorism also differs from more draconian forms of social engineering in that it poses as nonjudgmental, cloaking its exhortations in the pristine laboratory coat of science rather than caustic moral censure. It views people as mechanical and thus susceptible to some behavioral tinkering, and in this sense it is far less pessimistic or deterministic a view of man than the one offered by genetic science, for example. We're not ignorant; we are merely laboring under assumptions based on "imperfect information." We're not undisciplined losers intent on achieving instant gratification; we have simply adopted too many "time-inconsistent preferences" for our own good.

But if "choice architecture" is an appealing euphemism, it is also misleading, for the new behaviorism isn't interested in protecting people's freedom to choose; on the contrary, its core principle is the idea that only by allowing an expert elite to limit choice can individuals learn to break their bad habits.

Our current anxiety about the future, particularly at a time of acute economic crisis, makes the behaviorists' argument for a more expertly designed world all the more appealing. But coupled with Americans' desire for order and predictability is a long-standing fear of dependence—on government, on experts, on anything that sets itself in opposition to common sense and conventional wisdom. What the behaviorists of the past recognized, and what many who promote behaviorist-inflected policies today assume, is that human beings tend to act the same—not that they are necessarily created equal.

As a result, behaviorists tend to value personal freedom in the abstract while in practice limiting that freedom to ensure that people behave in socially responsible ways. Contemporary behaviorists want to nudge us, but not merely to make us happier, better people. They have specific hopes for the social effects this nudging will achieve, whether those are higher savings rates, thinner Americans, or fewer smokers.

Whether they are called hidden persuaders, behavior modifiers, or choice architects, behaviorists' attempts to control others raise difficult questions about freedom and personal responsibility. As Skinner recognized, "Talking about feelings is safe because nothing important will ever be done about them. . . . Talking about changes in the social environment is dangerous stuff." Who holds the "choice architects" accountable for their designs? Whose judgment is being substituted for that of the individual? What happens to a society when a self-control elite begins regularly shaping decisions for the masses?

The central fear about behaviorists in the twentieth century, most effectively expressed by Vance Packard in his 1957 book *The Hidden Persuaders*, was that the controllers would trample freedom by controlling us (either through subliminal advertising messages or fascist, *Clockwork Orange*–style mind control). And in 1969, cognitive psychologist and president of the American Psychological

Association George A. Miller warned his fellow psychologists of the dangers of investing the power of social control in the hands of a bureaucratic elite.

Today the questions we should ask are more subtle: Should we use science and social policy to protect people from themselves, and if we do, what does it mean to redefine freedom as merely freedom from bad habits and their unhealthy, unproductive effects? This kind of freedom is what Watson had in mind when he wrote in the conclusion of his 1924 book, *Behaviorism*, of our need for a new kind of freedom, a "behavioristic freedom."

This form of freedom is freedom *from* something rather than *for* something. It is freedom from "bad" habits (smoking, overeating, not saving for retirement) and their effects, and thus the "freedom" to be more productive, efficient citizens—citizens who might eventually become habituated to the idea that complicated choices are best left to government to sort out for them. In the terms outlined by Isaiah Berlin, negative liberty (freedom from constraint by others) was more important than positive liberty (freedom to realize your potential). The new behaviorists use the language of positive liberty while imposing constraints that would undermine individual freedom.

Behaviorism is an appealing philosophy for our time because it is deeply hopeful about our ability to change while simultaneously placing blame for our present problems on the accident of our surroundings, not on our own weaknesses. We are not inherently good or bad, self-controlled or weak-willed. We are all simply products of our environment. Our often poor response to the moral hazards of daily life (Should I exercise or eat that pizza? Should I buy that sweater I really can't afford or save my money?) are not really our fault, but the fault of our poorly designed social milieu (Pizza Hut lards their food with salt and fat to make it irresistible! The store offered me instant credit!). As behavioral economist Dan Ariely argues, the "one main lesson" readers should draw from the research in his best-selling book *Predictably Irrational* is that "we are all pawns in a game whose forces we largely fail to comprehend."

Contemporary behaviorists see no need for indoctrination or sub-liminal persuasion to right this wrong. On the contrary, modern behaviorism's goal is to make us feel as if we have embraced healthy behaviors and better choices on our own. Contemporary behavior-ists genuinely believe that people will make the right decisions if they are shown the correct path to take; barring that, they want the government to regulate the unhealthy things (trans fats, easy credit) that make us lose our will in the first place. As one behav-iorist rephrased the enduring question, "Know thyself": "Know thy behaviors, know thy environment, and know the functional rela-tionship between the two."

And yet, which path provides better protection for freedom—the inculcation of individual virtue or the exercise of social control? The new behaviorists are focused on results; they believe man's inherent irrationality can be tamed by scientific solutions, applied by a tech-nocratic elite, to create a better world. But just as individuals can be seized by irrational impulses and succumb to harmful short-term interests, so too can bureaucracies, as history reminds us. As well, there is the risk that we will become so comfortable with the ben-efits of this kind of control (the conveniences and ease our "choice architects" devise) that we will allow what Harvey Mansfield has called "rational control" to trump individual virtue.

At the heart of today's behaviorist approach is a notion at once appealing and hubristic: the idea that we can create social norms simply by applying the findings of social science on a broad scale (as opposed to the more complicated norms that develop organically, over time, and admittedly often imperfectly, in communities that then spread to the culture more broadly). It is not a coincidence that the view of human nature promoted by today's behaviorists—that we are all irrational creatures suffering from imperfect information—suits well a progressive politics that invests its hopes in a technocratic elite that is eager to use policy to shape people's personal choices.

Americans' anxious hopefulness about improving ourselves has proven fertile ground for behaviorist ideas in the past; as the recent emergence of behavioral science suggests, it still does. As the authors of the latest best-selling behavioral economics manifesto, *Super-freakonomics*, reassure us, "People aren't 'good' or 'bad.' People are people, and they respond to incentives. They can nearly always be manipulated—for good or ill—if only you find the right levers."

Viewed from this angle, behaviorism offers a more troubling—at times hopeless—view of human nature. Behaviorists would have us give up on the messy, uncertain work of building character and focus instead on changing the circumstances that encourage bad behavior. The behaviorist enterprise has always been an attempt to change people, and to do so by limiting their freedom to some degree, even if those limits are applied for our own good.

By describing our many behavioral missteps and offering solutions to nudge us in one direction rather than another, the new behaviorists hope to make us happier, healthier, and—most important—more productive. But this well-intentioned effort fails to grapple with a more vexing question: what if the things that make us irrational, weak-willed, and passionate are also what make us deeply, appealingly human?

25

Cyber-Anonymity

Ron Rosenbaum

But [Glenn] Beck is just soooo ugly. eeeewwwww
Posted By: | September 06, 2009 at 05:38 PM

Michelle Obama is more "like" soooooooo ugly!!
Posted By: Toxic Avenger | September 06, 2009 at 05:47 PM
—Anonymous commenter exchange on The Politico Website

These are the bastards trying to choke the breath out
of American debate. These are the perverts gang-raping
the Goddess of Liberty. These are the traitors who claim that
anyone who doesn't think like they do isn't a True American.
—Anonymous comment posted on liberal blog
Daily Kos September 5, 2009

You say Obama seems to think peace will ensue after the Jews
make various concessions in Israel. You see the J Street Jew issue
only as related to Israel. What about the Wall Street Whites?
What about the Business Billionaires like Buffet [sic]. He surrounds
himself with the Jews he wants dead, the whites he wants enslaved,
and the Billionaires whose money he covets. What is it about Black
Liberation Theology and Black Nationalism you don't get? It is
payback time baby, and the nation will die. He HATES us.
—Comment posted on conservative blog, The American Thinker

"MAN IS LEAST himself when he talks in his own person. Give him a
mask and he will tell you truth." So said Oscar Wilde. The problem

with applying this insight to the culture of the Internet is not that the mask reveals the truth, but that the truth revealed by the anonymous "screen name" is a deeply disturbing vision of the face beneath the mask: a face frequently twisted with self-righteous hatred, fear, and paranoia.

Few would disagree that the tone and content of political argument on the Web has become more toxic and divisive in the past decade. By threatening to drive out dissent and alienate ordinary citizens with its vitriolic personal attacks, it is shutting down the free interchange of ideas and arguments that is the hallmark of a democratic polity.

However agitated our debates may have been in the past, something has changed for the worse. The online conversation in particular has become a vicious internecine civil war, noxious and polarizing. And I think I know why: the snake in the garden is the cyber-disinhibition—the loss of restraint, the rhetorical race to the bottom—that is both enabled and encouraged by the use of anonymous screen names.

The original promise of the Web was that it would permit the flowering of a true intellectual democracy. The Web, especially that part of it known as the blogosphere, would give voice to the voiceless, providing a platform and an audience previously monopolized by self-proclaimed elite professionals. The Web would be the triumph of the amateur, of the lionized but seldom-heard-from ordinary citizen. From their unfiltered dialogue an inspiring exchange of ideas would ineluctably arise that would fulfill the Jeffersonian ideal of citizen democracy.

The blogosphere has certainly changed the character of political conversation, but in problematic ways. First, it has put the neighborly conversation that once took place over a picket fence or at the VFW dance on a vast and impersonal stage, before an audience that eggs on the most extreme ranters—those who seemingly have the leisure to spend their entire day haranguing the ether and harassing anyone who disagrees. Second, it provides a mask of anonymity that may have initially been intended to free blog commenters from the threat of exposure, but that now effectively immunizes them not just from exposure but from accountability, responsibility, and shame.

Such anonymity not only enabled and exacerbated the ugliness online. It made the ugliness the point. And it soon became the path by which ordinary cyber-disinhibition has devolved into cyber-derangement.

No one who has a glancing acquaintance with online "commenter culture" would disagree that political conversation has become a fever swamp of juvenile vituperation and personal abuse. Political discourse on the Web has become an ideological gang war wherein howling digital lynch mobs hound and repress the idiosyncratic views that once were the hallmark of democratic conversation—all of them ruled by the prime directive of the Web, namely, that any person who disagrees with you is not just wrong or misinformed but a repulsive and evil subhuman who deserves virtual lynching and slanderous obloquy.

I recently came upon a prime example of this dehumanizing tendency in a contribution to the Huffington Post by a Hollywood actor whose name was not familiar to me, although he seemed to assume both that he was famous and that he had a wickedly funny wit. He could not have embodied the Prime Directive more effectively, as attested by the flock of anonymous commenters who paid slavish tribute to him.

The poster proposed what he believed to be a hilarious experiment: transforming himself into a right-wing opponent of Obama's health-care proposals in order to understand how these alien life forms *think*. In defter hands this kind of imaginative exercise might have imparted some actual understanding and insight into the minds of his political adversaries. What he did instead was to describe in laborious, leaden, ham-handed terms the various tools he would need for this undertaking, which included:

▶ a rubber sledge hammer (for bashing myself in the temples to effect the signature glassy-eyes and hanging lower lip);

▶ an assortment of stick-on Hitler mustaches (to deface pictures of President Obama or to use as replacement beards for my Robert Bork action figure);

▶ penis reducer;

▶ a "God, guns and guts made America free" bib;

▶ a "Bible for Dummies" (big print);

▶ a Chia® Neil Cavuto;

▶ and a winking Sarah Palin endless video loop.

This rhetorical act of dehumanization perfectly embodies the Prime Directive that political opponents must be not just misguided but *ugly*—physically, morally, and mentally. The poster is apparently blind to the possibility that the opposition might consist of humans like himself who happen to have different views on health care. To the contrary, they must be malevolent and evil people who want the uninsured to die agonizing, untreated deaths. In short, he has become the mirror image of what he claims to despise—hanging lip, glassy eyes, and all.

Of course, this is not limited to the left. As a regular reader of right-wing comment threads (human nature is my beat), I came across this gem from a deranged conservative posted a day later:

> There is nothing about Obama that points to anything other than a power-driven narcissist intent on destroying what remains of what America once was and replacing it with a Marxist state in which he serves as president for life. Obama sees himself as Castro with cool or Saddam with nice shades. He is surrounded by a team of fellow travelers from Billy Ayers and J Wright behind the scenes through the Emanuel Brothers, Himmler (Rahm) and Mengele (Zeke) front and center. Now that they have the levers of power, their true intentions are completely unveiled.

This comment illustrates one of the most disturbing aspects of commenter culture: the revival of Nazis and Hitler in the form of ostensible anti-Nazi comments. "Godwin's Law" has ruled the Web from the beginning: all argument will eventually (and often quickly) descend to Hitler analogies.

For readers familiar with comment threads on political blogs and the anonymous abusers that drive them, what I am saying will not necessarily come as a surprise. Others may have merely glanced at some repellant comment threads and wisely chosen not to return, hoping perhaps that what they've seen is not representative.

Alas, it is representative. A veritable fountain of vitriol is gushing onto the screens of the land, and it reads like some kind of twisted self-hatred. One suspects that these poor souls didn't start out as the vicious ranters they've become: they are products of a digital culture that encourages and rewards the most extreme and violent expressions of rage.

And of course it's not just a phenomenon of the right. It was left blog commenters that brought us the idiot "Bushitler" conflation. And such crushing epithets as "Rethuglicans" and "Repugs" and "Repigs." Consider this comment on a fellow commenter in a discussion of journalistic partisanship: "clearly this guy is a crusty old fart who, like the republican party, has one foot in the grave. so long old man . . . thanks for the fantastic fucking mess you and your republican generation are leaving us with. but hey? at least gay people can't get married, right. fucking moron republicans . . ."

Yes, there are less abusive sites, more moderated—though not by the commenters' civility but by the site's gatekeepers. And the further they get from the political realm the more civil they are. But to view the new commenter culture red in tooth and claw on political sites is to see the hideous face behind the mask of the screen name.

Is this the true face of human nature "exposed by the mask" (in the nicely paradoxical phrase of Sir Peter Hall, founder of the Royal Shakespeare Company)? Or is the ugliness facilitated and enabled by the anonymity most posters assume, an ugliness that might not take root at all without the immunity from responsibility, accountability, and above all from shame that the screen name affords?

Why has ordinary cyber-disinhibition—the harshness lent to e-mail messages by the disjuncture of time and space, not being face-to-face with your interlocutor, and the inexpressiveness of cold, pixeled print—become cyber-derangement? Even those who know each other well can suffer from cyber-disinhibition; it is the exacerbation of abusiveness unleashed by the mask of anonymity that hides the link between one's identity and one's obscene online savagery in the slandering of strangers that has led to cyber-derangement. It is the rageaholics' cyber-porn.

There seems to be something very basic about the effect of these degrees of cyber-separation. But you can't blame the Web entirely: there is alas what seems like a kind of disease of human nature operative here. It's as if our worst instincts, like the shingles virus, could lie fallow for decades and then suddenly erupt in angry rashes.

And remember that this kind of rancid verbiage has consequences. The Web has become, for better or worse, a political power center and a shaper of outcomes in primaries and policy disputes. It has raised unknown candidates up and hounded established and powerful figures from office.

I have nothing against the rant as a literary form. I admire Swiftian invective when and if the attacker is both witty and willing to put his name behind his words. And yes, giving anonymity to dissenting speech or opinions that may be punished by repressive authority serves a purpose. But this is not about literary pseudonyms or pamphlets like *The Federalist Papers* written under the threat of tyranny. Besides, are we not more likely to assent to tyranny by hiding like cowards rather than putting our names unashamedly behind our words? Patrick Henry did not defy the king by crying out, "Give me liberty or give me a really sarcastic screen name."

Don't ask me for the alternative, by the way. There may be none. Not any *legal* remedies I'd support as a civil libertarian. But it's not about what's legal or illegal; it's about civilization vs. savagery, and the weapon used to combat it should not be the whip of the law but the lash of shame that such people should be made to feel. That is how civilized societies decide what is normal and acceptable behavior.

The writer Dan Gillmor suggests we look upon any anonymous screen name above an abusive comment as proclaiming, in capital letters, "I AM A CONTEMPTIBLE COWARD."

There is indeed an element of cowardice in hurling insults and then diving behind a rock to hide. Don't such anonymous abusers feel in their heart of hearts that they wouldn't put their real name on their repellant comments out of shame at being revealed as the source of such ugliness?

Apparently not. Allied with their immutable self-righteousness, they are branding themselves as cowards to outside observers, but it hasn't registered internally. They seem not to realize that by demonstrating they lack the nerve to stand behind their words, they make a prima facie case for their terminal timidity. Such an amazing lack of self-awareness I still find hard to explain—unless it is a perverse and addictive pleasure for such emotionally stunted personalities.

Despite the frequent charge that political polarization has driven the Internet to new lows, the change has come from the ground up. It didn't start with politicians and get taken up by the public at large. This is the dark side of a new populism in which the inflamed passions of the citizenry have driven the elites in both politics and the media to kowtow to them. Populism always had a divided soul, combining righteous anger against the unmerited power of big elites and a venomous (sometimes racist and anti-Semitic) conspiracy-minded underside.

As the Web has grown into a key power center during the past decade, all the more reason for concern about the vicious digital mobs who police and purge their own ranks of "unacceptable" views—and threaten to impose an unhealthy uniformity on left and right alike.

The resulting mob mentality was evident to me during the summer of 2009 as I watched footage of the howling, thuggish crowds at the health-care "Town Halls," some of whose members came carrying guns. This was the ugliness of commenter culture spilling off the screens and out into the streets—the dehumanizing hatred for those they disagreed with politically, bred in the mushroom cellars of the blog comment sections. Anyone who questioned the appropriateness, the judgment, or the motives involved in bringing a visible weapon to a "town hall" was berated by commenters with assertions about the right to carry arms—regardless of whether doing so in such circumstances was either stupid or meant to intimidate.

Indeed, there has been a definite rise in references to guns and violence in the right-wing comment sections. One of the more disturbing trends in anonymous commenter culture has been the increasing number of masked commenters who boast of the right of insurrectionary violence, which in some of their rants includes exhortations to shoot people whose health-care plan they don't like. It's a rancor that mirrors the worst excesses of left-wing blog discourse during the Bush years.

Lamentably, the language of murder has become normalized in commenter culture, as commenters step up their escalation of exhibitionist rage. I would not be surprised if the next political assassin turns out to have left a trail of vicious comments once his screen name is revealed. Either that or an unstable "lurker" will be incited to real violence by the verbal violence of commenter culture. There's a world of Travis Bickles out there, and they're not driving cabs. They're reading blogs.

26

Shariah in the West

Stephen Schwartz

ON OCTOBER 28, 2009, Luqman Ameen Abdullah, an African American Muslim, was killed in a shootout with agents of the FBI in Detroit. The dead man was one of twelve individuals sought for firearms violations and conspiracy to engage in theft and fraud. But they were also members of a little-known Islamist network dedicated to the establishment, through violence if necessary, of an enclave on U.S. territory to be governed by Islamic religious law, or Shariah. Their designated candidate to rule this separatist territory was the prominent black nationalist known in the 1960s as H. Rap Brown, and now as Jamil Abdullah Al-Amin, who at the time of the Detroit incident was serving a life term without parole at the U.S. federal prison in Florence, Colorado, for murdering a police officer in Georgia (along with other charges).

The conspiracy to establish Shariah in a secessionist enclave within America never, it seems, became a practical attempt. But fantasies of introducing Shariah in the United States have gained increasing attention as American society has come under assault, both globally and domestically, from radical Muslims. The most widely acknowledged case of Shariah imposition so far known originated at the Minneapolis–St. Paul International Airport and was revealed to the wider public in 2006. There, immigrant Somali Muslim cabdrivers would not take airport arrival passengers carrying alcohol or accompanied by dogs (including guide dogs for blind customers), on the grounds that for them to do so would violate Shariah. The Muslim drivers had begun their boycott on liquor and dogs about ten years previously, and airport customers had complained about the situation. In one incident sixteen drivers successively declined to carry "objectionable" passengers. The Somali cabdrivers applied to the Metropolitan Airports Commission for authorization to refuse service on religious grounds without being sent to the back of the airport taxi line and losing opportunities to make money.

The Metropolitan Airports Commission rejected the petition, but proposed a supposedly moderate compromise: drivers who would not carry alcohol or dogs could have a special light installed on their cabs indicating their enforcement of a ban. The commission produced this "solution" after consultation with the Muslim American Society (MAS), a radical Islamist group that favors introduction of Shariah into the United States. But while the commission imagined it was deliberating and acting fairly, the proposal for special taxis for Muslim drivers had potentially disastrous consequences. A public agency would have, for the first time, established a Shariah law interpretation on public property in the United States.

After deliberating, however, the commission found against the Somali cabbies and denied their request. The old rules continued in place: drivers who refused customers went to the back of the line. But nothing had been done to actively restrain the drivers from their discriminatory actions.

Americans have also recently learned of so-called honor murders committed by Muslims in the United States, and generally believe such crimes, usually carried out against family members, are a Shariah-based practice.

Early in 2009, Muzammil Hassan, forty-four, an immigrant from South Asia, was charged with second-degree murder in the killing and decapitation of his thirty-seven-year-old wife, Aasiya. The couple were prominent in the American Muslim community as proprietors of Bridges TV, a television station near Buffalo, New York, that broadcast Muslim content. Aasiya Hassan had complained to local authorities of domestic violence and had filed for divorce, obtaining a "stay-away" order against her husband. At the time of writing, Muzammil Hassan awaited trial in his wife's death. The crime seemed to many observers to be a so-called honor murder.

On October 20, 2009, an Iraqi immigrant girl, Noor Almaleki, age twenty, was run down and killed by a Jeep allegedly driven by her father, Faleh Hassan Almaleki, forty-eight, in an Arizona suburb. The father fled the United States but was captured in London. Reporters learned that Almaleki had taken his daughter to Iraq on "a family visit" in 2008 and had forced her into an arranged marriage with a man unknown to her. The father's explanation for the homicidal deed of which he stood accused was familiar: his daughter had dishonored his family by becoming "too Western," including working at a fast-food restaurant. At the time of writing, Faleh Almaleki was held in a jail in Phoenix, Arizona, on a suicide watch.

These incidents have been few but disturbing in America. The apparent invasion of Shariah law has been more pronounced in Europe. England has become the main field of confrontation over this issue. Differing polls and surveys have shown that up to 40 percent of British Muslims supposedly want the introduction of Shariah law in the country, while 41 percent opposed it and 19 percent were undecided. These figures, elicited by London's *Sunday Telegraph* in 2006, were not definitive. The potential opposition of 60 percent of British Muslims to introduction of Shariah was left unaddressed.

More important, the *Sunday Telegraph*'s description of Shariah was vague and appeared deliberately alarmist. No distinction was made in the reportage between Shariah as religious law involving the personal matters of Muslim observance, such as diet, form of prayer, charity, male circumcision, and burial—which is how most Muslims in the West view Shariah—and what the newspaper described as follows: "Islamic law is used in large parts of the Middle East, including Iran and Saudi Arabia, and is enforced by religious police. Special courts can hand down harsh punishments which can include stoning and amputation." The British non-Muslim public was left with the strong impression that nearly half of British Muslims sought the introduction of stoning and amputation as punishments in the country, with the threat that such would be applied to non-Muslims.

The scenario was nightmarish and, as a media projection, profoundly irresponsible. Unfortunately, this impression was reinforced by more accurate reporting on Shariah practice in Britain—specifically, on the emergence of informal "Shariah courts," which handle divorces for Muslim women who were married in Pakistan or India. If their marriages were not recorded with the British authorities, they cannot seek a U.K. divorce. These courts often leave wives at the mercy of their husbands on the pretext of reconciliation, but also charge the petitioners for divorce large sums to examine their cases. Proponents of the Islamic divorce system in Britain have called for governmental authority to back up the decisions of these improvised tribunals.

The 2006 *Sunday Telegraph* poll was organized after years of quiet penetration, as well as flamboyant radical agitation, in favor of Shariah-based practices in Britain. Shariah-compliant financial products, which do not invest on the basis of earning interest or in Islamically banned economic sectors involving alcohol, pork, gambling, or other vices, had been offered to British Muslims by British banks and investment houses since the early 1980s. By 1997, British financial institutions had similarly launched Shariah-compliant housing finance.

As the twentieth century ended, radical Shariah rhetoric in the West was exemplified by a British Muslim extremist, Egyptian-born Abu Hamza Al-Masri, who in 1999 justified the murder of Britons kidnapped in Yemen and stated that he organized military training for his followers inside Britain. He titled his organization Supporters of Shariah (SOS). His appearance was notable because of his loss of both hands and an eye, allegedly in Afghanistan, and use of prosthetic hooks at the ends of his arms. Abu Hamza Al-Masri defined terrorism as follows: "If it means killing a few people to stop the killing of more people it is justified." After a series of arrests, his dismissal as a mosque preacher, and other incidents, he was sentenced in 2006 for inciting murder and racial hatred. In 2008, the British authorities ruled that he could be extradited to the United States to face terrorism charges, but he remains in British custody while U.K. courts decide if his imprisonment in Oregon, while on trial, would violate his civil rights.

Al-Masri was a minor figure, notwithstanding his considerable media impact. A more alarming suggestion was voiced in 2008, in a television program, *Divorce Shariah Style*, broadcast by U.K. Channel 4. Sheikh Hassan, the senior judge and secretary of the oldest Islamic law body in Britain, the Shariah Council at Regents Park Mosque in London, said, "We know that if Shariah laws are implemented then you can change this country into a haven of peace. Because once a thief's hand is cut off, nobody is going to steal. If only once an adulterer is stoned, nobody is going to commit this crime at all. There would be no rapist[s] at all. This is why we say that, yes, we want to offer it to the British society. . . . And if they don't accept it, they would need more and more prisons."

Radical Shariah agitation has been less prominent in the Netherlands, Germany, and France. Dutch Muslim agitation against the politician Geert Wilders, who is frankly anti-Islam, has generated small but noisy demonstrations for Shariah to be introduced into Europe. Mohammed Bouyeri, the killer of the Dutch filmmaker Theo Van Gogh in 2004, was reported by Dutch media to have declared that the country's "parliament will be renamed a Sharia court and the chairman's gavel will fall to ratify Islamic [criminal] sentences." Such statements are obviously alarming to secular Europeans. But no Dutch poll has indicated a significant share of local Muslim opinion in favor of Shariah; nor has such a result appeared in Germany.

In France, *Le Monde des Religions*, a special-interest journal published by the leading Parisian daily, completed a poll of French Muslims in 2008 that showed a very different picture from that in Britain. On Shariah, 75 percent of those polled in France were opposed to its imposition: 38 percent said Islamic law does not apply in non-Muslim countries, while 37 percent declared that some elements of Shariah could be applied if they were adapted to French law. Only 17 percent claimed that Shariah should have jurisdiction in all countries, and 8 percent declined to comment.

Still, there is no doubt that Britain, the Netherlands, Germany, and France have experienced atrocious crimes such as so-called honor murders, forced marriage, and, in France, female genital mutilation. These horrific practices, while not specifically based in Shariah, have been vocally supported by fundamentalist clerics as well as by common practice in Saudi Arabia and other Arab countries. In this way, whether or not they are Islamic in essence, they have been assimilated into Islamic culture.

The Shariah debate in Western Europe has been badly complicated by the incompetent intervention of non-Muslim politicians, who, in their desire to appear tolerant, have offered opinions in favor of the introduction of Shariah into their countries. Such individuals have included, most notoriously, Archbishop of Canterbury Rowan Williams, head of the Anglican Communion, who in 2008 called for establishment of some (unspecified) aspects of Shariah alongside existing civil law in the United Kingdom. Williams commented that some form of official recognition for elements of Shariah was "unavoidable." His capitulatory gesture was soon echoed by a similar appeal from Britain's Lord Chief Justice, Baron Phillips of Worth Matravers. A leading Dutch conservative politician, Piet Hein Donner, had already declared, in 2006, that the Netherlands could adopt Shariah as law if two-thirds of its parliament voted to do so.

Late in 2007, a family court judge in Frankfurt caused a sensation when she (unnamed in media according to German practice) ruled that the Qur'an supported the right of husbands to beat their wives. The opinion was delivered in a case brought by a Moroccan woman against her Moroccan husband. The judge held that issuance of a protective order would be sufficient relief for the plaintiff, who withdrew an earlier demand for a divorce. An outcry against the opinion followed, from all German political parties of the right and left. After widespread debate on the case, the judge was threatened with professional sanctions.

In July 2008, another controversy began when German authorities announced that a new marriage law, to take effect at the beginning of 2009, would permit religious weddings to be solemnized without civil registration. But marriages in churches and mosques, if not registered civilly, would exclude the parties from recourse to the courts for divorce, rights of inheritance, and other civil remedies—

and might thus produce complaints by Muslim women before Shariah tribunals, as in Britain.

These problems were underscored late in 2008 when a politician representing the Free Democratic Party, Georg Barfuss, opined that Shariah could be established in his home state of Bavaria, if compatible with the Constitution.

And even in France, where one would expect that strong traditions of secular governance and the acceptance of it by most French Muslims would be a barrier to such developments, the authorities have so far failed to adequately resolve a court decision upholding the alleged Shariah-based right of a Muslim man to repudiate his wife on their wedding night when he perceived she was not a virgin.

In all these instances, from the remarks of Archbishop Williams to the controversy over a bride's virginity in France, non-Muslim public figures seemed motivated by ignorance and a patronizing attitude in "offering" Muslims a Shariah the believers themselves did not necessarily or uniformly desire.

Extreme critics of Islam have analyzed such events—attempts to impose Shariah on non-Muslims, so-called honor murders, and the naïveté of Western politicians in embracing some form of Shariah—as evidence that the West and its legal systems face imminent collapse. Such polemicists predict wholesale Islamization and waves of brutal Shariah penalties, plus more so-called honor crimes, and worse abuse of women, including imposition of body and face coverings. Above all, they argue that *all Muslims everywhere* wish for, or are commanded to work toward, the imposition of Shariah.

Unfortunately, neither the Shariah proponents, nor the fearmongers exercised by its specter, nor the political figures eager to placate Muslim opinion seem to know anything about Shariah and its real content.

To begin with, there is no evidence that any but a small minority of American Muslims favors any form of institutional Shariah in the United States. Unfortunately, the "Wahhabi lobby" of established American Muslim communal organizations, created and financed by Saudi Arabia, is dominated by acolytes of Islamic law, who have articulated their dream of a Shariah-ruled America. But aside from rare incidents such as the Detroit shootout, agitation for Shariah among American Muslims is seldom visible in the community. On the other hand, as in Western Europe, American Shariah fanatics have their friends in high places. Dalia Mogahed, a member of President Barack Obama's Council on Faith-Based and Neighborhood Partnerships, late in 2009 defended Shariah by claiming that her global polling, through the Gallup Organization, showed "the majority of women around the world associate sharia with 'gender justice.'" Presumably, her reference to "the majority of women" (as opposed to Muslim women) was a slip of the tongue. But there is no doubt that in her perspective, Shariah as public law guarantees Muslim women a dignity absent in the West.

Mogahed also commented benevolently regarding unidentified people, including non-Muslims, who believe "that the United States, and Britain, and other countries should be open to the concept of integrating Shariah into law in Muslim-majority societies." She added, "of course, most Muslim-majority societies do have Shariah as a part of their laws already." In reality, most Muslim-majority societies do not currently treat Shariah as a part of common public law, but as a separate corpus applicable only to exclusively religious matters. Shariah-dominated countries like Saudi Arabia, Iran, and Sudan represent exceptions, not the rule.

Most Muslims in the West accept a standard interpretation of Shariah, which has held throughout Islamic history that Muslim migrants to non-Muslim countries must accept the laws and customs of the lands to which they move. Traditional Muslim scholars emphasize that the Prophet Muhammad called on Muslims who leave Islamic territory "to listen to and obey the ruler, as long as one is not ordered to carry out a sin." No non-Muslim government requires Muslims to violate the rules of their religion by, for example, drinking alcohol, and most afford them liberties that are absent in Muslim countries.

Further, most Muslims living in the West, as in the French example, accept that Islamic law cannot be exported to countries without a Muslim majority. This is also a rule firmly based in Shariah. Most Muslims living in the West only see certain strictly personal matters, previously mentioned here, as subject to Shariah: diet, the form of prayer, payment of obligatory charity, male circumcision, and burial. These matters do not require the involvement of public institutions, except for coroners' offices at death. This traditional and moderate definition of Shariah—as a set of religious observances rather than public or criminal law—has been established in the Muslim world for centuries. But most American Muslims know little about Shariah. For example, the Minneapolis Somali cabdrivers were seemingly unaware that Islam does not bar non-Muslims from consuming alcohol, or Muslims from transporting such people, and that only certain rigid interpretations express disfavor of dogs as unclean.

In short, the call for introduction of Shariah in non-Muslim countries is a new and radical concept, without support in Islamic legal traditions. Realizing that any discussion of a Shariah regime in Western countries is not only deeply disturbing to Western non-Muslims but is also rejected by the great majority of Western Muslims, a small group of powerful fundamentalists, associated with the Egyptian theologian Yusuf Al-Qaradawi and the Swiss Muslim author Tariq Ramadan, have developed a new concept, "Shariah for Muslim minorities living in the West," or "parallel Shariah." Their intention is to erect a separate legal system in the Western countries that would have jurisdiction over Muslims, backed by the authority of the non-Muslim state. This group of "parallel Shariah" promoters admits that their aim is not, as it might seem, the protection of Muslims from discrimination, but rather the religious transformation of Western society through an Islamist version of the "long march through the institutions" adopted by the leftist radicals of the 1960s and 1970s.

But they, too, have little support among ordinary Western Muslims, and the concept has only caught on among Islamic fundamentalists. In the United States, Saudi-oriented Wahhabi clerics and their academic sympathizers generally observe a silence on the topic, and elsewhere, established Muslim leaders—in Britain, the Netherlands,

Germany, and France—support loyalty to local institutions as practiced by most of their congregants. Yet "parallel Shariah" appeals to
Western sensibilities regarding unfair treatment of Muslims, while
exploiting the general ignorance of Shariah among Western Muslims
themselves.

Some supporters of Shariah in Canada and the United Kingdom
have called for introduction of "Islamic mediation services" in
which Shariah decisions would be rendered through conciliation by
clerics, with enforcement by the non-Muslim authorities. But even
if such a legal paradigm were based on exclusively voluntary participation, the probability remains that such proceedings, in the U.K.
and Canadian Muslim communities today, would be governed by
fundamentalists.

What, then, is the threat of Shariah to Western liberty, and what
should be done about it? The problem is not one of a sudden radical Muslim takeover of the West. Rather, it resides with a small,
unpopular, but powerful Saudi-financed layer of top Muslim leaders
who seek to undermine Western canons of legal equality by introducing "parallel Shariah." While it may seem innocuous to some,
such a conception is pernicious in seeking to unduly increase the
influence in Western institutions of a single religion, Islam, while
driving Western Muslims apart from their non-Muslim neighbors.
This is a radical and seditious notion even if it does not call for a
violent assault on Western society.

Relations between religious communities and government authorities in the United States are based on a principle known as "reasonable accommodation." Under reasonable accommodation, for
example, employers are required to allow their workers to observe
religious holidays if they do not conflict with business needs.

"Parallel Shariah" exemplifies a demand for *unreasonable* accommodation of Islam in non-Muslim countries. Muslims living in the
West should be reminded, whether by their authentically moderate
leaders (who have played such a role in France), or by media—or, if
necessary, by Western governments—that their own religion calls
on them to accept Western law, to make no attempts to subvert it,

and to limit Shariah to purely religious matters. All other "Islamic" notions about Shariah in the West are tropes intended to radicalize Western Muslims. "Parallel Shariah" and "Islamic mediation" may not threaten the immediate freedoms of non-Muslims, but they are liable to endanger the liberties of Muslims themselves. Ultimately, any scheme to divide or dilute the universal protections of Western law will undermine the liberty of all.

27

Participatory Culture and the Assault on Democracy

Lee Siegel

UNTRAMMELED INDIVIDUALITY in popular culture used to be the stuff of vicarious daydreams. Today it is a real expectation. It's as if the conflict of rights vs. entitlements in the social realm had now been decided, in favor of the latter, in the realm of popular art and diversion.

As a result of that demand, we are now witnessing for the first time in history the advent of a true mass culture. Throughout the 1950s, 1960s, and 1970s, there was culture *for* the masses. It was turned out by the giant record companies, and by the book publishing companies, and by mass-circulation magazines like *Life, Look, Time,* and *Newsweek.* There were the Big Three television networks, and the handful of Hollywood studios and, compared with now, a limited number of radio stations, all commercial. But culture for the masses is not the same thing as culture *by* the masses.

No television viewer in 1957 could respond to *The Honeymooners* with a mash-up of the series—a re-editing—in which the viewer himself appears in a scene with Ralph Kramden. No one in 1969 could push a button, click a mouse, and become a "viral personality" recognized around the world. No one until about ten years ago could wake up in the morning, drag himself over to his computer before even getting dressed, and reach more people in his bathrobe with his private thoughts than William Faulkner ever did, even at the height of his renown. For the first time in history, we are all producers as well as consumers. This is mass culture.

It is no longer sufficient to live vicariously through a character in a film or television drama, or through the journey of a melody to which we surrender ourselves, or by immersing ourselves in the third-person experience of a figure in a novel. Now we want *access*. We demand *transparency*, not just in the political realm, but in culture, too—transparency being a powerful mode of access. Why accept Tolstoy's creation of Anna Karenina? The author holds the key to all her secrets and reveals them or not, as he chooses. Instead, the characters on a "reality" TV program helplessly reveal themselves seemingly by the pressure of our gaze—and often by our votes on their fate.

This is what I call participatory culture, which is composed of consumers *and* producers. From reality TV to blogs to the "most popular" lists that allow consumers to determine the producer's aesthetic choices, we live in an interactive—that is, participatory—world.

It was always certain musical occasions that made that type of participation possible, from ancient Dionysian rituals to the masque plays of Elizabethan times to, in our own era—if you will pardon an even greater leap—swing to Woodstock to rap. Now it's the more reflective arts, too. Consider the shift from third-person to first-person in contemporary fiction, and the rise of the memoir, which is of course written in the first person. It is much easier to inhabit an intimate, immediate "I" than a distant "he" or "she." First-person storytelling is as close to "participatory" as narrative gets, although websites exist now where you can rewrite famous novels. (You can save Madame Bovary and marry her, too. Good luck.) Indeed, the participatory turn accounts for the way rhythm has overtaken melody in popular music: it's easier to assimilate rhythm's sameness to your fantasies than to step out of yourself and follow melody's different changes. Rhythm is music's first person, as the close-up is film's. The same participatory dynamic rules video games, mash-ups, interactive websites, karaoke, and movieoke. Three-dimensional films such as James Cameron's *Avatar* make the audience feel that they are actually moving through the film's environment. The technology is said to be the next wave in filmmaking.

Participatory culture is an arena in which the hallowed American concept of "the people" determines, as never before, who shall create the artifacts of their diversion. The people also decide, as never before, what those artifacts shall be. I still wait for the *New Yorker* cartoon showing a group of headstones in a cemetery with the loving inscription "Most Emailed" on one of them. "Most popular" lists now guide the news judgment of newspaper and magazine editors. The cult of popularity has normalized the commodification of friends on social-networking sites like Facebook. It has made an indiscriminate hunger for popularity the only prerequisite for popularity—a willingness to use whatever is the most effective means of conformity to gravitate toward or attract the largest share of one type of market or another.

This is a sea change in the way we divert ourselves. To be sure, popular culture has always been almost synonymous with ratings: the top-ten hits, the best-seller list, the Nielsens, box-office reports. But the hallmark of great popular art used to be the way a performer put an original twist on a standard genre or formula. The last thing a budding young songwriter wished to do in 1964 was write an imitation of "I Want to Hold Your Hand." Now, if you put a talking cat on YouTube, within days the Web will bloom with thousands of talking geese, chickens, and goats. And they will all be saying the same thing. It used to be that performers strove to create excellence and originality within a popular style, in order to become popular. They competed against each other's work. In today's culture, you strive only to be popular—in order to become popular. You compete against other, measurable degrees of popularity. You strive to come as close to reproducing a successful "original" style as possible. You must sound more like everyone else than anyone else is able to sound like everyone else.

To put it another way, popular culture used to draw people to what they like. Popularity culture draws people to what everyone else likes. From "I love that thing he does!" to "Look at all those page views!" in just a few years.

This is the dynamic that first drove, for example, Wikipedia, the online encyclopedia that is a collaborative enterprise open to anyone who wishes to participate in it. During the early years of the project's existence, anybody could contribute to Wikipedia's entries. You didn't have to be a historian to add to the entry on Winston Churchill; you simply had to be interested in adding to the entry on Winston Churchill. Behind the anti-elitist rationale for such a magnitude of openness was a more fundamental principle: the more people who were allowed to participate in Wikipedia, the more people who would read Wikipedia. The result was an almost total chaos of misinformation, bitter squabbles among contributors, and litigation threatened by subjects who claimed that they were libeled by inaccurate facts. The "people's encyclopedia" is still a collaborative enterprise, but one that is monitored much more closely by an inner circle of editors.

The manipulation of participation in order to create popularity—with the result being a radical lowering of standards—is now rife throughout the culture. On CNN, you encounter I-reporters, non-journalists who are given a few precious minutes of airtime to report the news with, predictably, a colloquial, subjective slant. The dominant model for our culture and our politics now seems to be *American Idol*, with its invitation to viewers either to try to get on the show itself, or to use their votes to make or unmake the next pop culture superstar. Our current president, said to be the most poll-conscious politician ever to lead the country, seems to construct his very speeches along the participatory/popularity axis, as he presents irreconcilable viewpoints in order, not just to appeal to as many people as possible, but to give the illusion of national participation in his decisions. No wonder two reality-TV aspirants recently crashed a state dinner at the White House claiming they had been invited. In fact, they had not been invited, but they could be forgiven for thinking they had.

The most baleful potential of the new participatory and popularity culture is, on the one hand, to create people who are cut off from their fellow citizens, floating in a disconnected space where their imperial conception of self bears no relation to who they really are.

They do not respond to anything that either does not reflect their own experience, or that does not allow them to "produce" it, as well as to consume it. Behind this "access" and "transparency" thrives a low tolerance for facts that obstruct the ego, and a fanatical thirst to nourish one's *amour-propre* on public figures' slightest infractions. As in the enjoyment of reality television, public humiliation is becoming a national pastime for this new, disconnected, imperial self.

It is disconcerting that the people who watch *Survivor* and its many offshoots, as well as cable television's hourly deconstruction of public figures, do not realize that they are relishing a general contempt for individuality and for achievement that could easily boomerang back against themselves. The spectacle of such lack of self-awareness recalls Gershom Scholem's horror as he sat in a middle-class German audience in 1932 watching a performance of Bertolt Brecht and Kurt Weill's *Threepenny Opera*, a play that is filled with loathing for the middle class. "I was astonished," Scholem wrote, "when I saw that a middle-class audience that had lost all sense of its own situation was here cheering a play in which it was gibed and spat at with a vengeance."

Yet these products of our new participatory and popularity culture are also so uncertain of their relation to other people that they are extra vulnerable to approval, and susceptible to the most effective conformist strategy for gaining approval. Their egos are both larger than their environment and entirely submerged in it. *You must sound more like everyone else than anyone else is able to sound like everyone else.* Having created the illusion of a transparent, accessible, and manipulable world, the imperial self—like Chaplin confidently placing his foot where in fact there is no ground—disappears into it.

Scholem's terror as he sat in that audience was experienced during the post-WWII period by a generation of mostly Jewish émigrés when they encountered American popular culture. It is strange to read them now. Their sometimes absurdly paranoiac and hysterical reactions to, for example, American jazz—Theodor Adorno dismissed it as "the garbage fragments of a bourgeois culture"—were irrelevant at the time. They mistook for the slouching beast of a tyranny coming from within culture what was really the twilight of an incredibly rich and vital period in the American popular arts. In the introduction to the influential 1957 anthology *Mass Culture: The Popular Arts in America*, a volume heavily influenced by Frankfurt School critical theorists like Adorno, the sociologist Bernard Rosenberg summed up the intellectual response to mass culture after the war: "at its worst, mass culture threatens not merely to cretinize our taste, but to brutalize our senses while paving the way to totalitarianism." Rosenberg and others believed that this slow descent into tyranny was accomplished by robbing people of the right to think for themselves. Mass media imposed opinions and judgments on the individual, thus submerging the individual in the mob. As Herbert Marcuse wrote in his famous essay "Repressive Tolerance," "Under the rule of monopolistic media—themselves the mere instruments of economic and political power—a mentality is created for which right and wrong, true and false are predefined wherever they affect the vital interests of the society."

The "repressive tolerance" was the way commercial society absorbed the most autonomous and subversive social critique. Foucault meant much the same thing when, some twenty years later, he described modern society's tendency to control human behavior by publicly defining it through ever-evolving "freedoms," which were really methods of social construction and control. For many postwar thinkers, culture was the realm where the purveyance of thoughtless pleasure by corporate conglomerates was a crushing illusion.

The nightmare guiding this fear was J. L. Talmon's notion of "totalitarian democracy," in which citizens vote for elected representatives but do not participate in the state's most crucial decisions. The sham of commercial culture and representative democracy comprised one large deceit. For Adorno, Marcuse, Foucault, Talmon, and others, the answer to brutish, dehumanizing culture and politics was the dismantling of "the rule of monopolistic media" and the establishment of participatory culture, in which, presumably, access and transparency would be the order of the day.

The cunning of history indeed. In the postwar period, you could turn off the television, the radio, or the record player; decide not to go to a movie; put down a potboiler and pick up a literary novel. It turned out that the "monopolistic media" left a great deal of room for the cultivation of individual taste and freedom. Not Johnny Mercer or Elvis or the Beatles led the way to Auschwitz or Kolyma. Their original and idiosyncratic styles grew in the vast spaces in and around culture for the masses, like wildflowers in the shade of a public garden.

But with today's advent of participatory and popularity culture, culture never ends. The ever-present and almighty screen dominates your world. Information streams at you without end from every corner of society. Cable news whips people up into one politicized group or another. The "most popular" lists determine what you read—and a story about Britney Spears will be a lot more popular than a story about social injustice. One of the concerns that plagued *Mass Culture*'s editors and contributors was the worry over what modern people would do with their growing leisure time. A half century later, we are all caught up in the "prosuming"—Alvin Toffler's term for the new hybrid person who is both a producer and a consumer—interactive universe: the blogger or website owner, the Facebook person advertising his qualities, the eBay seller, the Match.com romantic aspirant, and so on.

For over a hundred years, high culture has been merging with popular culture. But now all *experience* is available as culture, which means that there are no criteria for judging these disjointed echoes of each other except their popularity. And what drives popularity is a routine's success in merging with the mass, in extending the most generic and derivative appeal. It also means that there is no escape from culture into a personal space.

For under the guise of increasingly democratic culture, commerce permeates every aspect of existence. There was always one chief difference between popular or high culture on the one hand, and commercial culture on the other. The former, even at their crassest and most profit-driven, were meant to be enjoyed disinterestedly. You were in the experience for the pleasure that comes either from high art's absorption of your attention or from popular art's gifts of diversion. In both cases, you were briefly sprung from the daily pressures of self-interest. You laid yourself and your ego aside, in one degree or another. In this more or less contemplative self-surrender, you found your true identity, your true self. For a moment, you were not driven by your ego, which is to a great degree driven by conventional social appetites.

Commercial culture, on the other hand, is all about the gratification of your self-interest, and it involves the total engagement of your ego. Assertiveness, initiative, full participation in every aspect of "the deal" that has a bearing on your self-interest—those qualities are what carry the day for a buyer or seller, not passive enjoyment of the situation unfolding before you. At the heart of a successful work of art, high or low, lies something wholly fresh and other, some type of original experience that draws out your own native originality as a person. At the heart of a transaction, however, is everday, socially constructed you. That is to say, at the heart of a successful transaction is the satisfaction of your self-interest. When culture becomes thoroughly commercialized in this way, we ourselves, not the media, are—to quote Marcuse again—"the mere instruments of economic and political power." No spaces for the cultivation of our individuality exist between us and the media monopolies or the sham elected representatives.

The essential liberal position is based on an idea—the idea of ever-expanding individual rights. It just so happens that the fantasy of a majestically sovereign and autonomous self is the heart and soul of American popular culture, a culture that is quintessentially liberal. The result is that the most serious threat to freedom in America today is the threat posed to democracy by the excesses of that culture. As our ever-expanding selves participate more in every cultural activity, the disinterestedness of play and of aesthetic pleasure gives way to crude self-assertion. And as everyone asserts their entitlement to participation, popularity replaces originality as a standard of excellence—you end up with what you might call an egalitarian antidemocracy, in which interactive crowds scorn and marginalize the democratic equalizer of true talent. That old bugbear of postwar sociology—the mob-self—is now a reality. In a participatory/popularity culture, the freedom to think and act for ourselves becomes harder and harder to achieve. The tyrannical majority so feared by Adorno, Foucault, Talmon, and others is all around us, and within us.

28

The U.N. Women's Treaty as a Threat to Freedom

Christina Hoff Sommers

THE CONVENTION on the Elimination of All Forms of Discrimination against Women (CEDAW—pronounced *see-daw*) was drafted by a United Nation's committee in the late 1970s, adopted by the U.N. General Assembly, and submitted to its member states in 1979. Nearly every nation on earth has long since ratified what has come to be known as "the Women's Treaty." The only holdouts are three Islamic states (Iran, Sudan, and Somalia), a few Pacific islands, the Vatican . . . and the United States.

America's failure to ratify CEDAW has not been for lack of high-level political support. President Jimmy Carter submitted it to the Senate for ratification in 1980. Many powerful legislators of both parties have favored it. U.S. adoption is supported not only by women's groups such as the National Organization for Women but also by broad-based groups, including Washington's heaviest hitters. Even the Audubon Society has endorsed CEDAW.

Some ascribe the U.S.'s failure to ratify the treaty to one man— the late Sen. Jesse Helms of North Carolina, who waged an indefatigable campaign against CEDAW. To Helms, CEDAW was "a terrible treaty negotiated by radical feminists with the intent of enshrining their radical anti-family agenda into international law." As chairman of the Senate Foreign Relations Committee (1995–2001), he refused even to hold hearings on the matter. Helms vowed that the Women's Treaty "will never see the light of day on my watch."

Helms's watch is now long over and CEDAW supporters can see daylight. President Obama and Vice President Biden are strong supporters of CEDAW. So are senators John Kerry, now chairman of the Foreign Relations Committee, and Barbara Boxer, chairwoman of the subcommittee with jurisdiction over CEDAW. Secretary of State Hillary Clinton is an enthusiast, as is Harold Koh, former dean of the Yale Law School, now the State Department's chief legal advisor. An influential advocate of "transnational jurisprudence," Koh invokes the sad irony that "more than half a century after Eleanor Roosevelt pioneered the drafting of the Universal Declaration of Human Rights, her country has not ratified . . . CEDAW." On May 29, 2009, the State Department notified the Senate that ratification of CEDAW is a priority of the administration.

The prospect that the Senate will at long last give serious consideration to CEDAW has energized dozens of activist groups and summoned forth an impressive volume of reports, fact sheets, petitions, position papers, and talking points praising the treaty's merits. There is even a pro-CEDAW rap song. U.S. ratification of CEDAW seems to be inevitable.

Except that it is not. For many years, Senator Helms's adamant opposition to CEDAW made support an easy gesture for many senators who may have shared his qualms but not his temerity. Now that ratification is a live prospect, the views of ordinary citizens, not just interest groups, will begin to be heard. The ratification debates will involve many heated claims and abstruse legal issues, but two overarching questions will decide the matter: First, will ratification materially improve the well-being of women throughout the world? Second, what will be its effects, for better or worse, on America itself?

Vice President Biden and Senator Boxer are emphatic on the question of how CEDAW would affect American laws and customs—*not at all.* In 2002 (when Senator Biden chaired the Foreign Relations Committee) the two made a simple and stirring case for the treaty in a *San Francisco Chronicle* op-ed. They reminded readers of honor killings in Pakistan, bride burnings in India, and female genital mutilation in sub-Saharan Africa. By signing the treaty, they said, the United

States would demonstrate its commitment to helping women secure their basic rights and increase our leverage with countries that are notoriously oppressive to women. And, contrary to fears of critics, CEDAW would have no effect on American law.

Koh made the same argument in a 2002 article in the *Case Western Reserve Journal of International Law*. He invoked recent atrocities against women in Afghanistan, Bosnia, and Haiti and pointed to many ways CEDAW has been used in countries like Nepal, Tanzania, and Sri Lanka to protect women from the predations of domestic violence and sex trafficking. He also emphasized CEDAW's negligible domestic impact: "The treaty provisions are entirely consistent with the letter and spirit of the United States Constitution and laws, both state and federal."

CEDAW opponents see the treaty's foreign and domestic consequences in exactly opposite terms. American ratification would do little to help women in oppressive nations and societies, they say. Signatories like Saudi Arabia, Burma, and North Korea have done almost nothing to reform their laws, policies, and traditional practices—even when admonished by the U.N.'s CEDAW compliance committee ("the Committee" to insiders). By contrast, the United States takes treaty obligations seriously: if we ratified CEDAW we would be morally committed to abide by its rules. But many of those rules are antithetical to American values, and any good-faith effort to incorporate them into American law would conflict with our traditions of individual freedom.

Amnesty International (along with other human rights groups) insists that these critics are wrong to suggest that CEDAW would conflict with American laws or traditions. On the contrary, says its "fact sheet," the treaty would not be "self-executing"—once ratified, it would not become the law of the land until our legislators took action to make it law. Furthermore, Amnesty explains, the United States could ratify it subject to caveats.

Amnesty is correct that a nation can ratify a treaty such as CEDAW with caveats—called "reservations, understandings, and declarations" ("RUDs"). But legal experts disagree about the power of RUDs to insulate the United States from provisions of a treaty it has committed itself to honor. CEDAW itself states, "A reservation incompatible with the object and purpose of the present Convention shall not be permitted" (Article 28-2). And as the National Organization for Women (somewhat indiscreetly) reported on its website on August 31, 2009, "Representatives from groups who have advocated for ratification over the years, suggest that RUDs have little meaning and could potentially be removed from the treaty at some point."

Amnesty is right to say that CEDAW is not self-executing and that the CEDAW Committee has no enforcement authority of its own. But the Committee is emphatic that CEDAW is obligatory, not hortatory: "Countries that have ratified or acceded to the Convention are legally bound to put its provisions into practice." Moreover, many legislators—and judges—will feel obligated to bring our laws in line with a treaty we have agreed to honor.

But according to Biden, Boxer, Koh, and others, American laws are already in full or nearly full compliance with the Women's Treaty. If so, the treaty would be of marginal domestic consequence. This, however, brings us to the most striking feature of the CEDAW debates: the treaty's most engaged and knowledgeable proponents—activist women's groups—*disagree* with the for-export-only argument emphasized by the public officials who are championing its ratification. Instead, they emphatically agree with conservative critics that CEDAW could be used to transform American laws and practices.

The Feminist Majority Foundation has released a video explaining how American women can use CEDAW to effect a "sea change" in our laws. NOW agrees. CEDAW is an opportunity for American women to secure rights the U.S. Constitution has not delivered. As Janet Benshoof, president of the Global Justice Center, recently explained, "If CEDAW were fully implemented in the United States it would revolutionize our rights." Referring to the treaty, she said, "American women need legal tools to fight patriarchy."

Politicians and human rights groups appear to be downplaying the domestic implications in order to get the necessary sixty seven votes for passage. What is certain is that, once CEDAW is ratified, the feminist groups and lawyers who have forthrightly declared their ambitions would no longer be confined to law journals and feminist websites. They would be the new "mainstream." And they would have new allies; U.N. officials and international NGOs would join them in cultivating American pastures under the legal and moral authority of the Women's Treaty. To see what would be in store, we must turn to the treaty's own text and intellectual provenance.

In the early 1970s, the U.N. General Assembly declared 1975 to be "International Women's Year" and authorized the first World Conference on Women. Thousands converged on Mexico City for both the official U.N. conference and a parallel conference held a few miles away called the Tribune. The U.N. conference was formal, orderly, and decorous. The Tribune, by contrast, was a raucous affair, attracting some four thousand feminist activists, writers, and intellectuals. The fifteen hundred American participants included such luminaries as Betty Friedan, Gloria Steinem, Angela Davis, and Bella Abzug.

Foreign Affairs gave a detailed account of some of the many quarrels that broke out between Western feminists and women's activists from the developing world. The Westerners held the view that "all women are subject to colonization," and in their speeches spoke of themselves as members of an inferior "caste." The Third World women were taken aback by facile comparisons between the sometimes uncomfortable circumstances of privileged middle-class Americans and those of the impoverished, often essentially enslaved women in their own countries. And they were alarmed by the bitter gender politics.

When members of the official U.S. delegation from the U.N. conference came across town to visit the Tribune, the male delegates were harangued, shouted down, and driven out. "The Third World women were outraged," said *Foreign Affairs*. The women from the developing countries accused the Westerners of "denigrating woman's maternal role" and weakening marriage. Soon women from the

Soviet Union joined the fray and made it clear that they did not share the Western feminist goal of eliminating gender roles.

Disputes over femininity, family, and motherhood were nothing new to the women's movement. Since its beginning in the early eighteenth century, reformers have held radically different views on gender roles. "Egalitarian feminists" stressed the essential sameness of the sexes and sought to liberate women from conventional social roles. By contrast, "social feminists" were not opposed to gender distinctions. Indeed they embraced them, looking for ways to give wives and mothers greater power, respect, and influence in the public sphere as well as more protection from abuse and exploitation in their domestic roles.

Social feminism has always enjoyed a distinct advantage over its more radical sister: great majorities of women like it. It clearly had a following among some of the non-Western and Soviet women at the Mexico women's conference in 1975. And an updated version of it informs the lives of most American women today. They want the same rights and opportunities as men—but few have the same life priorities as men.

Postwar America certainly needed a feminist correction. In the fifties and early sixties, women were locked out of most fields and allotted second-class status in courts, in education, and in the workplace. So-called Second Wave feminists like Friedan, Abzug, and Steinem urged American women to live "not at the mercy of the world, but as builder and designer of that world." And women listened. By the 1980s, American women were generally enjoying freedoms and opportunities far beyond those of any women in history.

But the Second Wave feminists suffered a serious setback. After scoring a series of landmark legal victories in the 1960s and early 1970s, they failed to pass the Equal Rights Amendment. In 1975, the ERA seemed to be on a fast track to ratification. But as political scientist Jane Mansbridge explains in her meticulous study, *Why We Lost the ERA*, Americans became disenchanted when they began to appreciate the radical worldview of its feminist sponsors.

Egalitarian feminists who dream of a fully androgynous society are to be found today in university women's studies programs, law schools, and the network of activist organizations that sprang into being in those heady days. For them, the fact that so many seemingly free and educated women continue to aspire to conventional female roles is evidence that women are still captive to a repressive patriarchal system.

The egalitarians are small in number but they are not without influence. Journalists and legislators listen to them, and if someone in academia commits the solecism of suggesting the possibility of innate sex differences, they strike with fury: former Harvard President Larry Summers is only their most famous victim. But the defeat of the ERA reduced them to guerrillas in the intellectual hills. What they now see in CEDAW is the opportunity to return to revolutionary leadership on the broad political plains. It is not for nothing that the Women's Treaty is sometimes called a "global ERA."

The treaty requires signatory countries to remove all barriers that prevent women from achieving full equality in all spheres of life—law, politics, education, employment, marriage, and "family planning." It defines discrimination against women to be "any distinction, exclusion or restriction made on the basis of sex" (Article 1). Some of its more specific provisions are highly laudable, such as its requirement that signatories "suppress all forms of traffic in women and exploitation of prostitution" (Article 6). Others are, from an American standpoint, unexceptionable, such as the requirement that signatories "accord to women equality with men before the law" (Article 15-1). *But CEDAW's central provision, Article 5(a), is pure 1970s egalitarian feminism.* This provision, celebrated by feminist legal scholars for its radicalism and sheer audacity, is the key to understanding what the Women's Treaty wants:

> States Parties shall take all appropriate measures: (a) To modify the social and cultural patterns of conduct of men and women, with a view to achieving the elimination of prejudices and customary and all other practices which are based on the idea of the inferiority or the superiority

of either of the sexes *or on stereotyped roles for men and women* (author's emphasis). (Article 5[a])

Throughout the treaty, the drafters show a determination to eradicate gender stereotypes, especially those that associate women with caregiving and motherhood. The treaty instructs states "to ensure that family education includes a proper understanding of maternity as a social function and the recognition of the common responsibility of men and women in the upbringing and development of their children" (Article 5[b]). It calls for "elimination of any stereotyped concept of the roles of men and women at all levels and in all forms of education . . . in particular, by the revision of textbooks and school programmes" (Article 10[c]). States are advised to provide paid maternity leave as well as a network of child-care facilities. And the battle against stereotypes requires special efforts to guarantee equal results in the workplace and in government. "Temporary special measures aimed at accelerating de facto equality between men and women shall not be considered discrimination" (Article 4-1). Signatory governments are also required to ensure women's "right to equal remuneration . . . in respect of work of equal value" (Article 11-1[d]) (which means "comparable worth" policies according to the CEDAW Committee).

If the United States were to ratify CEDAW, we would be subject to an initial evaluation of our compliance with its provisions, followed by regular four-year progress reviews by the CEDAW Committee, which consists of twenty-three experts of "high moral standing and competence in the field covered by the Convention." They are elected by signatory nations including Cuba, Burma, and Nigeria where elementary women's rights are routinely violated. Countries under review submit detailed reports outlining their progress toward fulfilling the treaty's requirements. Their representatives then meet with the Committee, where they are questioned, challenged, sometimes rebuked, and provided with official recommendations for improvement.

Today any country, no matter how free and democratic, is out of compliance with the treaty as long as significant gender roles are still discernible in its institutions. If, for example, more women than men are taking care of children, the Committee recommends ways to turn things around, usually with government-imposed quotas and "awareness raising" campaigns. The U.N. publishes detailed accounts of exchanges between the Committee and countries under review. It is hard to read them and not conclude that the United States would be in for a rough time.

Consider what happened when Iceland went up for scrutiny in July 2008. Iceland is a very small country but it has one of the most extensive gender-equity bureaucracies in the world. As Hanna Gunnsteinsdottir, head of Iceland's Department of Equality and Labor, tried to explain to the CEDAW Committee, her country has equity ministers, equity councils, equity advisors, and a Complaints Committee on Gender Equality whose rulings are binding. Every other year, a state-mandated "National Symposium on Gender Equity" educates citizens about sex-role stereotyping. More than 80 percent of Icelandic women are in the labor force, and parents enjoy paid maternity and paternity leave, including one month of pre-birth leave. Its current prime minister is the first openly lesbian head of government. Iceland would appear to be a model of egalitarianism. But it falls short.

The Committee praised the island nation for its "strides" toward gender parity. But Hanna Beate Schopp-Schilling, an expert from Germany, was concerned that for all of the government's gender and equity committees, the Parliament itself had not formed a committee on gender equity. The expert from Algeria wanted to know why so few women were full professors at the University of Iceland. Magalys Arocha Dominguez, a gender authority from Cuba, was unhappy to find that many Icelandic women held part-time jobs and spent much more time than men taking care of children. She was also displeased by survey findings that Iceland's women were allowing family commitments to shape their career choices. "What government measures have been put in place to change these patterns of behavior?"

CEDAW proponents such as Vice President Biden, Senator Boxer and Harold Koh praise its work with women in the developing world; in practice, the Committee devotes disproportionate energies to monitoring developed democracies. It recently advised Spain to organize a national "awareness raising campaign against gender roles in the family." Finland was urged "to promote equal sharing of domestic and family tasks between women and men." Slovakia's instructions were to "fully sensitize men to their equal participation in family tasks and responsibilities." Liechtenstein was closely questioned about a "Father's Day project" and reminded of the need to "dismantle gender stereotypes."

Much is uncertain about CEDAW, but this we know. If we ratify the treaty, there will be a three-ring circus each time the United States comes up for review. American laws, customs, and private behavior will be evaluated by twenty-three U.N. gender ministers to see if they are compliant with a feminist philosophy that is thirty years out of date.

The Committee will pounce on all facets of American life that do not evince statistical parity between the sexes. That many American mothers stay home with children or work part-time will be at the top of their list of "discriminatory practices." Committee members like Cuba's Magalys Arocha Dominguez will want to know what our government has done to change our patterns of behavior. The American delegation will then enter a "consultative dialogue" with the Committee to develop appropriate remedies.

Although the delegates' remedies will not be "self-executing," they will get plenty of help from organizations like NOW, the Feminist Majority, and the National Women's Law Center. Groups that Americans know nothing about will take CEDAW as a legal mandate to implement their worldview. One such organization is the National Council for Research on Women (NCRW), a network of more than one hundred women's research and policy centers. The NCRW's website features a list of abiding injustices that make its work "crucial":

▶ Women are still massively underrepresented in the sciences.

▶ There are too few female tenured professors.

▶ Women are underrepresented in corporate leadership.

▶ Women are *still* underpaid.

▶ Too few women lawyers make partner.

▶ Men still dominate the airwaves.

The hundreds of feminist scholars and activists in the NCRW realize that closing these gender gaps is not a matter of removing barriers—those were taken down in the 1970s. For committed egalitarians, innocent explanations for remaining differences—differences many would regard as freely chosen—are ruled out *a priori*. That there are fewer women than men in engineering, on corporate boards, or on Sunday morning political talk shows must be the result of "unconscious bias," "hostile climates," and "internalized oppression" of women. CEDAW would give the activists and lawyers of NCRW, NOW, and the Feminist Majority the license to reeducate and resocialize their fellow citizens—an opportunity that has eluded them under the Constitution. And don't count on the American Civil Liberties Union to speak up on behalf of freedom. Its Women's Rights Project now sets its agenda, and CEDAW ratification is at the top of the list.

But let's say, just for the sake of argument, that RUDs might provide some reasonable protection from the ministrations of the Committee. Why should the United States lend its authority to a human rights instrument that treats the conventions of femininity as demeaning to women? Few women *anywhere* want to see gender roles obliterated. The late Elizabeth Warnock Fernea was an expert on feminist movements in the contemporary Muslim world. In her travels through Saudi Arabia, Morocco, Turkey, and Iraq she met great numbers of advocates working to improve the status of women—and who were proud of women's roles as mother, wife, and caregiver. Fernea called it "family feminism" but it was classic social feminism—the style of women's liberation that hard-line

egalitarians disdain but that great majorities of women find enno-
bling and empowering.

Harold Koh suggests that by abjuring "the Women's Rights Treaty"
Americans are betraying the legacy of Eleanor Roosevelt. But Koh is
confused about Roosevelt's legacy. She was a lifelong, dyed-in-the-
wool social feminist, energetically committed to women's rights
and also to the protection, not elimination, of their social roles and
callings. She saw men and women as different but equal. And no
woman, she said, should feel "humiliated" if she gives priority to
home and family.

Gender researchers in the NCRW organizations will say that
Roosevelt was captive to the prejudices of her time. But it is more
likely that this deeply humane and large-souled woman, whose
vision helped create the Universal Declaration of Human Rights,
also had a 20/20 vision of where women's emancipation might lead.
Social feminism appears to be the universal feminism of women.
Ideologues do not like it. Why, then, should we give them the moral
high ground—over ourselves and many others who yearn to be as
free as we have become?

29

The Illusion of Innocence

Shelby Steele

MANY HAVE ARGUED that the political liberalism coming out of the 1960s quickly became—despite all its good intentions—a threat to freedom in America. I think this is true, but not the entire truth. Since the 1960s there has been a force at work—let's call it a great urgency in the American social order—that has given us a liberalism that short shrifts to freedom. This liberalism is more an effect than a cause. And its threat to freedom is essentially a by-product of its desire to achieve the "good"—"to end poverty in our time," to integrate the schools, to bring diversity to our institutions, to overcome all manner of social and economic inequities, and now even to universalize health care. So many beguiling ideas of the "good." Thus, the real threat to freedom is not as much the *instrument* of post-sixties liberalism as this almost visceral urgency in society to be identified with the "good." Out of this urgency comes the perverse "moral courage" to disregard the disciplines of freedom.

What is this urgency that threatens freedom?

The answer begins in the fact that civilized societies have an inherent moral accountability. The sins of one generation not only stigmatize subsequent generations but also make these ensuing generations responsible for reforming their forbears' misdeeds—misdeeds they themselves never committed. Think of Germany. Will there ever be a day when the Holocaust against the Jews will be forgotten, when German children can be born into innocence? Can we ever hear the German language spoken without hearing—as unfair as it may be today—a Nazi echo?

Stigma is the mechanism that carries moral accountability from one generation to another. Thus, white Americans—even newly arrived white immigrants—live under suspicion of being racists though they may harbor no racist sentiments whatsoever. Actual guilt or innocence is not the point. Moral stigmas operate by association, and by casting a society's sins as aspects of its God-given character. So the postwar stigmatization of Germany asserts that Germans have a characterological attraction to fascistic evil against which the world will always have to be on guard. White Americans are stigmatized as characterologically racist. When evil is a feature of the collective character, moral accountability for that evil is permanent—whether or not the evil is active or latent in society. Moral stigmas are most often unfair to individuals within a stigmatized group—for example, the white who is not a racist—but they can also be civilizing forces for the group as a whole.

And it is simply the case that when a society or group acknowledges a sin, it becomes stigmatized with that sin. There is an irony here because in doing the honorable thing one becomes stigmatized. But viewed another way, the acknowledgment reflects a determination to civilize society, and the stigma simply—and rather ruthlessly— enforces that determination. Only defeat in war forced Germany to acknowledge its horrendous sin. Then came the stigmatization— the idea of characterological German evil. The civil rights movement so disrupted American society in the 1950s and 1960s that white entitlement, as a legitimate way of life in America, was finally defeated. The 1964 Civil Rights Act was, effectively, a white American acknowledgment of the nation's long and immoral indulgence in white supremacy. For this honorable, if belated, acknowledgment, white America was immediately stigmatized as racist—and thus made morally accountable.

When societies and groups openly acknowledge their misdeeds, they implicitly agree to stigmatization as penitence.

But what leads a society or group to finally acknowledge its inhumanity to its fellow man? It is certainly not a guilty conscience, since the society will have long ago developed the rationalizations to live comfortably with its evil. White supremacy, for example, was an ideology that let whites oppress others *innocently*. Its very purpose was to put the white oppression of colored inferiors beyond the reach of moral judgment. We are not subjugating blacks, whites could say; we are merely enforcing God's natural hierarchy of races. The idea of God-given superiority (Hitler's Aryan supremacy is another example) allows the superior to repress the inferior out of a kind of noblesse oblige—as if the repression was a service to God and God's enterprise of shaping the world in his image.

Societies acknowledge their misdeeds only when their illusion of superiority is finally shattered so their oppression of others is seen not as a noble obligation but as a banal and self-serving hypocrisy. Without the ideology of white supremacy, segregation becomes visible as a staggering hypocrisy. It denies individual freedom to blacks in a society founded on the creed of individual freedom. So it is not the specter of past and present evils that finally drives societies to concede their inhumanity to others. This kind of acknowledgment happens only when these evils become broadly visible as hypocrisies. Societies can live easily with their evils but not with their open hypocrisies. Segregation was an evil for one hundred years. But the great achievement of the civil rights movement was to finally establish it as an open hypocrisy.

Why? Because to confirm segregation as a white American hypocrisy was to confirm it as a lie. If, for example, black inferiority was actually God's will, segregation would be a silly redundancy—so much effort and so many cruel repressions (including terrorism and murder) to keep down a people already consigned to inferiority by God. The hypocrisy—the lie—was that segregation was *innocent* because it only reflected God's natural hierarchy of races. But then why the oppression? Hypocrisy is pretending to be what you are not. And with segregation many (not all) white Americans pretended to be innocent even as they colluded with oppression—thus, the lie. But when segregation was established as a lie in the 1960s, all focus shifted from the argument over segregation to a demand for accountability from white America. Suddenly the hypocrite—not his victim—was on the hot seat, and segregation's inherent evil was simply a given in the case against him.

The point is that when a hypocrisy becomes established in a society, it becomes an extremely powerful transformative force—socially, culturally, and politically. Those associated with a hypocrisy that has become conventional wisdom are changed forever. And this was the fate of white America after the sixties. Few groups in history have taken their proven hypocrisy more to heart than white Americans. Yet there was really very little choice. If a society rejects responsibility for a hypocrisy it has already acknowledged, then it undermines or destroys its legitimacy as a society. This is why established hypocrisies are so transformative. They hold the legitimacy of the society and all its institutions in the balance: work to overcome this hypocrisy or risk illegitimacy. With segregation white America had been caught out in a lie, and this threatened the legitimacy of the American government itself. How could the authority of this government be legitimate once the scope of American hypocrisy around race was acknowledged? And in the sixties there were riots from one end of America to the other that asserted precisely the illegitimacy of American authority.

So the great urgency in the American social order mentioned above—the urgency that gave us post-sixties liberalism and the will to disregard freedom—is the loss of moral authority and legitimacy that came into American life after American hypocrisy was confirmed in the sixties. To acknowledge one's hypocrisy is to lose one's innocence—not a genuine innocence but a presumed innocence. America had always enjoyed a kind of naïve faith in its own innocence, its sense of itself as a fundamentally good nation of good and open people. This innocence was always a theme of the American identity, something that set Americans apart as they strolled foreign streets. It is a blessing of confidence for a country to think of itself in this way. It is a kind of exceptionalism. And this "blessing of confidence" is exactly the innocence that America began to lose to its hypocrisies in the 1960s.

And there were many hypocrisies that came to light in the sixties. When it was clear that blacks would succeed in establishing segregation as an American hypocrisy, the floodgates opened. Women came next. They had demanded equality for as long as blacks. Abigail Adams, in letters to her husband John, had urged him to make sure that equality for women was expressly written into the Constitution. But this was not an American possibility at the time, and women languished without the vote for another century and more. And there was the relegation of women to the domestic realm that technological advances and expanding prosperity began to make redundant in the 1950s. By the mid- and late 1960s the fate of American women was shaping up to be yet another instance of great American hypocrisy.

Then there were the Mexican farm workers, the Eskimos, the native Hawaiians and—most poignantly—the Native Americans who had fought whites for three centuries before finding themselves relegated to reservations. And it wasn't just a case of everyone with a beef piling on. It was a deepening and expanding of the idea of American hypocrisy. Here was case after case in which America had pretended to be what it was not—a free and open and fair society.

And looming over all of this was Vietnam—a war conducted by the world's greatest power against a small Asian country five thousand miles away. Here was the immense American "military-industrial complex" at war in a small country of yellow people, engineering coups behind the scenes and picking puppet dictators on the one hand, and claiming to be the world's beacon of freedom on the other. Whatever one may feel about this war—and however history may ultimately judge it—in the sixties it fit perfectly the emerging template of American hypocrisy.

So Vietnam expanded the specter of American hypocrisy far beyond the predictable complaints of the famously alienated— blacks, women, and other minorities. It caused an entire generation of white middle-class American youth to become enveloped in the belief—the faith, really—that hypocrisy was the central truth of American life. And our failure in Vietnam, our slogging along year after year in the purgatory of war, only further established this war as a grand exhibition of American hypocrisy—a trope, a metaphor for the American soul. Vietnam represented a final compounding of American hypocrisies into nothing less than a vision of American characterological evil.

Here was the idea that America was not an inherently good country but an inherently evil one. And of course the evidence was everywhere: racism and sexism at home, imperialism abroad. Even the environment was suddenly being seen as a victim of American hypocrisy. This is when America irrevocably lost its innocence. This is when whites were collectively stigmatized as racists and white men as sexists and warmongers. The entire American way of life became stigmatized as shallow, bigoted, conformist, and greedy— given to military adventurism abroad and empty consumerism at home. In the imagery of this period America was kitschy and materialistic one minute and supremacist and murderous the next. In any event, our presumed innocence as a nation—our faith in our fundamental fairness and decency—was soundly defeated. In its place came the idea of our characterological evil.

This was the confluence of charges that soon led to something new in American life—a "counterculture" that essentially defined itself in opposition to American hypocrisy. Vietnam had enabled middle-class white youth to feel themselves the victims of American hypocrisy—of a government that "lies"—much as blacks and other minorities had always felt. But of course the counterculture went much further than its antiwar position. Armed with the idea of characterological American evil, it invented itself along several themes: war is always wrong; material wealth is always decadent; sexual mores are inauthentic; feeling is more truthful than reason; poverty has both innocence and integrity; blackness carries wisdom, whiteness is trite; nature is truth, the city perverse; truth is always relative; and so on. A compendium of mostly bad ideas, but ideas unified by their assertion of "authenticity" in the face of America's notorious hypocrisy.

I mention the counterculture because it illustrates the same great mistake that American politics made in the 1960s. When America

began to lose the illusion of its innocence in the sixties—as hypocrisy was established as the nation's characterological evil—our culture and our politics were confronted with a choice. We could have
shored up our wobbly legitimacy as a democracy by returning to the
principles and disciplines of freedom, the long betrayal of which is
what led to the crisis of the sixties in the first place. We could have
determined to at last become a democracy of individuals, and set to
work building fairness into every corner of American life. In other
words, we could have absorbed one of the great lessons of the 1960s:
that we are in fact not an innocent society, unless one considers slavery, segregation, the confiscation of Indian lands, and second-class
citizenship for women to be aberrations from an otherwise perfect
innocence. We are a society of rough-and-ready human beings that
has been *humanized* not by an innate innocence but by the force of
law and the rigors of the Constitution (despite our many betrayals
of both).

So our first choice is simply to accept that we cannot count on
our innate innocence as a way to a better society. The genius of our
Constitution is its understanding that discipline, not innocence, is
what makes for a better social order. If segregation was a moral failure it was more importantly a failure of democratic discipline—an
indulgence in bigotry over democratic principle and the law. In this
first choice our great labor would be fairness, a recommitment to
freedom's disciplines.

The other choice we had coming out of the 1960s—the choice
that American liberalism actually followed—was to try to recover
this self-same illusion of American innocence that the sixties had
just exploded. Smarting from "the fall"—the implication of characterological evil—brought on by so much documented hypocrisy, this
choice went with denial rather than acceptance. We would redeem
our democracy and win back our legitimacy through a kind of self-
insistence. We might or might not lift up those we had oppressed, but
we would make a great display of social activism—a display of con-
trition on the one hand and of a determination to right past wrongs
on the other—that would advertise our fundamental innocence no

matter the results we achieved. This choice, in other words, was to invest in our innocence as the force that would both redeem and transform modern America. The sixties was a chance at self-acceptance, and thus a chance for a realistic vision of the future. But this was not to be.

American liberalism in the 1960s shifted its focus from freedom—its great historical mission—to redemption, to showing an America innocent of its past evils and hypocrisies. It put its faith in innocence rather than in the law. Yet the civil rights movement had been a movement of classic freedom-focused liberalism. Martin Luther King had fought for freedom, individual rights, and equality under the law. But post-sixties liberalism had little patience for freedom. To simply work toward fairness in society was too passive a mission. Worse, with freedom there could be no guarantee of results, and this liberalism wanted results above all else so that it could actually demonstrate that American society and its institutions were becoming innocent of America's past. A classically liberal focus on freedom and fairness was simply inadequate to the true goal of this new liberalism—to seize political power in the name of redeeming America of its past.

Add to this the fact that any politics claiming freedom as its great cause had become stigmatized in the sixties with all of America's past sins. After all, hadn't Americans been rapturous about freedom even as they had abided slavery and segregation? So how could freedom suddenly restore America's moral authority and legitimacy? Wasn't talk of freedom and fairness really only code for a return to hypocrisy?

Moreover, modern American conservatism has been nothing if not a freedom-focused politics, and so it has endured the same stigmatization as freedom itself. In post-1960s America it is simply a sophistication to believe that mere freedom is not enough to redeem America of its past. In fact, conservatives, precisely because they celebrate freedom, are presumed to do so because they really want to preserve the hierarchies and inequalities of old. Liberalism's great post-sixties cultural victory has been to infuse American culture with the idea that freedom—and its contemporary politics of conservatism—are *morally* inadequate to the demands of the times. Call a man a conservative, and you have called him a bigot and a hypocrite. Call him a liberal, and even the failed policies he supports flatter him because they display his good intentions, his innocence of the vile American past.

So the 1960s gave us a liberalism that uses innocence as a formula for power—innocence of the American past as entitlement to power. (Conversely, modern conservatism is presumed not to be innocent of that past, and therefore not entitled to power.) This is an activist liberalism that wants to intervene and socially engineer big, dramatic "good works" that are virtual exhibitions of innocence. It is different from the New Deal liberalism of the 1930s in that it never asks anything of the people it seeks to help. This is how it proves its innocence—by giving but never asking. It isn't truly after actual accomplishment in the real world as much as the self-aggrandizement of feeling innocent—that sweet little narcissism of seeing oneself above the shames of the past.

The first "good work" of this liberalism was the Great Society that President Johnson claimed would "end poverty in our time." Then came welfare grants aimed primarily at blacks (as victims) that asked absolutely nothing of them except that they not be married. Often an abstract vision of innocence would be announced, like "school integration," and there would follow a draconian program of school busing to engineer this vision into reality. Today "diversity" is a vision of innocence that American institutions from corporations to the military slavishly pursue through heavy-handed regimens of double standards and preferential treatment. The "Green" movement and the "climate change" movement—whatever the actual reality of the problems they address—are framed as assertions of new American innocence against old America's hypocrisies. And once this innocence-versus-hypocrisy framework is in place there is the inevitable reach for power, the call for government action. In this liberalism, the government is the champion of innocence against America's characterological evil—public power as the force for innocence against the hypocrisies of private power.

The pretense of modern liberalism is that it always stands ready to snatch America from the gravitational pull of its own characterological evil, its hypocrisy. This is its great sanctimony. So it is always doing us a favor when it names "a good" and then abridges freedom to chase that "good." Yet school busing all but destroyed the neighborhood school in America. Diversity means that today all black high school seniors—by dint of their skin color alone—are *prohibited* from freely competing with their white and Asian peers for admission to college. All agree that health care today needs reform, yet liberalism's focus on "the good"—synonymous with the "public option"—over freedom is likely to give us "universal" mediocrity rather than higher-quality care.

Modern liberalism thrives by using America's past hypocrisies as leverage against the timeless principles of freedom today. It is a liberalism of "moral" leverage and muscle, not a discipline of principle. It bullies freedom with the idea of an impossible innocence. Yet it takes its fire from one idea above all others: that it is the answer to America's characterological evil. But neither evil nor innocence is the whole American truth. The civil rights movement did not succeed because America finally became innocent; it succeeded because America finally became principled.

In the 1960s America was shamed into an obsession with innocence. Yet, ironically, this innocence has much in common with white supremacy. Both are concepts of supremacy. Both seek power at the expense of freedom—the power to build a "good" and new world in their name. But the idea of American innocence is as bogus as the idea of white supremacy. Both are vanities that try to supersede freedom. America was humbled by its indulgence in white supremacy, and it will be again by its lust for innocence.

30

Orthodoxy and Freedom in International Aid

Dennis Whittle

IN SEPTEMBER 1986, I joined the World Bank and was instantly terrified. At age twenty-five, I was one of the youngest high-level staff members in the bank, and I had only a master's degree rather than the PhD that nearly all my colleagues had earned. Furthermore, I had ended up at the World Bank almost by accident. An aimless student, I had followed my girlfriend to graduate school and applied to the bank almost on a lark.

My first months at work left me feeling not just underqualified but overwhelmed and confused. My first "mission" to a developing country rendered me almost mute with fear, and I was unable to produce even a cursory aide-mémoire of what I had done there. I could not get my arms around the bank's framework of project cycles and structural adjustment reviews. I felt stupid and inferior for the next seven years of my career.

In retrospect, those years of fear and insecurity prevented me from becoming comfortable with much of the accepted wisdom of my field. But they also ironically freed me to be open to a number of painful but fruitful innovations that would not have emerged from within the orthodoxy.

My initial assignment was in the Africa department, where I was to work on a structural adjustment program for Niger. My new colleagues had compiled a list of measures they believed Niger should take in different sectors (deregulate energy prices, increase funding for basic education, etc.) and were preparing to discuss them with the government. I recognized all these recommendations as instances of the general principles I had learned in grad school, but there seemed something mechanistic about them—as if the prescriptions were disembodied from the context and country.

"Do you have any books here about Niger?" I asked a colleague (this was before the Internet was in popular use).

"What do you mean?" she replied.

"Well, I kind of feel that I should know something about the country before I work on these recommendations or go discuss them with the government." My colleague was truly stumped for a few minutes. Finally, she went to our office library and hunted around and found an old State Department guide to Niger. I took it back to my office and noted that it was twenty years old.

The next month, I went with the team to Niger, where my job was to meet with the head of the public works sewer and sanitation division. I dutifully delivered our message about the need to increase funding for operation and maintenance through higher prices. But I never visited any of the sanitation installations or talked to any of the local engineers to get their perspectives, and there was no discussion about what the best course or sequence of action would be to address their budget and service problems effectively.

A few months later, I was assigned to the Indonesia department, where I was to work on agriculture projects. My new boss handed me a list of projects and asked me which one I would like to work on. The first that caught my eye was called *Irrigation XXIX*.

"So what does the XXIX signify?" I asked my boss.

"Oh, that is the twenty-ninth repeater project we have done using the same design over the past decade," he replied. "Those projects are easy for our engineers to design, since we don't change them very much."

I knew virtually nothing about irrigation and was intimidated by the talk of engineers, so my eye went down the page until I saw "Estate Tree Crops VIII." This was the eighth iteration of a project to help finance the creation of plantations of palm oil, rubber, and coconut. There was a parallel set of projects designed to help small farmers plant and process the same crops. For reasons I can't recall, I chose to work on these projects.

Quickly I discovered two things. First, there were a large number of colonial-era plantation managers overseeing these projects. These managers had spent long years in countries like Malaysia finely tuning the tree species, planting, fertilization, and harvesting practices to maximize yields per hectare. Second, these projects had a history of poor performance. Not only was there graft and missing hectares of trees, but there was a lot of resistance from small farmers to participate in the projects. Still, new projects of the same design were getting under way.

I soon traveled to Indonesia with a team to look at some of the existing projects and begin designing a new one. One day, we were touring a field tended by a very proud small farmer. As we came to the end of the first row of rubber tree seedlings, my colleague grabbed one of the seedlings and angrily tore it from the ground.

"This is not the proper spacing. We have told you ten times that the trees must be planted three meters apart."

The farmer's face fell. "But sir, I like to plant them further apart so I can grow food crops between them, so I can get food and income in between rubber harvests."

"No," my colleague replied. "That is not the way."

I was sickened by this exchange, and back in Jakarta I naïvely reported it to my boss. The next day, my colleague who had torn the seedling from the ground came down on me like a ton of bricks. "Never, ever, contradict me like that. I have been doing this work for twenty years, and you couldn't tell a rubber tree from a coconut tree."

Later, a team from the Indonesian Ministry of Finance assisted by Harvard University, began informally to question the design of our tree crops projects. One of their advisors, who had spent months in the field over the past year, reported that our projects optimized the returns to land, but not to the farmers themselves. They argued that the spacing we had observed in the field were the results of years of experimentation by farmers, who wanted more space between trees so they could grow other crops they needed to both feed their families and provide more robust sources of income. Our tree crops experts dug in their heels, however, and refused to even acknowledge the notion that there might be a tension between the incentives. The ensuing disagreement led to a four-year standoff in which almost no further projects were implemented.

During this four-year standoff, I worked on a general study of the agriculture sector as a whole. The recommendations we came up with were formulaic—and eerily analogous to those I had helped formulate in Niger. We urged the government to deregulate the price of fertilizer, sharply limit restrictions on land use, abolish the government's rice distribution company, and decrease export tariffs on timber. Though many of these were by any measure desirable, they took little account of the political realities or the history of the regulations and institutions in place.

The Indonesian government at that time disliked confrontation, and delayed a discussion of the first draft of the report. Instead, we were visited by a small group of the government's independent foreign advisors. These advisors had (at least) equal academic qualifications as our team, but they had worked in Indonesia for twenty years. They argued that some things could not be done for political reasons, and that to push too hard would be counterproductive. They also argued that, in the Indonesian context, some regulations normally considered "distorting" had a beneficial effect, at least in the short run.

The bank's response was to circle the wagons. We brought the full force and weight of the bank to bear through lengthy and costly research and analyses to prove that the independent advisors were wrong. After about nine months, we prevailed, and the government agreed to accept our recommendations (though they failed to implement many of them). One of the advisors confessed to me years later that he had been hospitalized because of the stress he was under during this struggle.

Later, I moved over to the macroeconomics unit in Jakarta, which was led by an excellent economist who is rightfully credited with helping the Indonesian government design some very effective reforms. Much of our day-to-day work revolved around a huge computerized model of the economy that purported to generate estimates of how much investment was needed to achieve a certain growth rate. But the reality was that this model, for all its intimidating complexity, was a simple accounting framework. We did not really understand the things that led to increased productivity, so we could not model it. Yet the "high priest" of the model had much status in the office, and we spent a lot of time and energy feeding the model instead of trying to gain insights into what made the economy really tick.

By the end of my time in Indonesia, in early 1992, I was tired and ready to leave the World Bank and do something different. In March, however, I got a call from a guy at headquarters saying that Russia had just joined the World Bank and asking if I was interested in joining the new Russia department.

"But I don't know anything about Russia," I told him. I had studied no Russian language or history in school, and had read little Russian literature beyond the classics.

"Well, none of us knows anything about Russia," he replied. "So you will fit right in."

Because of Russia's unique context and heritage of central planning, we faced a host of novel problems for which the bank had few established solutions. Our usual approaches by and large failed for the first year, and so we were required to try completely new things. One bank team working on housing reform even decided to produce a television series about life in a condominium association. This was far outside the range of our normal work and yet may have done more to help Russians adapt to a market economy than anything else we did. The five years I spent in Russia were one continuous exercise in experimentation. Though things often failed, the experience taught us all that it was more important to try to get at the root of a problem and solve it rather than apply simple, generic solutions.

One day I asked a colleague, who had previously worked for Gosplan, how on earth their planning system worked. "Not very well," he replied. "It worked so poorly, in fact, we had to hire smarter and smarter people just to keep the economy from collapsing. And in the end we failed." These words left a deep mark on me, and I later came to realize that the bank was not much different. Though it preached market economics, it operated in a top-down, centrally planned way that required it to hire "smarter and smarter" experts each year.

After five exhausting years in Russia, I was taking a break skiing in Colorado when I got a message from the new vice president in charge of strategy. "Call me ASAP," the message said.

I rang him in Washington and told him I was on vacation. "What is so urgent?" I asked.

"The president wants you to be head of new products," he replied. "Don't ask any questions, just come back to Washington."

A few days later, I was ushered in to see Jim Wolfensohn, the bank's relatively new president. He asked me if I was going to take the job.

"Well," I replied, "can I first ask you a question? What are new products?"

"That's the whole problem," he barked. "We haven't had any new products for the last fifty years, and that's why people are protesting against us in the streets!"

I got a small budget and a few empty offices. I had one consultant, with little bank experience, and no clear mandate or power other than to innovate. So I set about trying to fill the offices, while jockeying for position in the newly reorganized bureaucracy and trying to develop written guidelines that staff could follow to create new products. I consulted a couple of consultant reports about how to do innovation inside companies and dutifully set up an online "ideas box" to collect ideas from staff. For nine months, I spun my wheels and nothing worked. We had file cabinets full of ideas, but few new products because I could not figure out how to get them approved by the bureaucracy.

Finally, I gathered a group of former colleagues and we decided to do the following: we threw away all the rules and procedures I had spent months elaborating. We sent out a note to all bank staff saying that anyone with a good idea to improve economic, environmental, or social conditions in our client countries could come to the atrium on a specific day and pitch that idea to a jury panel. The only rules were that the team had to be composed of at least two people from separate departments, that the written materials could not exceed four pages, and that the verbal pitch could not exceed fifteen minutes. And we promised to make decisions within a week, even though we had no idea how we were going to do this.

This event in May 1998, which came to be known as the Innovation Marketplace, was a huge success. One hundred and ten teams set up booths with posters depicting their ideas in the enormous foyer of the bank's headquarters, which was normally empty and eerily quiet. Eleven jury panels (each comprising a bank manager, a private company executive, and a nonprofit leader) roamed the floor to hear the teams' pitches. Hundreds of bank staff and even some members of the public visited the booths, each with five votes that could be cast for their favorite ideas. The passion of the staff pitching the ideas, as well as their creativity in illustrating their points, was remarkable. One normally staid staff member working on malaria had a Plexiglas cube filled with mosquitoes, and he told the judges he would take off the top and let the mosquitoes out if they did not fund his malaria initiative—a stunt unheard of in the bank, but one that was highly effective.

A mere eight hours from the beginning of the competition, the jury panel selected eleven winners to receive funding ranging from fifty thousand to eight hundred thousand dollars to jump-start their ideas. While not all of the winning ideas panned out, many (including the malaria initiative) proved to be of strategic importance for the bank in the next twelve to eighteen months. It was impressive that such a rapid and low-overhead process could generate such results.

What struck me even more was the conversation I had at the end of the day with one of the people, a senior economist, who did not win. He was choked up, and I was worried he had a family crisis. The reason for the tears, he told me, was that he had been thinking about his idea for over ten years and had never before gotten anyone to listen to it. That day, he told me, someone listened to it for the first time, and though he won no funding, he had received good feedback and met some other colleagues who had a similar idea. He told me that he now felt free to join forces with his colleagues to work on the idea even without official permission or sanction. Though I had no way of assessing his chances, the fact that he had a newfound sense of freedom in his professional life was striking.

About eighteen months later, we went even further: we invited anyone in the world with a good idea to fight poverty to compete in an event called the Development Marketplace. Out of over eleven hundred proposals from eighty countries, we invited three hundred finalists to Washington in early 2000 to compete for $5 million in funding. The scene in the atrium this time was even more compelling. One team comprised two older women from Uganda who had never been outside their home province. They were competing against a team of scientists from NASA and a team of Supreme Court justices from Latin America.

"Is it true that the World Bank president is going to hear our idea?" the two Ugandan women asked.

"Yes, it is," I answered, in what was surely the highlight of my career.

The bank's president did come to their booth and hear their proposal, and at the end of the second day they were overjoyed to hear their names called as one of the winners. (They won about eighty thousand dollars to start a microcredit scheme that would provide new mothers with enough income to buy the medicine and vitamins their children needed.) The guys from NASA did not win, but were happy to have had a chance to promote their idea about using satellite imagery to improve crop rotation in the developing world. The team from the Supreme Court did win, and marched up to the stage proudly to accept their funding for an initiative to train judges in how to adjudicate cases involving indigenous land rights.

All told, the jurors selected about forty teams for funding. Like the Innovation Marketplace eighteen months before, the Development Marketplace had been all about ideas and action, not problems and impediments. Furthermore, it did not matter who you were— whether you were a senior economist at the bank, a government official, or two women from the village. All that mattered was whether you had a good idea and the potential to make it happen.

At the end, a woman from South Africa came up to me and said, "We did not win."

"Well, I'm sorry about that," I replied, "but maybe we will have another one of these competitions in another year or two."

"Well just because the World Bank didn't fund our project doesn't mean that no one else will. And I can't afford to wait two years anyway."

She was asking for a true marketplace—one that operated continuously, that gave regular access to anyone regardless of position or credentials, that ensured ideas would be heard and evaluated on their merit. Given the structure of the aid industry, the question itself was almost heresy. Didn't she know that development required specialized agencies with top experts studying problems, devising solutions, and then funding them directly? That it implied the need for limiting voice primarily to those who had gained privileged status within the bureaucracy? The existing aid system was not only closed and hierarchical, but it also enforced an orthodoxy about which types of ideas were considered valid or appropriate.

Two of us on the team spent the next six months thinking intensively about the South African woman's question. During this time, we were being promoted rapidly up the ranks inside the bank, and in the process our work was taking us more and more into the guts of the bureaucracy and further and further away from the idea of a marketplace for aid. Ironically, even though the bank itself preached a heavily market-oriented gospel to its clients, its own DNA was top-down and more akin to central planning.

In the end, we resigned completely from the bank to launch Global-Giving, a 24/7 online marketplace for aid projects. We had no idea exactly what this meant at first, not to mention the fact that neither of us knew anything about how to develop or operate a website. All we knew is that anyone should be eligible to propose an idea or project, and anyone should be able to fund it—with the minimum possible interference or intermediation from us. Our situation was the opposite of orthodoxy, and it was terrifying for a couple of years.

Slowly GlobalGiving began to gain momentum, attracting both project ideas and funding from around the world. By 2009, many millions of dollars had begun to flow through the GlobalGiving marketplace, connecting tens of thousands of donors (both large and small) to project leaders in over seventy countries. Most gratifyingly, GlobalGiving also began to spawn many similar initiatives, including online peer-to-peer microcredit marketplaces and marketplaces focused on specific issues such as education.

Well-functioning market mechanisms are the opposite of institutional orthodoxy. Such mechanisms increase access, innovation, learning, and efficiency in the quest for ideas that will improve economic, social, and environmental conditions in the developing world. The effectiveness of future development aid will turn on the degree to which such market mechanisms are adopted more broadly.

Marketplaces require rules and regulations and even structures, too. One of the challenges will be to maintain effective feedback loops within the marketplaces themselves. Such feedback loops must minimize the tendency toward accepting "the way things are done." Instead, feedback must force a continual reexamination of whether not only the products of the marketplace but the marketplace structure *itself* is delivering the best impact. Adaptation based on results must be part of the core DNA of these marketplaces if they are to avoid the straightjacket of orthodoxy.

Contributors

Anne Applebaum is a columnist for the *Washington Post* and *Slate*, covering U.S. and international politics. She also writes regularly for a range of newspapers and magazines in Britain and the United States, including the *New York Review of Books*, the *New Republic*, and the *Daily Telegraph*. She was the foreign editor, then deputy editor, of the *Spectator* and covered the collapse of communism in 1989 for the *Economist*. Her most recent book, *Gulag: A History*, which narrates the history of the Soviet concentration camp system, won the 2004 Pulitzer Prize for nonfiction; it has appeared in more than two dozen translations. She currently resides in Warsaw, where she is at work on a new book about the imposition of totalitarianism in postwar Central Europe.

Bruce Bawer was born in New York City in 1956, received a PhD in English from Stony Brook University in 1983, and moved to Europe in 1998. He has been a literary critic for the *New Criterion* (1983–93), film critic for the *American Spectator* (1986–90), columnist for the *Advocate* (1994–99), and is a longtime *Hudson Review* contributor. He has written for *City Journal*, the *Wilson Quarterly*, the *New Republic*, the *American Scholar*, the *New York Times*, the *Washington Post Book World*, the *Wall Street Journal*, the *Chronicle of Higher Education*, *Salon*, and the Pajamas Media website. His books include the essay collections *Diminishing Fictions* (1988), *The Screenplay's the Thing* (1992), *The Aspect of Eternity* (1993), and *Prophets and Professors* (1995); the poetry collection *Coast to Coast* (1993); and *Stealing Jesus: How Fundamentalism Betrays Christianity* (1997). *A Place at the Table: The Gay Individual in American*

Society (1993), which challenged both antigay prejudice and gay-left orthodoxy, was a watershed in the gay rights movement, and in 1999 was named by columnist Dale Carpenter as the decade's most important book on homosexuality. *While Europe Slept: How Radical Islam Is Destroying the West from Within* (2006) was a *New York Times* best seller, appeared in several languages, and was a National Book Critics Circle Award finalist. His latest book, *Surrender: Appeasing Islam, Sacrificing Freedom* (2009), is now in paperback. Bawer has also translated several books, writes and translates for Human Rights Service at www.rights.no, and blogs at www.brucebawer.com.

Adam Bellow is currently vice president/executive editor at Harper-Collins. He has also been an executive editor at Doubleday (Random House) and was formerly editorial director of the Free Press (Simon & Schuster). A native New Yorker, he grew up on the Upper West Side (with its attendant intellectual deformities) and graduated from Princeton University in 1980 with a degree in comparative literature. He also did graduate work at the University of Chicago (political philosophy) and Columbia University (history) before entering publishing in 1989. His editorial interests range broadly across history, politics, religion, philosophy, and other branches of social science, but he is best known for publishing conservatives, and played a key role in the conservative intellectual revolt of the 1980s and 1990s. His essays and articles have appeared in the *Atlantic*, the *New York Times*, the *Wall Street Journal*, *Newsweek*, the *Los Angeles Times*, and *World Affairs*. He is also the author of *In Praise of Nepotism: A History of Family Enterprise from King David to George W. Bush* (2004).

Peter Berkowitz is the Tad and Dianne Taube Senior Fellow at the Hoover Institution, Stanford University, where he chairs the Task Force on National Security and Law and cochairs the Task Force on the Virtues of a Free Society. He is the author of *Virtue and the Making of Modern Liberalism* (1999) and *Nietzsche: The Ethics of* *an Immoralist* (1995). He is the editor of several Hoover Institution Press books: *The Future of American Intelligence* (2005); *Terrorism, the Laws of War, and the Constitution: Debating the Enemy Combatant Cases* (2005); *Varieties of Progressivism in America* (2004); *Varieties of Conservatism in America* (2004); and *Never a Matter of Indifference: Sustaining Virtue in a Free Republic* (2003). With coeditor Tod Lindberg, in 2004 he launched Hoover Studies in Politics, Economics, and Society, a series of concise books published in cooperation with Rowman and Littlefield. He has written on a range of subjects for a variety of publications, including the *Atlantic, Haaretz, National Review,* the *New Republic, Policy Review,* the *Times Literary Supplement,* the *Wall Street Journal,* the *Washington Post,* the *Weekly Standard,* and the *Yale Law Journal.* He taught constitutional law and jurisprudence at George Mason University School of Law from 1999 to 2007, and political philosophy in the government department at Harvard University from 1990 to 1999. He holds a JD and a PhD in political science from Yale University, an MA in philosophy from the Hebrew University of Jerusalem; and a BA in English literature from Swarthmore College.

Max Borders is a writer living in the Research Triangle area, North Carolina, with his wife and three-year-old son. Formerly managing editor of Tech Central Station, Max continues to write nonfiction and opinion journalism. Max earns part of his living developing films as an executive at Free To Choose Network, an organization committed to building popular support for personal, political, and economic freedom. Before that he was a policy analyst and new media director for a North Carolina think tank. In 2008, the Charles G. Koch Foundation selected Max to join a group of rising classical liberal intellectuals to the Koch Associates Program—a continuing education program in organization theory, free-market economics, and nonprofit management. He is now a mentor for the program. In past lives, Max has worked as program director for a DC-area research and education institute, taught philosophy to undergrads, and written about technology for a Big Five consulting firm. He has an MA in philosophy from University College London and a BA from Appalachian State University. Currently, Max is working on an online marketplace for social change projects. His myriad experiences in higher education, public policy, and private enterprise keep him fascinated by the intersection of theory and practice.

Richard A. Epstein is the James Parker Hall Distinguished Service Professor of Law at the University of Chicago, where he has taught since 1972. He has also been the Peter and Kirstin Bedford Senior Fellow at the Hoover Institution since 2000 and a visiting professor at New York University Law School since 2007. Prior to joining the University of Chicago Law School faculty, he taught law at the University of Southern California from 1968 to 1972. He received an LLD, hc, from the University of Ghent in 2003. He has been a member of the American Academy of Arts and Sciences since 1985 and a Senior Fellow of the MacLean Center for Clinical Medical Ethics at the University of Chicago Medical School, also since 1983. He served as editor of the *Journal of Legal Studies* from 1981 to 1991, and of the *Journal of Law and Economics* from 1991 to 2001. He was a director of the John M. Olin Program in Law and Economics at the University of Chicago from 2001 to 2008. He is the author of several books, which include *Takings: Private Property and the Power of Eminent Domain* (1985), *Simple Rules for a Complex World* (1995), *Overdose: How Excessive Government Regulation Stifles Pharmaceutical Innovation* (2006), and *How Progressives Rewrote the Constitution* (2006). He has written numerous articles on a wide range of legal and interdisciplinary subjects.

Jessica Gavora is a Washington, DC, writer on politics and feminism. She has written widely about feminism and federal gender equity law in sports and education. Her acclaimed critique of gender equity in American education, *Tilting the Playing Field: Schools, Sports, Sex and Title IX*, was published in May 2002. In addition to writing about politics and culture, Gavora served as the chief speechwriter for Attorney General John Ashcroft and a senior policy advisor at the Department of Justice. She has also written speeches and articles for a number of political candidates and elected officials. Gavora received her master's degree in American foreign policy and international economics from the Johns Hopkins School of Advanced International Studies (SAIS) in 1993. She is a graduate of Marquette University with degrees in political science and journalism. She was born in Fairbanks, Alaska, and has eight brothers and sisters and fifteen nieces and nephews. She lives in Washington with her husband, Jonah Goldberg; her daughter, Lucy; and dog, Cosmo.

Michael Goodwin is the chief political columnist for the *New York Post* and nypost.com, writing on national, international, and New York issues in a full-page column that appears each Wednesday and Sunday. Goodwin also offers commentary on the Fox News Channel and various radio stations. Before joining the *Post* in 2009, he was the political columnist for the *New York Daily News*. Goodwin also served as the *Daily News'* executive editor and editorial page editor. In 1999, he led the editorial board to its first Pulitzer Prize in fifty-eight years for a series of editorials revealing corruption at the famed Apollo Theatre. His editorial board also received the George Polk Award in 2000 for securing basic rights for migrant farm workers. Goodwin is the coauthor of *I, Koch*, a 1985 unauthorized biography of New York's former mayor Edward I. Koch. In 2005, Goodwin edited a series of essays called "New York Comes Back," which focused on the impact of the Koch mayoralty. That book accompanied a museum exhibit Goodwin helped organize. Goodwin began his career as a reporter and City Hall bureau chief for the *New York Times*. He served for three years as an adjunct professor at Columbia University's Graduate School of Journalism and was a juror for the Pulitzer Prizes. He also hosted a public affairs program on a New York TV station. Born in Lewistown, Pennsylvania, Goodwin earned a BA in English literature from Columbia. He and his family live in New York.

Daniel Hannan has been Conservative MEP (Member of the European Parliament) for the South East of England since 1999. Local

Conservatives voted him to the top of the regional list for the 2004 and 2009 European elections. He is Secretary-General of the Alliance of European Conservatives and Reformists—the only bloc in Brussels that campaigns against closer integration. In March 2009, Daniel's speech in the European Parliament attacking Gordon Brown attracted one-and-a-half million views within seventy-two hours, and went on to become the most watched political clip in British history. In 2009, Daniel was awarded the prize for International Legislator of the Year by the American Legislative Exchange Council, and Speech of the Year by *Spectator* magazine. Daniel is the author of seven books about the European Union and, more recently, of *The Plan: Twelve Months to Renew Britain*, which has become the best-selling political tract in Britain, and which sets out a comprehensive platform for the decentralization of power. He writes for the *Daily Telegraph*, the *Mail on Sunday*, and the *Spectator*, and blogs every day at www.hannan.co.uk. His blog attracts two hundred thousand hits a week from eighty thousand unique users. In 2009, his blog won the Bastiat Prize for Online Journalism. Daniel speaks French and Spanish and loves Europe, but believes that the European Union is making us poorer, less democratic, and less free. He wants to take powers back from Brussels, and then to pass them down to local councils or, better yet, individual citizens.

Alexander Harrington is founder and artistic director of the Eleventh Hour Theatre Co., for which directed his own translation of Aeschylus's *Agamemnon; The Burial at Thebes; Richard II; Henry IV, Parts 1 & 2*; and *Henry V*; and his own adaptation of Dostoevsky's *The Brothers Karamazov* (published in the New York Theatre Experience's anthology *Playing with Canons*). Harrington and the Eleventh Hour are frequent guest artists at La MaMa E.T.C.; the Culture Project and HERE have also presented their work. Other directing credits include *Billy Budd, Twelfth Night, Much Ado about Nothing*, and the premieres of Edward Einhorn's *Linguish* (New York International Fringe Festival); Kathryn Sanders's *So Alone, Last Night in Paris*, and

Surprises from a Cloud; John A. Adams's *In the Shadow of a Dream*; and Lella Heins's *Finder Keeper, Lion Taming in Miami,* and *Tender Loving Care* (as a part of evening of Heins's short plays at the Medicine Show theatre), and *The Theory of Color*. Harrington has adapted and directed Chekhov's "The Kiss" and Sherwood Anderson's "The Philosopher" for the stage (both produced for Lincoln Center Theatre Directors Lab/the Culture Project festivals). As scholar and critic, Harrington's work has appeared in *Dissent* magazine, *First of the Month, Upstart Crow, Shakespeare Criticism,* and *Literary Themes for Students: War and Peace*. Harrington teaches acting Shakespeare at HB studio and has taught at Clemson University and NYU's Gallatin School. He was an original member of the Lincoln Center Theater Directors Lab and a participant in the Actors Studio Playwrights/Directors Unit.

Mark Helprin was raised on the Hudson and in the British West Indies. After receiving degrees from Harvard College and Harvard's Graduate School of Arts and Sciences, he did postgraduate work at the University of Oxford, Princeton, and Columbia. He has served in the British Merchant Navy, the Israeli infantry, and the Israeli Air Force. His stories, essays, and commentary have appeared in the *New Yorker,* the *Atlantic Monthly,* the *New Criterion, Commentary,* the *Wall Street Journal,* the *Washington Post,* the *New York Times, National Review, American Heritage, Forbes ASAP,* and many other publications here and abroad. Senior Fellow of the Claremont Institute for the Study of Statesmanship and Political Philosophy, Fellow of the American Academy in Rome, Member of the Council on Foreign Relations, former Guggenheim Fellow, and advisor on defense and foreign relations to presidential nominee Robert Dole, he has been awarded, among other prizes, the National Jewish Book Award and the Prix de Rome. Translated into dozens of languages, his books include *A Dove of the East & Other Stories; Refiner's Fire; Ellis Island & Other Stories; Winter's Tale; A Soldier of the Great War; Memoir from Antproof Case; Swan Lake, A City* *in Winter* and *The Veil of Snows* (illustrated by Chris Van Allsburg); *The Pacific & Other Stories*; *Freddy and Fredericka*; and the nonfiction *Digital Barbarism*.

Christopher Hitchens was born in 1949 and educated at the Leys School, Cambridge and Balliol College Oxford. He worked as a journalist and reviewer in London before immigrating to the United States in 1981. In Washington, DC, where he makes his home, he has at different times been the correspondent of the *Nation, Harper's*, the *New Statesman*, the *Spectator*, and the *Times Literary Supplement*. He has reported from more than sixty different countries. He is currently a columnist for *Vanity Fair* magazine and a book reviewer for the *Atlantic*. His books include studies of George Orwell, Thomas Jefferson, Thomas Paine, the Anglo-American relationship, and the island of Cyprus. He has also written a number of books and articles critical of religious belief, including a critique of Mother Teresa and a study titled *God Is Not Great*.

Robert D. Kaplan is a senior fellow at the Center for a New American Security in Washington, DC, and a national correspondent for the *Atlantic*. From 2006 to 2008, he was the Class of 1960 Distinguished Visiting Professor in National Security at the United States Naval Academy, Annapolis. He is the best-selling author of twelve books on international affairs and travel, which have been translated into many languages. His latest work is *Hog Pilots, Blue Water Grunts: The American Military in the Air, at Sea, and on the Ground*. In the 1980s, Kaplan was the first American writer to warn in print about a future war in the Balkans. Former President Clinton and President George W. Bush are both readers of Kaplan's books. Besides the *Atlantic Monthly*, Kaplan's essays have appeared on the editorial pages of the *New York Times*, the *Wall Street Journal*, the *Washington Post*, and the *Los Angeles Times*. He has been a consultant to the U.S. Army's Special Forces Regiment, the U.S. Air Force, and the U.S. Marines. He has lectured at military war colleges, the FBI, the National Security Agency, the Pentagon's Joint

Staff, major universities, the CIA, and business forums. Kaplan has delivered the Secretary of State's Open Forum Lecture at the U.S. State Department.

James Kirchick is a contributing editor of the *New Republic*, an online columnist for the *New York Daily News*, and a contributing writer to the *Advocate*. He is a frequent contributor to newspapers, magazines, and policy journals across the country, including the *Los Angeles Times*, the *Wall Street Journal*, the *Washington Post*, Politico, the *Weekly Standard*, *Commentary*, *Policy Review*, and *Out*. He has been a Phillips Foundation Journalism Fellow and is a recipient of the National Lesbian and Gay Journalists' Association Journalist of the Year Award.

Greg Lukianoff is a constitutional lawyer and the president of the Foundation for Individual Rights in Education (FIRE). He is a regular blogger for the Huffington Post and has published articles in the *Chronicle of Higher Education*, the *Los Angeles Times*, *Reason* magazine, *Fraternal Law*, *Inside Higher Ed*, the *Boston Globe*, the *New York Post*, as well as numerous other publications. Lukianoff is a frequent guest on local and nationally syndicated radio and television programs—including *CBS Evening News*, *The O'Reilly Factor*, *The Abrams Report*, and *Hannity and Colmes*—and has testified before the U.S. Senate about free speech issues on America's campuses. Lukianoff is a graduate of American University and of Stanford Law School, where he focused on First Amendment and constitutional law. In 2008 he became the first-ever recipient of the Playboy Foundation Freedom of Expression Award. Before joining FIRE, Lukianoff interned at the ACLU of Northern California and the Organization for Aid to Refugees in Prague, Czech Republic, and was the development manager of the EnvironMentors Project in Washington, DC. Along with Harvey A. Silverglate and David French, he is a coauthor of FIRE's *Guide to Free Speech on Campus*. Lukianoff is also a fiction writer and a proud member of the board of directors of Philadelphia's Theater Exile.

Barry C. Lynn is director of the Markets, Enterprise, and Resiliency Project, and a senior fellow at the New America Foundation. He is author of *Cornered: The New Monopoly Capitalism and the Economics of Destruction* (2009) and *End of the Line: The Rise and Coming Fall of the Global Corporation* (2005). His groundbreaking work on the growing fragility of industrial systems has attracted wide attention, and Lynn has presented his theories to senior officials in Japan, Germany, Britain, France, Taiwan, and the European Commission, as well as the U.S. Treasury Department. Lynn's work on the political and economic effects of the revolutionary changes in our antimonopoly laws has attracted wide attention, especially in the Conservative and Liberal Democratic parties in Britain. Lynn has consulted extensively with Fortune 500 businesses, labor and industrial unions, and academic groups. His articles have appeared in publications including *Harper's*, the *Financial Times*, *Harvard Business Review*, and the *National Interest*. Lynn was executive editor of *Global Business Magazine* for seven years, and worked as a correspondent in Peru and Venezuela for the Associated Press and Agence France Presse. He was born in Miami, and lives in Washington with his wife and two sons.

David Mamet is author of the plays *Race, November, Romance, Boston Marriage, Oleanna, Glengarry Glen Ross* (1984 Pulitzer Prize and New York Drama Critics Award), *American Buffalo, The Old Neighborhood, A Life in the Theater, Speed-the-Plow, Edmond, Lakeboat, The Water Engine, The Woods, Sexual Perversity in Chicago, Reunion*, and *The Cryptogram* (1995 Obie Award). Translations and adaptations: *The Voysey Inheritance* by Harvey Granville-Barker; *Red River* by Pierre Laville; *The Cherry Orchard, Three Sisters*, and *Uncle Vanya* by Anton Chekov; and *Faustus*. Films: *The Postman Always Rings Twice, The Verdict, The Untouchables, House of Games* (writer/director), *Oleanna* (writer/director), *Homicide* (writer/director), *The Spanish Prisoner* (writer/director), *Hoffa, Wag the Dog, The Edge, The Winslow Boy* (writer/director), *Hannibal, State and Main* (writer/director), *Heist* (writer/director), *Spartan* (writer/director), and *Redbelt* (writer/director). Mamet is also the author of *Warm and Cold*, a book for children with drawings by Donald Sultan, and two other children's books, *Passover* and *The Duck and the Goat*; *Writing in Restaurants, Some Freaks*, and *Make-Believe Town*, three volumes of essays; *The Hero Pony* and *The China Man* (books of poems); *Three Children's Plays*; *On Directing Film*; *The Cabin*; and the novels *The Village, The Old Religion*, and *Wilson*. His most recent books include the acting books, *True and False* and *Three Uses of the Knife*; *The Wicked Son*; and *Bambi vs. Godzilla*. Mamet was also a cocreator of the four-season running, hit CBS television series The Unit, and is a cofounder and member of the Atlantic Theater Company.

Katherine Mangu-Ward is a senior editor at *Reason* magazine and Reason.com. Previously, Mangu-Ward worked as a reporter for the *Weekly Standard* magazine and as a researcher at the *New York Times* op-ed page. She was a 2005 Phillips Foundation Journalism Fellow. Her work has appeared in the *Wall Street Journal*, the *Washington Post*, the *Los Angeles Times*, the *New York Times* online, and numerous other publications. Mangu-Ward is a graduate of Yale University, where she received a BA in political science and philosophy. She lives in Washington, DC, with her husband.

Tara McKelvey is a frequent contributor to the *New York Times Book Review* and author of *Monstering: Inside America's Policy on Secret Interrogations and Torture in the Terror War*, which former National Security Advisor Zbigniew Brzezinski has described as "a shocker . . . an indictment of an administration in which no senior official has been held accountable for acts that stained America's escutcheon." She has been a research fellow at New York University School of Law's Center on Law and Security, an Ochberg Fellow with the Dart Center for Journalism and Trauma, a Hoover Media Fellow at Stanford University's Hoover Institution, and most recently a fellow in the Templeton-Cambridge Fellowship in Religion and Science program and in Johns Hopkins University's International Reporting Project.

Mark T. Mitchell received his PhD in government (political theory) in 2001 from Georgetown University. He currently teaches political theory at Patrick Henry College in Purcellville, Virginia. In 2008–9 he was a fellow at the James Madison Program in American Ideals and Institutions at Princeton University. Mitchell is the author of *Michael Polanyi: The Art of Knowing* (2006) and *The Politics of Gratitude: Scale, Place, Community, and the American Future* (forthcoming). He is coeditor of a book on the thought of Wendell Berry titled *The Humane Vision of Wendell Berry* (forthcoming). His writing has appeared in various academic and popular journals, including the *Journal of Religious Ethics, Humanitas, Modern Age,* the *Intercollegiate Review, Perspectives in Political Science,* and the *Political Science Reviewer.* In 2009, Mitchell cofounded an online magazine called *Front Porch Republic,* which gathers together a group of popular writers from both the left and right to explore and promote notions such as limits, sustainability, community, and stewardship of the natural world.

Michael C. Moynihan is a senior editor of *Reason* magazine and a producer at Reason TV. Before joining *Reason,* Moynihan was a resident fellow at the Swedish policy institute Timbro and edited the English-language website Stockholm Spectator. He is currently a visiting fellow at Timbro. His writing has appeared in the *Los Angeles Times, Utne Reader,* the *New York Post,* the *Chicago Sun-Times,* the *Weekly Standard, Wilson Quarterly,* Politico, *Commentary,* and numerous other publications. In Europe, Moynihan has written for *Expressen, Aftonbladet, Neo, Sveriges Television,* and *Göteborgs-Tidningen.* Moynihan is a graduate of the University of Massachusetts, Amherst. He lives in Washington, DC.

Chris Norwood, an award-winning author and journalist, is the founder of Health People: Community Preventive Health Institute in the South Bronx. She started Health People as a women's AIDS peer education program in 1990; since then, Health People has gone forward to fight a range of chronic disease—especially diabetes and asthma—along with AIDS by training South Bronx residents affected by ill health to become leaders and educators to successfully fight disease and death in their own community. Health People has also shown that empowering people to build their own health and the health of their community results in them rebuilding their lives; dozens of men and women Health People trained as volunteer peer educators—including those with AIDS, a background of addiction, and little education—have gone on to complete their education and work full-time. Health People believes giving people the chance to build their own solutions is vital for all ages; its unique Kids-Helping-Kids mentoring program trains older teens with sick, missing, or deceased parents to be mentors for younger children in the same difficult situations. In 2005, Norwood was selected for a groundbreaking group Nobel Peace Prize nomination that honored one thousand women around the world for their local work. Her books include *About Paterson: The Making and Unmaking of an American City*—about America's first industrial city—and *Advice for Life: A Woman's Guide to AIDS*. She is a graduate of Wellesley College.

Glenn Harlan Reynolds is the Beauchamp Brogan Distinguished Professor of Law at the University of Tennessee, where he teaches, among other subjects, constitutional law and Internet law. He is the author of *The Appearance of Impropriety*, *An Army of Davids*, and numerous articles in publications such as the *Atlantic Monthly*, the *Wall Street Journal*, *Forbes*, and the *Columbia Law Review*. He is the founder of the pioneering political/technical blog InstaPundit .com, and a regular columnist for the *Washington Examiner*.

Naomi Schaefer Riley is an affiliate scholar at the Institute for American Values. She was, until recently, the deputy taste editor of the *Wall Street Journal*, where she covered religion, higher education, and philanthropy for the editorial page. Her book, *God on the Quad: How Religious Colleges and the Missionary Generation Are Changing America*, was published in 2005. Prior to joining the *Journal*, she founded *In Character*, a magazine published by the

John M. Templeton Foundation. Her writing has also been published in the *Boston Globe*, the *New York Times*, the *Los Angeles Times*, and the *Chronicle of Higher Education*, among other publications. She has received the Phillips Foundation Journalism Fellowship and the Intercollegiate Studies Institute Journalism Fellowship. She is the winner of the 2006 American Academy of Religion's Newswriting Contest for Opinion Writing. Riley graduated magna cum laude from Harvard University. She lives in the suburbs of New York with her husband and two children.

Christine Rosen is senior editor of the *New Atlantis: A Journal of Technology & Society*, where she writes about the social impact of technology, bioethics, and the history of genetics. Rosen is the author of *Preaching Eugenics: Religious Leaders and the American Eugenics Movement* (2004), a history of the ethical and religious debates surrounding the eugenics movement in the United States. Her most recent book is *My Fundamentalist Education*, which tells the story of the Christian fundamentalist school she attended as a child in St. Petersburg, Florida. Since 1999, Rosen has also been an adjunct scholar at the American Enterprise Institute for Public Policy Research, where she has written about women and the economy, feminism, and women's studies. Rosen's opinion pieces and essays have appeared in publications including the *New York Times Magazine*, the *Wall Street Journal*, the *New Republic*, the *Washington Post*, the *American Historical Review*, the *Weekly Standard*, *Commentary*, the *New England Journal of Medicine*, the *Wilson Quarterly*, and *Policy Review*. She earned a BA in history from the University of South Florida in 1993, and a PhD in history from Emory University in 1999. Rosen lives in Washington, DC, with her husband, Jeffrey, and their children.

Ron Rosenbaum is the author of seven books, including *The Shakespeare Wars: Clashing Scholars, Public Fiascoes, Palace Coups*; *Explaining Hitler: The Search for the Origin of His Evil*; and *The Secret Parts of Fortune*, a collection of his essays and reporting, which have appeared in the *New York Times Magazine*, *Harper's*, the *New Yorker*, the *New York Observer*, and others. He is currently a cultural columnist at Slate.com and is working on a book about the mechanics and morals of nuclear war in the twenty-first century, as well as a short biography of Bob Dylan. He was cowriter of the award-winning PBS Frontline documentary *Faith and Doubt at Ground Zero*. He has been the lone liberal blogger on a conservative blog site for three years.

Stephen Schwartz is executive director of the Center for Islamic Pluralism (CIP), a transnational network of moderate Muslims, at www.islamicpluralism.org. Although brought up without religion, he has been Muslim since 1997, and is active in interfaith activities involving Muslims, Christians, and Jews. His books include *The Two Faces of Islam: Saudi Fundamentalism and Its Role in Terrorism* (2002), which introduced the non-Muslim reading audience around the world to the extremist Wahhabi sect that inspired Al-Qaeda. In 2008, his volume *The Other Islam: Sufism and the Road to Global Harmony*, on Islamic spirituality, was published. CIP issued a major study in 2009 titled *A Guide to Shariah Law and Islamist Ideology in Western Europe, 2007–2009*. Schwartz's other works include a collection of writings on Muslim-Jewish relations in the Balkans, *Sarajevo Rose* (2005), and *Kosovo: Background to a War* (2000). Schwartz's writings on Islam have been translated and widely read in Muslim countries. He served from 1989 to 1999 as a staff writer at the *San Francisco Chronicle*. His articles have been printed in the *Wall Street Journal*, the *Globe and Mail* (Toronto), the *Weekly Standard*, the *Spectator* (London), the *New Criterion*, and many other leading periodicals.

Lee Siegel has written about culture and politics for numerous publications, including *Harper's*, the *Atlantic Monthly*, the *New Yorker*, *New York*, *Time*, the *New York Times*, and the *Wall Street Journal*. He has been the television critic for the *New Republic*, where he was also a senior editor; art critic for Slate; and book critic for the

Nation. He is the author of three books: *Falling Upwards: Essays in Defense of the Imagination; Not Remotely Controlled: Notes on Television;* and, most recently, *Against the Machine: How the Web Is Reshaping Commerce and Culture—and Why It Matters.* In 2002, he received the National Magazine Award for Reviews and Criticism.

Christina Hoff Sommers is a resident scholar at the American Enterprise Institute. Before joining AEI, she was a professor of philosophy at Clark University, where she specialized in moral theory. Her academic articles have appeared in publications including the *Journal of Philosophy* and the *New England Journal of Medicine,* and those on social and political subjects in the *Wall Street Journal,* the *New York Times,* the *Washington Post,* the *New Republic,* the *Weekly Standard,* the *Atlantic,* and the *American.* She is probably best known for her critique of late twentieth century feminism, *Who Stole Feminsim?* Sommers is the editor of *Vice and Virtue in Everyday Life,* a leading college ethics textbook, and the newly published *The Science on Women in Science.*

Shelby Steele is the Robert J. and Marion E. Oster Senior Fellow at the Hoover Institution, specializing in race relations, multiculturalism, and affirmative action. Steele received the Bradley Prize (2006) for contributions to the study of race in America, and the National Humanities Medal (2004). In 1991, his work on the documentary *Seven Days in Bensonhurst* was recognized with an Emmy Award, a Writer's Guild Award, and a San Francisco Film Festival Award. Steele received the National Book Critics' Circle Award (1990) for *The Content of Our Character: A New Vision of Race in America.* Other books: *A Bound Man: Why We Are Excited About Obama and Why He Can't Win* (2007); *White Guilt: How Blacks and Whites Together Destroyed the Promise of the Civil Rights Era* (2006); and *A Dream Deferred: The Second Betrayal of Black Freedom in America.* Steele writes extensively for major publications including the *New York Times* and the *Wall Street Journal.* He is a contributing editor at *Harper's* magazine and an in-demand speaker, and he has appeared on national news programs including *Nightline* and *60 Minutes*. Steele is a member of the National Association of Scholars, the national board of the American Academy for Liberal Education, the University Accreditation Association, and the national board at the Center for the New American Community at the Manhattan Institute. Steele holds a PhD in English from the University of Utah, an MA in sociology from Southern Illinois University, and a BA in political science from Coe College.

Dennis Whittle is CEO of GlobalGiving, which he cofounded in late 2000 after a career in the official aid sector. GlobalGiving is the world's leading marketplace for international philanthropy. It allows qualified community-based groups around the world to post projects, and anyone in the world to fund them. Updates are posted directly to the site and automatically sent to donors, who can provide feedback and ask questions. Tens of thousands of individual donors, as well as many leading Fortune 500 companies, use GlobalGiving. From 1997 to 2000, Dennis co-led the World Bank's Corporate Strategy and Innovation units, including the team that created the Development Marketplace. From 1992 to 1997, he led a variety of initiatives in the bank's Russia program, including housing reform and energy efficiency projects. From 1987 to 1992, Dennis was an economist in the World Bank's Jakarta office, advising the Indonesian Ministries of Finance and National Development, and managing projects in the agriculture and forestry sectors. Before joining the World Bank in 1986, Dennis worked in the Philippines with the Asian Development Bank and with USAID. Dennis graduated with honors in religious studies from the University of North Carolina–Chapel Hill, where he was a Morehead Scholar, and did his graduate work in development studies and economics at Princeton University's Woodrow Wilson School. Dennis also completed the Advanced Management Program at Harvard Business School.